THE NEW FOLGER LIBRARY SHAKESPEARE

Designed to make Shakespeare's great plays available to all readers, the New Folger Library edition of Shakespeare's plays provides accurate texts in modern spelling and punctuation, as well as scene-by-scene action summaries, full explanatory notes, many pictures clarifying Shakespeare's language, and notes recording all significant departures from the early printed versions. Each play is prefaced by a brief introduction, by a guide to reading Shakespeare's language, and by accounts of his life and theater. Each play is followed by an annotated list of further readings and by a "Modern Perspective" written by an expert on that particular play.

Barbara A. Mowat is Director of Research *emerita* at the Folger Shakespeare Library, Consulting Editor of *Shakespeare Quarterly*, and author of *The Dramaturgy of Shakespeare's Romances* and of essays on Shakespeare's plays and their editing.

Paul Werstine is Professor of English in the Graduate School and at King's University College at Western University. He is a general editor of the New Variorum Shakespeare and author of *Early Modern Playhouse Manuscripts and the Editing of Shakespeare*, as well as many papers and essays on the printing and editing of Shakespeare's plays.

Folger Shakespeare Library

The Folger Shakespeare Library in Washington, D.C., is a privately funded research library dedicated to Shakespeare and the civilization of early modern Europe. It was founded in 1932 by Henry Clay and Emily Jordan Folger, and incorporated as part of Amherst College in Amherst, Massachusetts, one of the nation's oldest liberal arts colleges, from which Henry Folger had graduated in 1879. In addition to its role as the world's preeminent Shakespeare collection and its emergence as a leading center for Renaissance studies, the Folger Shakespeare Library offers a wide array of cultural and educational programs and services for the general public.

EDITORS

BARBARA A. MOWAT
Director of Research emerita
Folger Shakespeare Library

PAUL WERSTINE
Professor of English
King's University College at the University of Western Ontario, Canada

FOLGER SHAKESPEARE LIBRARY

Troilus and Cressida

By

WILLIAM SHAKESPEARE

EDITED BY BARBARA A. MOWAT
AND PAUL WERSTINE

SIMON & SCHUSTER PAPERBACKS
NEW YORK LONDON TORONTO SYDNEY

Simon & Schuster Paperbacks
A Division of Simon & Schuster, Inc.
1230 Avenue of the Americas
New York, NY 10020

Washington Square Press New Folger Edition October 2007
This Simon & Schuster paperback edition August 2011

SIMON & SCHUSTER PAPERBACKS and colophon are registered trademarks of Simon & Schuster, Inc.

For information regarding special discounts for bulk purchases, please contact Simon & Schuster Special Sales at 1-866-506-1949 or business@simonandschuster.com.

The Simon & Schuster Speakers Bureau can bring authors to your live event. For more information or to book an event, contact the Simon & Schuster Speakers Bureau at 1-866-248-3049 or visit our website at www.simonspeakers.com.

Manufactured in the United States of America

15 14 13 12 11 10 9 8

ISBN 978-0-7432-7331-2

From the Director of the Folger Shakespeare Library

It is hard to imagine a world without Shakespeare. Since their composition four hundred years ago, Shakespeare's plays and poems have traveled the globe, inviting those who see and read his works to make them their own.

Readers of the New Folger Editions are part of this ongoing process of "taking up Shakespeare," finding our own thoughts and feelings in language that strikes us as old or unusual and, for that very reason, new. We still struggle to keep up with a writer who could think a mile a minute, whose words paint pictures that shift like clouds. These expertly edited texts, presented here with accompanying explanatory notes and up-to-date critical essays, are distinctive because of what they do: they allow readers not simply to keep up, but to engage deeply with a writer whose works invite us to think, and think again.

These New Folger Editions of Shakespeare's plays are also special because of where they come from. The Folger Shakespeare Library in Washington, DC, where the Editions are produced, is the single greatest documentary source of Shakespeare's works. An unparalleled collection of early modern books, manuscripts, and artwork connected to Shakespeare, the Folger's holdings have been consulted extensively in the preparation of these texts. The Editions also reflect the expertise gained through the regular performance of Shakespeare's works in the Folger's Elizabethan Theater.

I want to express my deep thanks to editors Barbara Mowat and Paul Werstine for creating these indispensable editions of Shakespeare's works, which incorporate the best of textual scholarship with a richness of commentary that is both inspired and engaging. Readers who want to know more about Shakespeare and his plays can follow the paths these distinguished scholars have tread by visiting the Folger itself, where a range of physical and digital resources (available online) exist to supplement the material in these texts. I commend to you these words, and hope that they inspire.

Michael Witmore
Director, Folger Shakespeare Library

From the Director of the Folger Shakespeare Library

[illegible]

Contents

Editors' Preface

In recent years, ways of dealing with Shakespeare's texts and with the interpretation of his plays have been undergoing significant change. This edition, while retaining many of the features that have always made the Folger Shakespeare so attractive to the general reader, at the same time reflects these current ways of thinking about Shakespeare. For example, modern readers, actors, and teachers have become interested in the differences between, on the one hand, the early forms in which Shakespeare's plays were first published and, on the other hand, the forms in which editors through the centuries have presented them. In response to this interest, we have based our edition on what we consider the best early printed version of a particular play (explaining our rationale in a section called "An Introduction to This Text") and have marked our changes in the text—unobtrusively, we hope, but in such a way that the curious reader can be aware that a change has been made and can consult the "Textual Notes" to discover what appeared in the early printed version.

Current ways of looking at the plays are reflected in our brief prefaces, in many of the commentary notes, in the annotated lists of "Further Reading," and especially in each play's "Modern Perspective," an essay written by an outstanding scholar who brings to the reader his or her fresh assessment of the play in the light of today's interests and concerns.

As in the Folger Library General Reader's Shakespeare, which this edition replaces, we include explanatory notes designed to help make Shakespeare's language clearer to a modern reader, and we place the notes on the page facing the text that they explain. We also follow the earlier edition in including illustrations—of objects, of clothing, of mythological figures—from books and manuscripts in the Folger Library collection. We provide fresh accounts of the life of Shakespeare, of the publishing of his plays, and of the theaters in which his plays were performed, as well as an introduction to the text itself. We also include a section called "Reading Shakespeare's Language," in which we try to help readers learn to "break the code" of Elizabethan poetic language.

For each section of each volume, we are indebted to a host of generous experts and fellow scholars. The "Reading Shakespeare's Language" sections, for example, could not have been written had not Arthur King, of Brigham Young University, and Randall Robinson, author of *Unlocking Shakespeare's Language,* led the way in untangling Shakespearean language puzzles and shared their insights and methodologies generously with us. "Shakespeare's Life" profited by the careful reading given it by the late S. Schoenbaum; "Shakespeare's Theater" was read and strengthened by Andrew Gurr, John Astington, and William Ingram; and "The Publication of Shakespeare's Plays" is indebted to the comments of Peter W. M. Blayney. We, as editors, take sole responsibility for any errors in our editions.

We are grateful to the authors of the "Modern Perspectives"; to the Huntington and Newberry Libraries for fellowship support; to King's University College for the grants it has provided to Paul Werstine; to the Social Sciences and Humanities Research Council of Canada, which provided him with a Research Time

Stipend for 1990–91; to R. J. Shroyer of the University of Western Ontario for essential computer support; to the Folger Institute's Center for Shakespeare Studies for its sponsorship of a workshop on "Shakespeare's Texts for Students and Teachers" (funded by the National Endowment for the Humanities and led by Richard Knowles of the University of Wisconsin), a workshop from which we learned an enormous amount about what is wanted by college and high-school teachers of Shakespeare today; to Karen Bjelland for helpful conversations; to Alice Falk for her expert copyediting; and especially to Stephen Llano, our production editor at Washington Square Press. Among the texts we consulted, we found David Bevington's Arden *Troilus and Cressida* (1998) and Anthony B. Dawson's New Cambridge *Troilus and Cressida* (2003) particularly helpful.

Our biggest debt is to the Folger Shakespeare Library—to Gail Kern Paster, Director of the Library, whose interest and support are unfailing (and whose scholarly expertise is an invaluable resource), and to Werner Gundersheimer, the Library's Director from 1984 to 2002, who made possible our edition; to Deborah Curren-Aquino, who provides extensive editorial and production support; to Jean Miller, the Library's former Art Curator, who combs the Library holdings for illustrations, and to Julie Ainsworth, Head of the Photography Department, who carefully photographs them; to Peggy O'Brien, former Director of Education at the Folger and now Director of Education Programs at the Corporation for Public Broadcasting, who gave us expert advice about the needs being expressed by Shakespeare teachers and students (and to Martha Christian and other "master teachers" who used our texts in manuscript in their classrooms); to Allan Shnerson and Mary Bloodworth for their expert computer support; to the staff of the Research Division, especially Karen Rogers (whose help is crucial), Mimi Godfrey (with special thanks for research assistance), Kathleen Lynch, Carol Brobeck, Liz Pohland, Owen Williams, and Caryn Lazzuri; and, finally, to the generously supportive staff of the Library's Reading Room.

Barbara A. Mowat and Paul Werstine

Shakespeare's *Troilus and Cressida*

For the dramatic speech and action of *Troilus and Cressida,* Shakespeare turned to two of the most prominent authors in his culture. The first was Homer, who had inspired much of Greek and Latin literature as author of the *Iliad* and the *Odyssey,* the epic poems treating the Trojan War and its aftermath. The second was Geoffrey Chaucer, who, as author of *The Canterbury Tales* and the great romance of the Trojan War *Troilus and Criseyde,* was the only English writer granted status comparable to the titans of classical literature. Homer's heroes, especially Achilles and Hector, are so magnificent that they attract the interest and intervention of the gods of the classical world. These gods contend with each other over the fates of their favorites, and sometimes even join the fight with them on the battlefield between the walls of Troy and the ships of the Greek invaders. The Greeks and the Trojans battle over Helen, the queen of Sparta and wife of Menelaus; she was taken from him by Paris, a son of Priam, king of Troy, and now is held within the city's impenetrable gates and walls. Helen, every bit as magnificent as her male counterparts, is, in Homer, innocent of inconstancy because she is the victim of a divine spell.

Chaucer's young Trojan prince Troilus and the widow Criseyde, with whom he falls in love, are fitting company for the Homeric heroes among whom Chaucer places them. However immature Troilus is at the beginning of the romance, his love for Criseyde matures him and ennobles his character, so that by the time they consummate their love, she can imagine him providing her the protection of a wall of steel. During their long affair, he loves her with great constancy. And he continues to love her after she is sent away by the Trojan council to the Greeks, to whom her father has already fled, and even after her betrayal of him when the Greek Diomedes prevails on her to accept him as her lover. While Criseyde turns out finally to be false, Chaucer and the rather clumsy and inexperienced narrator he creates both seem highly sympathetic to her in her vulnerable state. Up to the moment of her inconstancy, the poem is lavish in providing readers with details of her domestic situation and of her states of mind and feeling in a way that draws us close to her. Only Chaucer's Pandarus and Diomedes seem to anticipate their Shakespearean counterparts, both men ruthless in exploiting Criseyde's fears.

None of Shakespeare's characters are the exemplars of heroism, constancy, or greatness found in Homer's and Chaucer's creations. In part, their diminishment in Shakespeare's play may result from his transformation of them from epic and romance to drama. By convention in epic, the characters associate with the gods and thereby share the glory of these divinities; by convention in drama, the gods do not appear, and the characters therefore cannot exceed the limits of their humanity. By convention too in both romance and epic, the characters are presented to us by admiring narrators; by convention in drama, the characters must speak for themselves. But the shift in genre from epic and romance to drama cannot in itself account for the shrinking of the Homeric and Chaucerian characters to their Shakespearean size.

Instead, Shakespeare shapes the action of his play and the speeches of his characters so as to diminish the characters. The leaders of the Greek army, General Agamemnon and his councillors Nestor and Ulysses, talk endlessly as they scheme to get their chief warrior Achilles again to fight. Their schemes involve deception and cheap theatricality, and Greek officers and warriors alike are presented as fitting subjects for the cynical Thersites to lash mercilessly with his tongue. On the Trojan side, when the leaders meet to discuss whether to keep Helen, Hector provides powerfully reasonable arguments for delivering her up to the Greeks and then, on a seeming whim, sides with the others in continuing the war to keep her. In Shakespeare's version, all the Greeks and Trojans, Paris excepted, doubt that Helen is worth the lives lost in their war for her. Just as Paris dotes on Helen, so Troilus on Cressida. Yet in contrast to Chaucer's Troilus, Shakespeare's fails to mature in response to his love and remains in adolescent self-absorption, almost indifferent to Cressida's plight when she is forced out of Troy and made to go to her father in the Greek camp. For her part, Shakespeare's Cressida shows nothing of the thoughtful reflection of her Chaucerian predecessor; it is replaced in her by calculation and manipulation of her suitors. Apparently, Shakespeare chose to part ways with Homer and Chaucer by throwing onto their characters a relentlessly satirical light, one that makes his play a savage attack on the ideals that serve as cover for greed, violence, and lust.

After you have read *Troilus and Cressida*, we invite you to read the essay printed after it, "*Troilus and Cressida:* A Modern Perspective," written by Professor Jonathan Gil Harris of George Washington University.

SEAVEN BOOKES

OF THE ILIADES OF

HOMERE, PRINCE

OF POETS,

¶ *Translated according to the Greeke, in iudgement* of his best Commentaries

by

George Chapman Gent.

Scribendi recte, sapere est & principium & fons

LONDON.

Printed by *Iohn Windet*, and are to be solde at the signe of the Crosse-keyes, neare *Paules* wharffe.

1598.

Title page of Homer's *Iliad,* translated by George Chapman (1592).
(From the Folger Library collection.)

Reading Shakespeare's Language: *Troilus and Cressida*

For many people today, reading Shakespeare's language can be a problem—but it is a problem that can be solved. Those who have studied Latin (or even French or German or Spanish), and those who are used to reading poetry, will have little difficulty understanding the language of Shakespeare's poetic drama. Others, though, need to develop the skills of untangling unusual sentence structures and of recognizing and understanding poetic compressions, omissions, and wordplay. And even those skilled in reading unusual sentence structures may have occasional trouble with Shakespeare's words. Four hundred years of "static" intervene between his speaking and our hearing. Most of his immense vocabulary is still in use, but a few of his words are no longer used and many of his words now have meanings quite different from those they had in the sixteenth and seventeenth centuries. In the theater, most of these difficulties are solved for us by actors who study the language and articulate it for us so that the essential meaning is heard—or, when combined with stage action, is at least *felt*. When we are reading on our own, we must do what each actor does: go over the lines (often with a dictionary close at hand) until the puzzles are solved and the lines yield up their poetry and the characters speak in words and phrases that are, suddenly, rewarding and wonderfully memorable.

Shakespeare's Words

As you begin to read the opening scenes of a play by Shakespeare, you may notice occasional unfamiliar words. Some are unfamiliar simply because we no longer use them. In the opening act of *Troilus and Cressida,* for example, one finds the words *indrenched* (i.e., drowned), *tortive* (i.e., twisted), *importless* (i.e., trivial), and *oppugnancy* (i.e., opposition). Words of this kind, more frequent in *Troilus and Cressida* than in most of Shakespeare's plays, are explained in notes to the text.

In *Troilus and Cressida,* as in all of Shakespeare's writing, more problematic are the words that are still in use but that now have a different meaning. In the opening scenes of *Troilus and Cressida,* for example, the word *porridge* is used where we would say "soup," *fair* where we would say "beautiful," *morrow* where we would say "morning," and *ward* where we would say "defend." Such words will be explained in the notes to the text, but they will become familiar the more of Shakespeare's plays you read.

Some words are strange not because of the "static" introduced by changes in language over the past centuries but because these are words that Shakespeare is using to build a dramatic world that has its own space, time, and history. In the Prologue to *Troilus and Cressida,* for example, Shakespeare quickly constructs the recent background to the Trojan War, some episodes of which are the subject of his play. He gives an account of Greek "princes orgulous," wearing "crownets regal," sailing for "Phrygia" in order "to ransack Troy" because it is the city "whose strong immures" secure "Helen, Menelaus' queen," "ravished" by "wanton Paris." Shakespeare then describes the "Dardan plains," where the Greeks have pitched their "brave pavilions" within sight of "Priam's six-gated city." These words and names and the world they create will become increasingly familiar as you get further into the play.

Shakespeare's Sentences

In an English sentence, meaning is quite dependent on the place given each word. "The dog bit the boy" and "The boy bit the dog" mean very different things, even though the individual words are the same. Because English places such importance on the positions of words in sentences, on the way words are arranged, unusual arrangements can puzzle a reader. Shakespeare frequently shifts his sentences away from "normal" English arrangements—often to create the rhythm he seeks, sometimes to use a line's poetic rhythm to emphasize a particular word, sometimes to give a character his or her own speech patterns or to allow the character to speak in a special way. When we attend a good performance of the play, the actors will have worked out the sentence structures and will articulate the sentences so that the meaning is clear. When reading the play, we need to do as the actor does: that is, when puzzled by a character's speech, check to see if words are being presented in an unusual sequence.

Often Shakespeare rearranges subjects and verbs (i.e., instead of "He says" we find "Says he"). In *Troilus and Cressida,* when Cressida's servant Alexander, speaking of Hector, tells her that "to the field goes he" (1.2.11), Alexander is using such a construction. So is the Greek councillor Nestor when he says "In the reproof of chance / Lies the true proof of men" (1.3.33–34). The "normal" order would be "he goes" and "the true proof of men lies in the reproof of chance." Shakespeare also frequently places the object before the subject and verb (i.e., instead of "I hit him," we might find "Him I hit"). Cressida provides an example of this inversion when she says "this maxim out of love I teach" (1.2.299); she offers another more elaborate example by saying "Words, vows, gifts, tears, and love's full sacrifice / He offers" (1.2.289–90). The "normal" order would be "I teach this maxim" and "He offers words, vows, gifts, tears, and love's full sacrifice."

Inversions are not the only unusual sentence structures in Shakespeare's language. Often in his sentences, words that would normally appear together are separated from each other. Again, this is frequently done to create a particular rhythm or to stress a particular word, or else to draw attention to a needed piece of information. Take, for example, the Greek general Agamemnon's "Distinction, with a broad and powerful fan, / Puffing at all, winnows the light away" (1.3.27–28). Here the subject ("Distinction") is separated from its verb ("winnows") by the phrases "with a broad and powerful fan" and "Puffing at all." Or take the Greek warrior-king Ulysses' accusation against Achilles:

> The great Achilles, whom opinion crowns
> The sinew and the forehand of our host,
> Having his ear full of his airy fame,
> Grows dainty of his worth[.]
>
> (1.3.146–49)

In this case the subject of the sentence ("Achilles") is separated from the verb ("grows") by a clause ("whom opinion crowns / The sinew and the forehand of our host") and then by a phrase ("Having his ear full of his airy fame"). Both the clause and the phrase deserve the emphasis they receive because they indicate how Achilles has grown so full of self-regard. In order to create sentences that seem more like the English of everyday speech, one can rearrange the words, putting together the word clusters ("Distinction winnows," "Achilles grows dainty"). The result will usually be an increase in clarity but a loss of rhythm or a shift in emphasis.

Often in *Troilus and Cressida,* rather than separating basic sentence elements, Shakespeare simply holds them back, delaying them until other material to which he wants to give greater emphasis has been presented. Shakespeare puts this kind of construction in the mouth of Ulysses when he begins to address his general, Agamemnon:

> Thou great commander, nerves and bone of Greece,
> Heart of our numbers, soul and only sprite,
> In whom the tempers and the minds of all
> Should be shut up, hear what Ulysses speaks.
> (1.3.57–60)

The basic sentence elements (the verb and its object "hear what Ulysses speaks") are here delayed while Ulysses shows elaborate deference to Agamemnon. This attitude could hardly be more appropriate to the occasion, because Ulysses is preparing to deliver a speech on the theme of the importance of respect for authority.

Sometimes Shakespeare fashions speeches that combine both the delay and the separation of basic sentence elements. One such example marks a speech by Troilus:

> . . . when my heart,
> As wedgèd with a sigh, would rive in twain,
> Lest Hector or my father should perceive me,
> I have, as when the sun doth light a-scorn,
> Buried this sigh in wrinkle of a smile[.]
> (1.1.35–39)

This time the subject and verb ("I have buried") must wait for Troilus's detailed presentation of his emotional state in a subordinate clause ("when my heart, / As wedgèd with a sigh, would rive in twain") that then incorporates a second clause ("Lest Hector or my father should perceive me"). When at last subject and verb do appear, the two parts of the verb ("have buried") are separated from each other by yet another clause that is used by Troilus to characterize his facial expression ("as when the sun doth light a-scorn").

Finally, in many of Shakespeare's plays, sentences are sometimes complicated not because of unusual structures or interruptions but because Shakespeare omits words and parts of words that English sentences normally require. (In conversation, we, too, often omit words. We say "Heard from him yet?" and our hearer supplies the missing "Have you.") Frequent reading of Shakespeare—and of other poets—trains us to supply such missing words. When, for example, Pandarus asks Cressida "Do you know a man if you see him?" she answers with an incomplete or elliptical sentence that has no main clause: "Ay, if I ever saw him before and knew him" (1.2.67–69). It is easy for the reader or listener to supply the omitted main clause "I know a man" before the "if" in Cressida's reply because three of these four words ("know a man") immediately precede the "if" in Pandarus's question. Such omissions as this one give the dialogue the flavor of casual conversation. However, elliptical sentences can also function to convey a note of formality or high seriousness, as in Hector's challenge to the Greek warriors, which is read out by Aeneas. It begins with a sentence that omits both subject and verb:

Kings, princes, lords,
If there be one among the fair'st of Greece
That holds his honor higher than his ease,
That seeks his praise more than he fears his peril,
That knows his valor and knows not his fear,

That loves his mistress more than in confession
With truant vows to her own lips he loves
And dare avow her beauty and her worth
In other arms than hers—to him this challenge.
(1.3.272–80)

In this case, the reader or listener does not face much difficulty inferring a possible subject and verb to supplement the sentence's last four words: "to him [Hector delivers] this challenge."

Shakespearean Wordplay

Shakespeare plays with language so often and so variously that entire books are written on the topic. Here we will mention only two kinds of wordplay, metaphors and puns. A metaphor is a play on words in which one object or idea is expressed as if it were something else, something with which the metaphor suggests it shares common features. For instance, when Ulysses is scheming to award Ajax the chance to fight Hector, Ulysses plans to have the Greeks metaphorically "dress him [Ajax] up in voices" if he wins (1.3.390). Here "voices"—that is, declarations of approval—are presented as the elaborate clothes in which someone who is being elevated to a superior position is attired. Troilus also uses metaphor to express his desire for Cressida: "Her bed is India; there she lies, a pearl" (1.1.102). She is, for him, a highly valued gem ("pearl") that can transform any ordinary domestic object ("bed") into a place of untold wealth ("India"—the East or West Indies). Later Nestor creates an elaborate and extended metaphor that compares different kinds of men to different kinds of ships:

In the reproof of chance
Lies the true proof of men. The sea being smooth,
How many shallow bauble boats dare sail
Upon her patient breast, making their way
With those of nobler bulk!
But let the ruffian Boreas once enrage
The gentle Thetis, and anon behold
The strong-ribbed bark through liquid mountains cut,
Bounding between the two moist elements,
Like Perseus' horse. Where's then the saucy boat
Whose weak untimbered sides but even now
Corrivaled greatness? Either to harbor fled
Or made a toast for Neptune. Even so
Doth valor's show and valor's worth divide
In storms of Fortune.
(1.3.33–47)

According to Nestor, those men who are capable of nothing but "valor's show" (that is, the mere appearance of courage) are no more than "shallow bauble boats" that "dare sail" only on a calm sea and that flee to harbor or sink (becoming "a toast for Neptune") when the north wind whips up a storm. However, true courage ("valor's worth") is a ship of "nobler bulk," a "strong-ribbed bark" that can endure the storm and "through liquid mountains cut." *Troilus and Cressida* is in large part made up of metaphoric language, offering the reader the challenge and the richness of complex poetry.

A pun is a play on words that sound the same but that have different meanings (or on a single word that has more than one meaning). Pandarus puns in complaining that his efforts to bring Troilus and Cressida together as lovers are unrewarded and have earned him the good will of neither: "I have had my labor for my travail, . . . gone between and between, but small thanks for my labor" (1.1.71–73). To make a pun on *travail,* Shakespeare exploits the fact that in his time the two words we now distinguish as *travail* and *travel* were used interchangeably, each word being an acceptable alternative spelling of the other. Thus Pandarus complains that he has no reward for his labor except for his toil and trouble (*travail*) and his *travel*, the journeys from Troilus to Cressida and back, as he has "gone between and between." Aeneas also puns as he delivers Hector's challenge to the Greeks, in particular to the "one among the fair'st of Greece / . . . That loves his mistress . . . / And dare avow her beauty and her worth / In other arms than hers" (1.3.273–80). The challenge puns on two meanings of *arms,* evoking both the limbs of the beloved mistress and the armor and weapons of the warrior who loves her. Several characters in *Troilus and Cressida* (and especially Thersites) are given language thick with puns, many of which will be pointed out in our notes to the text.

Implied Stage Action

Finally, in reading Shakespeare's plays we should always remember that what we are reading is a performance script. The dialogue is written to be spoken by actors who, at the same time, are moving, gesturing, picking up objects, weeping, shaking their fists. Some stage action is described in what are called "stage directions"; some is signaled within the dialogue itself. We must learn to be alert to such signals as we stage the play in our imaginations.

Often the dialogue offers an immediately clear indication of the action that is to accompany it. For example, when, in the presence of Ajax, Achilles invites Thersites to speak of Ajax, Thersites says "I say, this

Ajax—" (2.1.80–81), at which point Achilles cuts short Thersites' speech with the words "Nay, good Ajax." Achilles' warning indicates that Ajax is somehow attempting to silence Thersites. Although we cannot be sure exactly what kind of violence Ajax is about to unleash on Thersites—a punch or a kick—we are confident enough there is the threat of violence that we add the stage direction *"Ajax menaces him* [*Thersites*]*."* Again when Pandarus says to Cressida "Come, draw this curtain and let's see your picture. Alas the day, how loath you are to offend daylight" (3.2.46–48), it is clear that Pandarus is not referring to an actual picture behind a curtain but is using a commonplace metaphor to allude to Cressida's face covered by a veil. Therefore we add the word *veiled* to Cressida's entrance (line 38 SD) and add the stage direction *"He* [*Pandarus*] *draws back her veil"* to the dialogue just quoted. No matter how confident we are about the appropriateness of these particular additional stage directions, we place them in half-square brackets, just as we do all stage directions that we add to the early printed text, whether they are of our own creation or the work of earlier editors.

Occasionally in *Troilus and Cressida,* dialogue signals about stage action are not so clear. Take, for example, the fight in the lists between Ajax and Hector in Act 4. In both of the earliest printed texts, the dialogue and stage directions accompanying it appear as follows:

Alarum.

AGAMEMNON They are in action.
NESTOR Now, Ajax, hold thine own!
TROILUS Hector, thou sleep'st. Awake thee!
AGAMEMNON
His blows are well disposed.—There, Ajax!

Trumpets cease.

DIOMEDES
You must no more.
AENEAS Princes, enough, so please you.
AJAX
I am not warm yet. Let us fight again.
(4.5.127–33)

Here Agamemnon's first speech clearly indicates that the fight begins when the trumpets sound the call to arms ("*Alarum*"), and Ajax's request to "fight again" must signal that fighting has ceased. Yet the conduct and outcome of the fight and how it was staged seem quite impossible to specify in stage directions. Nestor's encouragement to Ajax to "hold thine own" (i.e., be a match for Hector) does not suggest that Ajax is enjoying any advantage at the moment Nestor speaks. However, at the next moment, when Troilus speaks ("Hector, thou sleep'st"), Hector appears at a clear disadvantage. Agamemnon's praise of Ajax ("His blows are well disposed.—There, Ajax!") may be taken as a response to Ajax's somehow getting the better of Hector, or, in contrast, it may show Agamemnon's surprised delight that Ajax is able finally to hold his own against an allegedly sleepy Hector. When Diomedes and Aeneas successively command an end to combat, are we to conclude that both adversaries are still fighting as vigorously after the trumpets have ceased as they were before, or that only Ajax or only Hector persists after his opponent has stopped attacking? In light of the great uncertainty regarding the progress of this contest, we have refrained from adding any stage direction beyond *"The fight begins"* just before Agamemnon's first speech. We leave it to the reader to engage with the dialogue and to draw whatever inferences, if any, seem most plausible about the encounter of Hector and Ajax in the lists. Directors and actors can experiment with various ways of combining the dialogue with stage action, as can the reader who has developed the skill of responding in imagination to complex dramatic cues.

It is immensely rewarding to work carefully with Shakespeare's language—with the words, the sentences, the wordplay, and the implied stage action—as readers for the past four centuries have discovered. It may be more pleasurable to attend a good performance of a play—though not everyone has thought so. But the joy of being able to stage one of Shakespeare's plays in one's imagination, to return to passages that continue to yield further meanings (or further questions) the more one reads them—these are pleasures that, for many, rival (or at least augment) those of the performed text, and certainly make it worth considerable effort to "break the code" of Elizabethan poetic drama and let free the remarkable language that makes up a Shakespeare text.

Shakespeare's Life

Surviving documents that give us glimpses into the life of William Shakespeare show us a playwright, poet, and actor who grew up in the market town of Stratford-upon-Avon, spent his professional life in London, and returned to Stratford a wealthy landowner. He was born in April 1564, died in April 1616, and is buried inside the chancel of Holy Trinity Church in Stratford.

We wish we could know more about the life of the world's greatest dramatist. His plays and poems are testaments to his wide reading—especially to his knowledge of Virgil, Ovid, Plutarch, Holinshed's *Chronicles,* and the Bible—and to his mastery of the English language, but we can only speculate about his education. We know that the King's New School in Stratford-upon-Avon was considered excellent. The school was one of the English "grammar schools" established to educate young men, primarily in Latin grammar and literature. As in other schools of the time, students began their studies at the age of four or five in the attached "petty school," and there learned to read and write in English, studying primarily the catechism from the Book of Common Prayer. After two years in the petty school, students entered the lower form (grade) of the grammar school, where they began the serious study of Latin grammar and Latin texts that would occupy most of the remainder of their school days. (Several Latin texts that Shakespeare used repeatedly in writing his plays and poems were texts that schoolboys memorized and recited.) Latin comedies were introduced early in the lower form; in the upper form, which the boys entered at age ten or eleven, students wrote their own Latin orations and declamations, studied Latin historians and rhetoricians, and began the study of Greek using the Greek New Testament.

Since the records of the Stratford "grammar school" do not survive, we cannot prove that William Shakespeare attended the school; however, every indication (his father's position as an alderman and bailiff of Stratford, the playwright's own knowledge of the Latin classics, scenes in the plays that recall grammar-school experiences—for example, *The Merry Wives of Windsor,* 4.1) suggests that he did. We also lack generally accepted documentation about Shakespeare's life after his schooling ended and his professional life in London began. His marriage in 1582 (at age eighteen) to

A stylized representation of the Globe theater.
From Claes Jansz Visscher, *Londinum florentissima Britanniae urbs* . . . [c. 1625].

Anne Hathaway and the subsequent births of his daughter Susanna (1583) and the twins Judith and Hamnet (1585) are recorded, but how he supported himself and where he lived are not known. Nor do we know when and why he left Stratford for the London theatrical world, nor how he rose to be the important figure in that world that he had become by the early 1590s.

We do know that by 1592 he had achieved some prominence in London as both an actor and a playwright. In that year was published a book by the playwright Robert Greene attacking an actor who had the audacity to write blank-verse drama and who was "in his own conceit [i.e., opinion] the only Shake-scene in a country." Since Greene's attack includes a parody of a line from one of Shakespeare's early plays, there is little doubt that it is Shakespeare to whom he refers, a "Shake-scene" who had aroused Greene's fury by successfully competing with university-educated dramatists like Greene himself. It was in 1593 that Shakespeare became a published poet. In that year he published his long narrative poem *Venus and Adonis;* in 1594, he followed it with *The Rape of Lucrece.* Both poems were dedicated to the young earl of Southampton (Henry Wriothesley), who may have become Shakespeare's patron.

It seems no coincidence that Shakespeare wrote these narrative poems at a time when the theaters were closed because of the plague, a contagious epidemic disease that devastated the population of London. When the theaters reopened in 1594, Shakespeare apparently resumed his double career of actor and playwright and began his long (and seemingly profitable) service as an acting-company shareholder. Records for December of 1594 show him to be a leading member of the Lord Chamberlain's Men. It was this company of actors, later named the King's Men, for whom he would be a principal actor, dramatist, and shareholder for the rest of his career.

So far as we can tell, that career spanned about twenty years. In the 1590s, he wrote his plays on English history as well as several comedies and at least two tragedies (*Titus Andronicus* and *Romeo and Juliet*). These histories, comedies, and tragedies are the plays credited to him in 1598 in a work, *Palladis Tamia,* that in one chapter compares English writers with "Greek, Latin, and Italian Poets." There the author, Francis Meres, claims that Shakespeare is comparable to the Latin dramatists Seneca for tragedy and Plautus for comedy, and calls him "the most excellent in both kinds for the stage." He also names him "Mellifluous and honey-tongued Shakespeare": "I say," writes Meres, "that the Muses would speak with Shakespeare's fine filed phrase, if they would speak English." Since Meres also mentions Shakespeare's "sugared sonnets among his private friends," it is assumed that many of Shakespeare's sonnets (not published until 1609) were also written in the 1590s.

In 1599, Shakespeare's company built a theater for themselves across the river from London, naming it the Globe. The plays that are considered by many to be Shakespeare's major tragedies (*Hamlet, Othello, King Lear,* and *Macbeth*) were written while the company was resident in this theater, as were such comedies as *Twelfth Night* and *Measure for Measure.* Many of Shakespeare's plays were performed at court (both for Queen Elizabeth I and, after her death in 1603, for King James I), some were presented at the Inns of Court (the residences of London's legal societies), and some were doubtless performed in other towns, at the universities, and at great houses when the King's Men went on tour; otherwise, his plays from 1599 to 1608 were, so far as we know, performed only at the

Globe. Between 1608 and 1612, Shakespeare wrote several plays—among them *The Winter's Tale* and *The Tempest*—presumably for the company's new indoor Blackfriars theater, though the plays seem to have been performed also at the Globe and at court. Surviving documents describe a performance of *The Winter's Tale* in 1611 at the Globe, for example, and performances of *The Tempest* in 1611 and 1613 at the royal palace of Whitehall.

Shakespeare wrote very little after 1612, the year in which he probably wrote *King Henry VIII.* (It was at a performance of *Henry VIII* in 1613 that the Globe caught fire and burned to the ground.) Sometime between 1610 and 1613 he seems to have returned to live in Stratford-upon-Avon, where he owned a large house and considerable property, and where his wife and his two daughters and their husbands lived. (His son Hamnet had died in 1596.) During his professional years in London, Shakespeare had presumably derived income from the acting company's profits as well as from his own career as an actor, from the sale of his play manuscripts to the acting company, and, after 1599, from his shares as an owner of the Globe. It was presumably that income, carefully invested in land and other property, which made him the wealthy man that surviving documents show him to have become. It is also assumed that William Shakespeare's growing wealth and reputation played some part in inclining the crown, in 1596, to grant John Shakespeare, William's father, the coat of arms that he had so long sought. William Shakespeare died in Stratford on April 23, 1616 (according to the epitaph carved under his bust in Holy Trinity Church) and was buried on April 25. Seven years after his death, his collected plays were published as *Mr. William Shakespeares Comedies, Histories, & Tragedies* (the work now known as the First Folio).

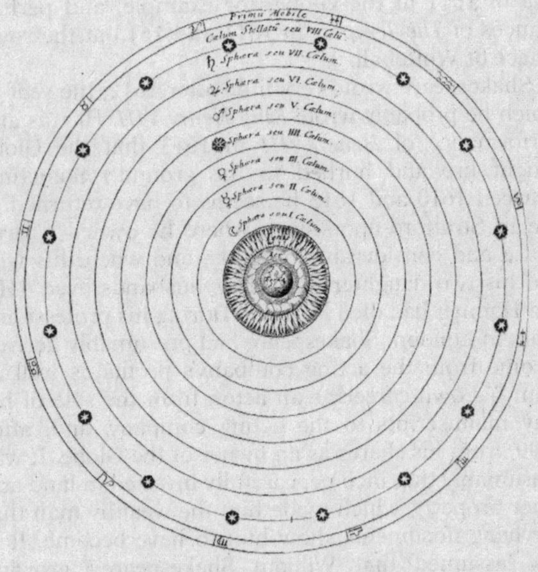

The Ptolemaic system. (1.3.89-90)
From Marcus Manilius, *The sphere of* . . . (1675).

The years in which Shakespeare wrote were among the most exciting in English history. Intellectually, the discovery, translation, and printing of Greek and Roman classics were making available a set of works and worldviews that interacted complexly with Christian texts and beliefs. The result was a questioning, a vital intellectual ferment, that provided energy for the period's amazing dramatic and literary output and that fed directly into Shakespeare's plays. The Ghost in *Hamlet,* for example, is wonderfully complicated in part because he is a figure from Roman tragedy—the spirit of the dead returning to seek revenge—who at the same time inhabits a Christian hell (or purgatory); Hamlet's description of humankind reflects at one moment the Neoplatonic wonderment at mankind ("What a piece of work is a man!") and, at the next, the Christian disparagement of human sinners ("And yet, to me, what is this quintessence of dust?").

As intellectual horizons expanded, so also did geographical and cosmological horizons. New worlds—both North and South America—were explored, and in them were found human beings who lived and worshiped in ways radically different from those of Renaissance Europeans and Englishmen. The universe during these years also seemed to shift and expand. Copernicus had earlier theorized that the earth was not the center of the cosmos but revolved as a planet around the sun. Galileo's telescope, created in 1609, allowed scientists to see that Copernicus had been correct; the universe was not organized with the earth at the center, nor was it so nicely circumscribed as people had, until that time, thought. In terms of expanding horizons, the impact of these discoveries on people's beliefs—religious, scientific, and philosophical—cannot be overstated.

London, too, rapidly expanded and changed during the years (from the early 1590s to around 1610) that Shakespeare lived there. London—the center of England's government, its economy, its royal court, its overseas trade—was, during these years, becoming an exciting metropolis, drawing to it thousands of new citizens every year. Troubled by overcrowding, by poverty, by recurring epidemics of the plague, London was also a mecca for the wealthy and the aristocratic, and for those who sought advancement at court, or power in government or finance or trade. One hears in Shakespeare's plays the voices of London—the struggles for power, the fear of venereal disease, the language of buying and selling. One hears as well the voices of Stratford-upon-Avon—references to the nearby Forest of Arden, to sheepherding, to small-town gossip, to village fairs and markets. Part of the richness of Shakespeare's work is the influence felt there of the various worlds in which he lived: the world of metropolitan London, the world of small-town and rural England, the world of the theater, and the worlds of craftsmen and shepherds.

That Shakespeare inhabited such worlds we know from surviving London and Stratford documents, as well as from the evidence of the plays and poems themselves. From such records we can sketch the dramatist's life. We know from his works that he was a voracious reader. We know from legal and business documents that he was a multifaceted theater man who became a wealthy landowner. We know a bit about his family life and a fair amount about his legal and financial dealings. Most scholars today depend upon such evidence as they draw their picture of the world's greatest playwright. Such, however, has not always been the case. Until the late eighteenth century, the William Shakespeare who lived in most biographies was the creation of legend and tradition. This was the Shakespeare who was supposedly caught poaching deer at Charlecote, the estate of Sir Thomas Lucy close by Stratford; this was the Shakespeare who fled from Sir Thomas's vengeance and made his way in London by taking care of horses outside a playhouse; this was the Shakespeare who reportedly could barely read but whose natural gifts were extraordinary, whose father was a butcher who allowed his gifted son sometimes to help in the butcher shop, where William supposedly killed calves "in a high style," making a speech for the occasion. It was this legendary William Shakespeare whose Falstaff (in *1* and *2 Henry IV*) so pleased Queen Elizabeth that she demanded a play about Falstaff in love, and demanded that it be written in fourteen days (hence the existence of *The Merry Wives of Windsor*). It was this legendary Shakespeare who reached the top of his acting career in the roles of the Ghost in *Hamlet* and old Adam in *As You Like It*—and who died of a fever contracted by drinking too hard at "a merry meeting" with the poets Michael Drayton and Ben Jonson. This legendary Shakespeare is a rambunctious, undisciplined man, as attractively "wild" as his plays were seen by earlier generations to be. Unfortunately, there is no trace of evidence to support these wonderful stories.

Perhaps in response to the disreputable Shakespeare of legend—or perhaps in response to the fragmentary and, for some, all-too-ordinary Shakespeare documented by surviving records—some people since the mid-nineteenth century have argued that William Shakespeare could not have written the plays that bear his name. These persons have put forward some dozen names as more likely authors, among them Queen Elizabeth, Sir Francis Bacon, Edward de Vere (earl of Oxford), and Christopher Marlowe. Such attempts to find what for these people is a more believable author of the plays is a tribute to the regard in which the plays are held. Unfortunately for their claims, the documents that exist that provide evidence for the facts of Shakespeare's life tie him inextricably to the body of plays and poems that bear his name. Unlikely as it seems to those who want the works to have been written by an aristocrat, a university graduate, or an "important" person, the plays and poems seem clearly to have been produced by a man from Stratford-upon-Avon with a very good "grammar school" education and a life of experience in London and in the world of the London theater. How this particular man produced the works that dominate the cultures of much of the world almost four hundred years after his death is one of life's mysteries—and one that will continue to tease our imaginations as we continue to delight in his plays and poems.

Shakespeare's Theater

The actors of Shakespeare's time performed plays in a great variety of locations. They played at court (that is, in the great halls of such royal residences as Whitehall, Hampton Court, and Greenwich); they played in halls at the universities of Oxford and Cambridge, and at the Inns of Court (the residences in London of the legal societies); and they also played in the private houses of great lords and civic officials. Sometimes acting companies went on tour from London into the provinces, often (but not only) when outbreaks of bubonic plague in the capital forced the closing of theaters to reduce the possibility of contagion in crowded audiences. In the provinces the actors usually staged their plays in churches (until around 1600) or in guildhalls. Though surviving records show only a handful of occasions when actors played at inns while on tour, London inns were important playing places up until the 1590s.

The building of theaters in London had begun only shortly before Shakespeare wrote his first plays in the 1590s. These theaters were of two kinds: outdoor or public playhouses that could accommodate large numbers of playgoers, and indoor or private theaters for much smaller audiences. What is usually regarded as the first London outdoor public playhouse was called simply the Theatre. James Burbage—the father of Richard Burbage, who was perhaps the most famous actor in Shakespeare's company—built it in 1576 in an area north of the city of London called Shoreditch. Among the more famous of the other public playhouses that capitalized on the new fashion were the Curtain and the Fortune (both also built north of the city), and the Rose, the Swan, the Globe, and the Hope (all located on the Bankside, a region just across the Thames south of the city of London). All these playhouses had to be built outside the jurisdiction of the city of London because many civic officials were hostile to the performance of drama and repeatedly petitioned the royal council to abolish it.

The theaters erected on the Bankside (a region under the authority of the Church of England, whose head was the monarch) shared the neighborhood with houses of prostitution and with the Paris Garden, where the blood sports of bearbaiting and bullbaiting were carried on. There may have been no clear distinction between playhouses and buildings for such sports, for the Hope was used for both plays and baiting, and Philip Henslowe, owner of the Rose and, later, partner in the ownership of the Fortune, was also a partner in a monopoly on baiting. All these forms of entertainment were easily accessible to Londoners by boat across the Thames or over London Bridge.

Evidently Shakespeare's company prospered on the Bankside. They moved there in 1599. Threatened by difficulties in renewing the lease on the land where their first playhouse (the Theatre) had been built, Shakespeare's company took advantage of the Christmas holiday in 1598 to dismantle the Theatre and transport its timbers across the Thames to the Bankside, where, in 1599, these timbers were used in the building of the Globe. The weather in late December 1598 is recorded as having been especially harsh. It was so cold that the Thames was "nigh [nearly] frozen," and there was heavy snow. Perhaps the weather aided Shakespeare's company in eluding their landlord, the snow hiding their activity and the freezing of the Thames allowing them to slide the timbers across to the Bankside without paying tolls for repeated trips over London Bridge. Attractive as this narrative is, it remains just as likely that the heavy snow hampered transport of the timbers in wagons through the London streets to the river. It also must be remembered that the Thames was, according to report, only "nigh frozen" and therefore as impassable as it ever was. Whatever the precise circumstances of this fascinating event in English theater history, Shakespeare's company was able to begin playing at their new Globe theater on the Bankside in 1599. After the first Globe burned down in 1613 during the staging of Shakespeare's *Henry VIII* (its thatch roof was set alight by cannon fire called for by the performance), Shakespeare's company immediately rebuilt on the same location. The second Globe seems to have been a grander structure than its predecessor. It remained in use until the beginning of the English Civil War in 1642, when Parliament officially closed the theaters. Soon thereafter it was pulled down.

The public theaters of Shakespeare's time were very different buildings from our theaters today. First of all, they were open-air playhouses. As recent excavations of the Rose and the Globe confirm, some were polygonal or roughly circular in shape; the Fortune, however, was square. The most recent estimates of their size put the diameter of these buildings at 72 feet (the Rose) to 100 feet (the Globe), but they were said to hold vast audiences of two or three thousand, who must have been squeezed together quite tightly. Some of these spectators paid extra to sit or stand in the two or three levels of roofed galleries that extended, on the upper levels, all the way around the theater and surrounded an open space. In this space were the stage and, perhaps, the tiring house (what we would call dressing rooms), as well as the so-called yard. In the yard stood the spectators who chose to pay less, the ones whom Hamlet contemptuously called "groundlings." For a roof they had only the sky, and so they were exposed to all kinds of weather. They stood on a floor that was sometimes made of mortar and sometimes of ash mixed with the shells of hazelnuts, which, it has recently been discovered, were standard flooring material in the period.

Unlike the yard, the stage itself was covered by a roof. Its ceiling, called "the heavens," is thought to have been elaborately painted to depict the sun, moon, stars, and planets. Just how big the stage was remains hard to determine. We have a single sketch of part of the interior of the Swan. A Dutchman named Johannes de Witt visited this theater around 1596 and sent a sketch of it back to his friend, Arend van Buchel. Because van Buchel found de Witt's letter and sketch of interest, he copied both into a book. It is van Buchel's copy, adapted, it seems, to the shape and size of the page in his book, that survives. In this sketch, the stage appears to be a large rectangular platform that thrusts far out into the yard, perhaps even as far as the center of the circle formed by the surrounding galleries. This drawing, combined with the specifications for the size of the stage in the building contract for the Fortune, has led scholars to conjecture that the stage on which Shakespeare's plays were performed must have measured approximately 43 feet in width and 27 feet in depth, a vast acting area. But the digging up of a large part of the Rose by archaeologists has provided evidence of a quite different stage design. The Rose stage was a platform tapered at the corners and much shallower than what seems to be depicted in the van Buchel sketch. Indeed, its measurements seem to be about 37.5 feet across at its widest point and only 15.5 feet deep. Because the surviving indications of stage size and design differ from each other so much, it is possible that the stages in other playhouses, like the Theatre, the Curtain, and the Globe (the outdoor playhouses where Shakespeare's plays were performed), were different from those at both the Swan and the Rose.

After about 1608 Shakespeare's plays were staged not only at the Globe but also at an indoor or private playhouse in Blackfriars. This theater had been constructed in 1596 by James Burbage in an upper hall of a former Dominican priory or monastic house. Although Henry VIII had dissolved all English monasteries in the 1530s (shortly after he had founded the Church of England), the area remained under church, rather than hostile civic, control. The hall that Burbage had purchased and renovated was a large one in which Parliament had once met. In the private theater that he constructed, the stage, lit by candles, was built across the narrow end of the hall, with boxes flanking it. The rest of the hall offered seating room only. Because there was no provision for standing room, the largest audience it could hold was less than a thousand, or about a quarter of what the Globe could accommodate. Admission to Blackfriars was correspondingly more expensive. Instead of a penny to stand in the yard at the Globe, it cost a minimum of sixpence to get into Blackfriars. The best seats at the Globe (in the Lords' Room in the gallery above and behind the stage) cost sixpence; but the boxes flanking the stage at Blackfriars were half a crown, or five times sixpence. Some spectators who were particularly interested in displaying themselves paid even more to sit on stools on the Blackfriars stage.

Whether in the outdoor or indoor playhouses, the stages of Shakespeare's time were different from ours. They were not separated from the audience by the dropping of a curtain between acts and scenes. Therefore the playwrights of the time had to find other ways of signaling to the audience that one scene (to be imagined as occurring in one location at a given time) had ended and the next (to be imagined at perhaps a different location at a later time) had begun. The customary way used by Shakespeare and many of his contemporaries was to have everyone onstage exit at the end of one scene and have one or more different characters enter to begin the next. In a few cases, where characters remain onstage from one scene to another, the dialogue or stage action makes the change of location clear, and the characters are generally to be imagined as having moved from one place to another. For example, in *Romeo and Juliet,* Romeo and his friends remain onstage in Act 1 from scene 4 to scene 5, but they are represented as having moved between scenes from the street that leads to Capulet's house into Capulet's house itself. The new location is signaled in part by the appearance onstage of Capulet's servingmen carrying napkins, something they would not take into the streets. Playwrights had to be quite resourceful in the use of hand properties, like the napkin, or in the use of dialogue to specify where the action was taking place in their plays because, in contrast to most of today's theaters, the playhouses of Shakespeare's time did not use movable scenery to dress the stage and make the setting precise. As another consequence of this difference, however, the playwrights of Shakespeare's time did not have to specify exactly where the action of their plays was set when they did not choose to do so, and much of the action of their plays is tied to no specific place.

Usually Shakespeare's stage is referred to as a "bare stage," to distinguish it from the stages of the past two or three centuries with their elaborate sets. But the stage in Shakespeare's time was not completely bare. Philip Henslowe, owner of the Rose, lists in his inventory of stage properties a rock, three tombs, and two mossy banks. Stage directions in plays of the time also call for such things as thrones (or "states"), banquets (presumably tables with plaster replicas of food on them), and beds and tombs to be pushed onto the stage. Thus the stage often held more than the actors.

The actors did not limit their performing to the stage alone. Occasionally they went beneath the stage, as the Ghost appears to do in the first act of *Hamlet*. From there they could emerge onto the stage through a trapdoor. They could retire behind the hangings across the back of the stage (or the front of the tiring house), as, for example, the actor playing Polonius does when he hides behind the arras. Sometimes the hangings could be drawn back during a performance to "discover" one or more actors behind them. When performance required that an actor appear "above," as when Juliet is imagined to stand at the window of her chamber in the famous and misnamed "balcony scene," then the actor probably climbed the stairs to the gallery over the back of the stage and temporarily shared it with some of the spectators. The stage was also provided with ropes and winches so that actors could descend from, and reascend to, the "heavens."

Perhaps the greatest difference between dramatic performances in Shakespeare's time and ours was that in Shakespeare's England the roles of women were played by boys. (Some of these boys grew up to take male roles in their maturity.) There were no women in the acting companies, only in the audience. It had not always been so in the history of the English stage. There are records of women on English stages in the thirteenth and fourteenth centuries, two hundred years before Shakespeare's plays were performed. After the accession of James I in 1603, the queen of England and her ladies took part in entertainments at court called masques, and with the reopening of the theaters in 1660 at the restoration of Charles II, women again took their place on the public stage.

The chief competitors for the companies of adult actors such as the one to which Shakespeare belonged and for which he wrote were companies of exclusively boy actors. The competition was most intense in the early 1600s. There were then two principal children's companies: the Children of Paul's (the choirboys from St. Paul's Cathedral, whose private playhouse was near the cathedral); and the Children of the Chapel Royal (the choirboys from the monarch's private chapel, who performed at the Blackfriars theater built by Burbage in 1596, which Shakespeare's company had been stopped from using by local residents who objected to crowds). In *Hamlet* Shakespeare writes of "an aerie [nest] of children, little eyases [hawks], that cry out on the top of question and are most tyrannically clapped for 't. These are now the fashion and . . . berattle the common stages [attack the public theaters]." In the long run, the adult actors prevailed. The Children of Paul's dissolved around 1606. By about 1608 the Children of the Chapel Royal had been forced to stop playing at the Blackfriars theater, which was then taken over by the King's company of players, Shakespeare's own troupe.

Acting companies and theaters of Shakespeare's time were organized in different ways. For example, Philip Henslowe owned the Rose and leased it to companies of actors, who paid him from their takings. Henslowe would act as manager of these companies, initially paying playwrights for their plays and buying properties, recovering his outlay from the actors. With the building of the Globe, however, Shakespeare's company managed itself, with the principal actors, Shakespeare among them, having the status of "sharers" and the right to a share in the takings, as well as the responsibility for a part of the expenses. Five of the sharers, including Shakespeare, owned the Globe. As actor, as sharer in an acting company and in ownership of theaters, and as playwright, Shakespeare was about as involved in the theatrical industry as one could imagine. Although Shakespeare and his fellows prospered, their status under the law was conditional upon the protection of powerful patrons. "Common players"—those who did not have patrons or masters—were classed in the language of the law with "vagabonds and sturdy beggars." So the actors had to secure for themselves the official rank of servants of patrons. Among the patrons under whose protection Shakespeare's company worked were the lord chamberlain and, after the accession of King James in 1603, the king himself.

In the early 1990s we seemed on the verge of learning a great deal more about the theaters in which Shakespeare and his contemporaries performed—or, at least, opening up new questions about them. At that time about 70 percent of the Rose had been excavated, as had about 10 percent of the second Globe, the one built in 1614. It was then hoped that more would become available for study. However, excavation was halted at that point, and it is not known if or when it will resume.

The Publication of Shakespeare's Plays

Eighteen of Shakespeare's plays found their way into print during the playwright's lifetime, but there is nothing to suggest that he took any interest in their publication. These eighteen appeared separately in editions called quartos. Their pages were not much larger than the one you are now reading, and these little books were sold unbound for a few pence. The earliest of the quartos that still survive were printed in 1594, the year that both *Titus Andronicus* and a version of the play now called *Henry VI, Part 2* became available. While almost every one of these early quartos displays on its title page the name of the acting company that performed the play, only about half provide the name of the playwright, Shakespeare. The first quarto edition to bear the name Shakespeare on its title page is *Love's Labor's Lost* of 1598. A few of these quartos were popular with the book-buying public of Shakespeare's lifetime; for example, quarto *Richard II* went through five editions between 1597 and 1615. But most of the quartos were far from best sellers; *Love's Labor's Lost* (1598), for instance, was not reprinted in quarto until 1631. After Shakespeare's death, two more of his plays appeared in quarto format: *Othello* in 1622 and *The Two Noble Kinsmen,* coauthored with John Fletcher, in 1634.

In 1623, seven years after Shakespeare's death, *Mr. William Shakespeares Comedies, Histories, & Tragedies* was published. This printing offered readers in a single book thirty-six of the thirty-eight plays now thought to have been written by Shakespeare, including eighteen that had never been printed before. And it offered them in a style that was then reserved for serious literature and scholarship. The plays were arranged in double columns on pages nearly a foot high. This large page size is called "folio," as opposed to the smaller "quarto," and the 1623 volume is usually called the Shakespeare First Folio. It is reputed to have sold for the lordly price of a pound. (One copy at the Folger Library is marked fifteen shillings—that is, three-quarters of a pound.)

In a preface to the First Folio entitled "To the great Variety of Readers," two of Shakespeare's former fellow actors in the King's Men, John Heminge and Henry Condell, wrote that they themselves had collected their dead companion's plays. They suggested that they had seen his own papers: "we have scarce received from him a blot in his papers." The title page of the Folio declared that the plays within it had been printed "according to the True Original Copies." Comparing the Folio to the quartos, Heminge and Condell disparaged the quartos, advising their readers that "before you were abused with divers stolen and surreptitious copies, maimed, and deformed by the frauds and stealths of injurious impostors." Many Shakespeareans of the eighteenth and nineteenth centuries believed Heminge and Condell and regarded the Folio plays as superior to anything in the quartos.

Once we begin to examine the Folio plays in detail, it becomes less easy to take at face value the word of Heminge and Condell about the superiority of the Folio texts. For example, of the first nine plays in the Folio (one-quarter of the entire collection), four were essentially reprinted from earlier quarto printings that Heminge and Condell had disparaged; and four have now been identified as printed from copies written in the hand of a professional scribe of the 1620s named Ralph Crane; the ninth, *The Comedy of Errors,* was apparently also printed from a manuscript, but one whose origin cannot be readily identified. Evidently, then, eight of the first nine plays in the First Folio were not printed, in spite of what the Folio title page announces, "according to the True Original Copies," or Shakespeare's own papers, and the source of the ninth is unknown. Since today's editors have been forced to treat Heminge and Condell's pronouncements with skepticism, they must choose whether to base their own editions upon quartos or the Folio on grounds other than Heminge and Condell's story of where the quarto and Folio versions originated.

Editors have often fashioned their own narratives to explain what lies behind the quartos and Folio. They have said that Heminge and Condell meant to criticize only a few of the early quartos, the ones that offer much shorter and sometimes quite different, often garbled, versions of plays. Among the examples of these are the 1600 quarto of *Henry V* (the Folio offers a much fuller version) or the 1603 *Ham-*

let quarto (in 1604 a different, much longer form of the play got into print as a quarto). Early-twentieth-century editors speculated that these questionable texts were produced when someone in the audience took notes from the plays' dialogue during performances and then employed "hack poets" to fill out the notes. The poor results were then sold to a publisher and presented in print as Shakespeare's plays. More recently this story has given way to another in which the shorter versions are said to be re-creations from memory of Shakespeare's plays by actors who wanted to stage them in the provinces but lacked manuscript copies. Most of the quartos offer much better texts than these so-called bad quartos. Indeed, in most of the quartos we find texts that are at least equal to or better than what is printed in the Folio. Many Shakespeare enthusiasts persuaded themselves that most of the quartos were set into type directly from Shakespeare's own papers, although there is nothing on which to base this conclusion except the desire for it to be true. Thus speculation continues about how the Shakespeare plays got to be printed. All that we have are the printed texts.

The book collector who was most successful in bringing together copies of the quartos and the First Folio was Henry Clay Folger, founder of the Folger Shakespeare Library in Washington, D.C. While it is estimated that there survive around the world only about 230 copies of the First Folio, Mr. Folger was able to acquire more than seventy-five copies, as well as a large number of fragments, for the library that bears his name. He also amassed a substantial number of quartos. For example, only fourteen copies of the First Quarto of *Love's Labor's Lost* are known to exist, and three are at the Folger Shakespeare Library. As a consequence of Mr. Folger's labors, scholars visiting the

Folger Library have been able to learn a great deal about sixteenth- and seventeenth-century printing and, particularly, about the printing of Shakespeare's plays. And Mr. Folger did not stop at the First Folio, but collected many copies of later editions of Shakespeare, beginning with the Second Folio (1632), the Third (1663–64), and the Fourth (1685). Each of these later folios was based on its immediate predecessor and was edited anonymously. The first editor of Shakespeare whose name we know was Nicholas Rowe, whose first edition came out in 1709. Mr. Folger collected this edition and many, many more by Rowe's successors.

An Introduction to This Text

The play we call *Troilus and Cressida* was printed in two somewhat different versions in the first quarter of the seventeenth century:

(1) In 1609 appeared *The Historie of Troylus and Cresseida,* a quarto (Q) that lacks a few short passages of the text with which most modern readers are familiar. Some of these passages are among the most difficult to read in the play, and may have been cut for that reason.

(2) The second version to see print is found in what we now call the First Folio of Shakespeare's plays, published in 1623 (F). Titled simply *The Tragedie of Troylus and Cressida,* F supplies the passages not in Q but lacks, sometimes apparently through error, several lines or pairs of lines that Q preserves. These two versions also differ from each other in their readings in about five hundred places. In a great many of these cases, the difference is limited to the choice of a single

THE

Famous Historie of

Troylus *and* Cresseid.

Excellently expressing the beginning of their loues, with the conceited wooing of *Pandarus* Prince of *Licia*.

Written by William Shakespeare.

LONDON
Imprinted by *G. Eld* for *R. Bonian* and *H. Walley*, and are to be sold at the spred Eagle in Paules Church-yeard, ouer against the great North doore.
1609.

Title page of a 1609 Quarto of *Troilus and Cressida*, copy STC22332. (From the Folger Library collection.)

THE TRAGEDIE OF
Troylus and Cresſida.

Actus Primus. *Scœna Prima.*

Enter Pandarus and Troylus.

Troylus.

CAll here my Varlet, Ile vnarme againe.
Why ſhould I warre without the wals of Troy
That finde ſuch cruell battell here within?
Each Troian that is maſter of his heart,
Let him to field, *Troylus* alas hath none.

Pan. Will this geere nere be mended?

Troy. The Greeks are ſtrong, & skilful to their ſtrength,
Fierce to their skill, and to their fierceneſſe Valiant;
But I am weaker then a womans teare;
Tamer then ſleepe, fonder then ignorance;
Leſſe valiant then the Virgin in the night,
And skilleſſe as vnpractis'd Infancie.

Pan. Well, I haue told you enough of this: For my part, Ile not meddle nor make no farther. Hee that will haue a Cake out of the Wheate, muſt needes tarry the grinding.

Troy. Haue I not tarried?

Pan. I the grinding; but you muſt tarry the bolting.

Troy. Haue I not tarried?

Pan. I the boulting; but you muſt tarry the leau'ing.

Troy. Still haue I tarried.

Pan. I, to the leauening: but heeres yet in the word hereafter, the Kneading, the making of the Cake, the heating of the Ouen, and the Baking; nay, you muſt ſtay the cooling too, or you may chance to burne your lips.

Troy. Patience her ſelfe, what Goddeſſe ere ſhe be,
Doth leſſer blench at ſufferance, then I doe:
At *Priams* Royall Table doe I ſit;
And when faire *Creſſid* comes into my thoughts,
So (Traitor) then ſhe comes, when ſhe is thence.

Pan. Well:
She look'd yeſternight fairer, then euer I ſaw her looke,
Or any woman elſe.

Troy. I was about to tell thee, when my heart,
As wedged with a ſigh, would riue in twaine,
Leaſt *Hector*, or my Father ſhould perceiue me:
I haue (as when the Sunne doth light a-ſcorne)
Buried this ſigh, in wrinkle of a ſmile:
But ſorrow, that is couch'd in ſeeming gladneſſe,
Is like that mirth, Fate turnes to ſudden ſadneſſe.

Pan. And her haire were not ſomewhat darker then *Helens*, well go too, there were no more compariſon betweene the Women. But for my part ſhe is my Kinſwoman, I would not (as they tearme it) praiſe it, but I wold ſome-body had heard her talke yeſterday as I did: I will not diſpraiſe your ſiſter *Caſſandra's* wit, but——

Troy. Oh *Pandarus*! I tell thee *Pandarus*;
When I doe tell thee, there my hopes lye drown'd:
Reply not in how many Fadomes deepe
They lye indrench'd. I tell thee, I am mad
In *Creſſids* loue. Thou anſwer'ſt ſhe is Faire,
Powr'ſt in the open Vlcer of my heart,
Her Eyes, her Haire, her Checke, her Gate, her Voice,
Handleſt in thy diſcourſe. O that her Hand
(In whoſe compariſon, all whites are Inke)
Writing their owne reproach; to whoſe ſoft ſeizure,
The Cignets Downe is harſh, and ſpirit of Senſe
Hard as the palme of Plough-man. This thou tel'ſt me;
As true thou tel'ſt me, when I ſay I loue her:
But ſaying thus, inſtead of Oyle and Balme,
Thou lai'ſt in euery gaſh that loue hath giuen me,
The Knife that made it.

Pan. I ſpeake no more then truth.

Troy. Thou do'ſt not ſpeake ſo much.

Pan. Faith, Ile not meddle in't: Let her be as ſhee is, if ſhe be faire, 'tis the better for her: and ſhe be not, ſhe ha's the mends in her owne hands.

Troy. Good *Pandarus*: How now *Pandarus*?

Pan. I haue had my Labour for my trauell, ill thought on of her, and ill thought on of you: Gone betweene and betweene, but ſmall thankes for my labour.

Troy. What art thou angry *Pandarus*? what with me?

Pan. Becauſe ſhe's Kinne to me, therefore ſhee's not ſo faire as *Helen*, and ſhe were not kin to me, ſhe would be as faire on Friday, as *Helen* is on Sunday. But what care I? I care not and ſhe were a Black-a-Moore, 'tis all one to me.

Troy. Say I ſhe is not faire?

Troy. I doe not care whether you doe or no. Shee's a Foole to ſtay behinde her Father: Let her to the Greeks, and ſo Ile tell her the next time I ſee her: for my part, Ile meddle nor make no more i'th'matter.

Troy. *Pandarus*! *Pan.* Not I.

Troy. Sweete *Pandarus*.

Pan. Pray you ſpeake no more to me, I will leaue all as I found it, and there an end. *Exit Pand.*

Sound Alarum.

Tro. Peace you vngracious Clamors, peace rude ſounds,
Fooles on both ſides, *Helen* muſt needs be faire,
When with your bloud you daily paint her thus.
I cannot fight vpon this Argument:

From the 1623 First Folio.
(Copy 75 in the Folger Library collection.)

word. Variation between Q and F, while a source of ongoing discussion among textual scholars and editors, makes very little difference to most readers.

Publication of both Q and F was unusually complicated in comparison to that of most of Shakespeare's plays. Q survives in two different states, each with its own title page, the second state alone containing the prefatory "A neuer writer, to an euer reader. Newes," printed in this edition in modern spelling on pages 3–5. The title page of the first state describes the play as a "Historie" published "*As it was acted by the Kings Maiesties* seruants at the Globe." The title page of the second state removes reference to the King's company of players and their Globe playhouse and describes the play as "The Famous Historie of Troylus *and* Cresseid. *Excellently expressing the beginning* of their loues, with the conceited wooing of *Pandarus* Prince of *Licia.*" Removal of reference to players and playhouse from the second state's title page is consistent with the assertions of the second state's "A neuer writer" that the play was "neuer stal'd with the Stage, neuer clapper-clawd with the palmes of the vulger." Scholars have differed widely in their interpretations of the contradiction between the first and second states as to whether *Troilus and Cressida* was ever staged.

Publication of the F version of the play was also complicated. Indeed, the play almost did not become part of the First Folio. A few copies of the book do not contain it, and it was never listed in the Folio's "Catalogue," or table of contents. There were two different attempts to include *Troilus and Cressida,* the second a great deal more successful than the first. Each attempt located the play in a different place in the book, and for each attempt typesetters employed a different kind of printer's copy. Originally, the play was to appear as the fourth of the tragedies, following *Coriolanus, Titus Andronicus,* and *Romeo and Juliet.* This intention is clear from the copies of the First Folio that contain a leaf that prints on one side the last page of *Romeo and Juliet,* numbered page "77," and on the other side the first page of *Troilus and Cressida,* unnumbered (as are the first pages of all the Folio's plays). On this leaf, the last page of *Romeo and Juliet* is crossed off in pen and ink to indicate that the leaf is to be canceled, rather than bound up with a finished book—an indication that was not always noticed or observed, as the survival of copies of the leaf demonstrates. Also printed at the same time was the leaf containing the second and third pages of F *Troilus,* as is indicated by their being numbered pages "79" and "80." These are the only pages of the F version to contain page numbers, although all the rest of the Folio plays are printed on pages that are numbered throughout (except for their first pages). The text of *Troilus and Cressida* found on these three pages is almost identical to that found in Q, except for some printer's errors and the correction of a few of the most obvious errors in Q, such as the omission of an entrance for Pandarus at 1.2.40 SD.

Before any more of *Troilus* could be printed, there was a change of plan and a relocation of the play within the book. Now *Troilus and Cressida* was placed between *Henry VIII,* the last of the history plays that constitute the middle section of the book, and *Coriolanus,* the first play in the concluding tragedies section. This is where *Troilus and Cressida* appears in the great majority of the extant copies of the First Folio. In these copies, in place of the canceled leaf on which *Troilus*'s first page was initially printed, there is a leaf that contains on one side "The Prologue" (which had not been printed in the first attempt) and on the other side the first page of the play. This second printing of this page was evidently set into type directly from its first printing, because the second printing contains errors introduced during the first. Following this reset first page come pages "79" and "80"; their appearance indicates that they were saved from the interrupted initial attempt to print the play. The rest of *Troilus and Cressida* then follows, printed on twenty-five unnumbered pages.

These twenty-five pages were evidently set from a different kind of printer's copy than that used in the first attempt. During that attempt, the typesetter seems to have worked simply to reproduce word for word the text of the play that appears in Q; if there were any pen-and-ink changes made to the typesetter's copy of Q, they were very few, and they could have been made without anyone's consulting a manuscript source. But the twenty-five pages printed in the second attempt contain so many more departures from and additions to the Q text that the printer must have had recourse to a manuscript version of the play in addition to Q. It would have been from this manuscript that the printer would also have acquired the Prologue, which is unique to F.

Precisely how this manuscript was used in the printing house has been the subject of debate. Some, including the present editors, favor the view that the last twenty-five pages of F were printed directly from a copy of Q that had been annotated with reference to a manuscript, perhaps with some of the additional short passages having been copied onto slips of paper that were interleaved among the pages of the Q copy. This view is based not only on the many errors shared by Q and F, but also on the reappearance of typographical peculiarities from Q in F. For example, of the fifty-five occurrences of the word *Troy* in the play's dialogue, it is printed in roman type forty-seven times in the same places in both Q and F; in the five places it is printed in italic in Q, it is also in italic in F; and there are only three places where the word is printed in roman in Q but in italic in F. It would seem, then, that F was set directly from printed copy, just as were a number of other plays—*A Midsummer Night's Dream, The Merchant of Venice,* and *Henry IV, Part 1,* to name only three. Despite such evidence, some scholars have raised an objection to this view. Citing the appearance of errors in F in places where Q is self-evidently correct, they argue that it is impossible that an annotator of Q would have deliberately replaced these Q readings with F's errors. Consider the following useful example; the quotation is from Q, with the variants from F added in pointed brackets:

> *Vlis.* Shee will sing any man at first sight.
> *Ther.* And any man may sing ⟨finde⟩ her, if hee can take her Cliff ⟨life⟩, she's noted.
>
> (5.2.11–14)

Admittedly, no intelligent annotator would have substituted the bracketed F readings for Q's words. However, it is entirely possible that the errors in F originate with the typesetter, not the annotator: study of typesetters' performance in reprinting quartos of other plays for the Folio shows that they were capable of straying from their perfectly clear printed copy in ways not unlike what we find in the passage quoted. Thus there is no need to qualify or abandon the inference that F was set from an annotated and perhaps interleaved copy of Q.

Usually, twentieth-century editors of Shakespeare determined their preferences regarding versions of a play according to their theories about the origins of the early printed texts. In the case of *Troilus and Cressida,* however, there emerged no consensus among editors about the kinds of manuscript lying behind Q or behind the annotations incorporated into the printing of F. For much of the twentieth century, it was argued that the manuscript used to annotate Q copy for F was Shakespeare's own draft of the play; some repetitions in F were interpreted as arising from his incompletely deleted first shots that had been replaced by second thoughts (see the Textual Notes at 4.5.110 and 5.3.123). In contrast, Q was thought to be based on a scribal transcript that preserved some of Shakespeare's revisions to the earlier version found in F. There followed an attempt to turn this account upside down and to establish that Q, rather than F, represented Shakespeare's own draft and that the manuscript used to annotate Q copy for F was Shakespeare's revision of his play. More recently, another editor has suggested that Q may derive from a transcript of the play, perhaps by Shakespeare, that contains some of his revisions, further speculating that F may derive from a different manuscript of Shakespeare's that contains other revisions.

While scholarly opinions about the manuscript sources of Q and F are very much at odds, we can be confident that the manuscript used to annotate Q copy for F came from the playhouse. Good evidence for this conclusion is the number of stage directions calling for sounds (sound calls) that are added to the F text. These can be found, for example, at 1.3.0, 1.3.216, 3.1.0, 3.3.0, 4.4.149, and 5.4.0. In several non-Shakespearean plays that survive in playhouse manuscripts, sound calls are one kind of stage direction that we find repeatedly added in the margin in the hands of theatrical personnel. Unfortunately, identification of the theatrical provenance of the manuscript used to annotate the copy of Q employed by the F printers does nothing to determine whether Q or F is the better text on which to base an edition. Among surviving theatrical manuscripts, we find both authorial and scribal copies of widely varying quality.

Our decision to select Q as the basis for this edition is based on our evaluation of the quality of the readings in the two versions, rather than on any of the conflicting accounts of the origins of Q and F. There are problems with both texts. Q prints many errors, a number of them apparently the result of careless copying or typesetting. One particularly bad passage occurs in 5.1.59–62, where Q mistakenly prints "faced" (corrected in F to "forced"), "her's" (corrected in F to "hee is"), "day" (corrected in F to "Dogge"), and "Moyle" (corrected in F to "Mule"). Another batch of Q errors appear to be examples of what is called *contextual variation.* This error occurs when the eye and attention of a scribe or compositor strays from the word to be copied toward another word in the immediate context, and the scribe or compositor erroneously copies or sets the other word. The transcript or the printed version then varies from the original under the influence of context. One striking example of such an error occurs at 5.1.15, where in Q Thersites orders Patroclus to "be silent, box," and F corrects Q's nonsensical "box" to the intelligible "boy." Q's choice of word occurs two lines above in the phrase "Surgeons box," and it is to be suspected that some agent in the transmission of Q from Shakespeare into print, whether a scribe or a compositor, allowed his eye to wander from "boy" to "box," and repeated "box" in error. Although there is no good evidence that deliberate changes were introduced into the text that Q preserves, Q shows so many careless errors that we, as editors, would prefer not to have to rely on Q.

But we feel that we must; for although F displays fewer careless errors than Q, F may also contain what can be interpreted as calculated but unnecessary attempts to improve and clarify the play's language. For example, in the following exchange F's intervention seems primarily to endow Thersites' speech with a touch of formality:

ACHILLES Why, but he is not in this tune, is he?
THERSITES No, but ⟨he's⟩ out of tune thus.
(3.3.314–15)

As another example, F's addition to 2.3.66–68 may be erroneous in its redundancy and ambiguity: "Agamemnon is a fool to offer to command Achilles, Achilles is a fool to be commanded ⟨of *Agamemnon,*⟩ Thersites is a fool to serve such a fool. . . ." It is obvious from the first clause who Achilles' would-be commander is. Furthermore, by introducing "of Agamemnon" into the second clause, F makes the reference "such a fool" in the third clause harder to read than it was in Q. In F, but not in Q, the phrase could refer either to Achilles, whom Thersites does serve and to whom the phrase clearly refers in Q, or to Agamemnon. However, it is to be acknowledged that this suspicion of F's reading holds the informal conversation of the dialogue accountable to strict stylistic and grammatical standards.

F's most striking error occurs at 5.1.21–24. In Q, Thersites concludes the curse he calls down on Patroclus of "the rotten diseases of the south" by naming "could palsies, rawe eies, durt rotten liuers, whissing lungs, bladders full of impostume, sciaticas, lime-kills ith' palme, incurable bone-ach, and the riueled fee simple of the tetter . . ."; F deletes most of the list, reducing it to "palsies, and the like." Clearly, some agent in the transmission of F had no qualms about discarding Shakespeare's language. It is therefore just possible that the rest of F's verbal substitutions and additions—those that are not corrections of obvious

Q errors—also proceed from such an agent's attempt to improve, sophisticate, or otherwise change Shakespeare. There is nothing so remarkable about the F-only readings that we feel compelled to invoke Shakespeare as the only conceivable source of them. The possibility that F is a sophisticated version not only may undercut many editors' confidence that F preserves Shakespeare's own revisions but also leads us, as editors, to prefer Q, which does not arouse the same kind of suspicions about wrong-headed attempts to enhance the text.

This edition therefore offers its readers the Q version of *Troilus and Cressida* and is based directly upon that printing.* But our text offers an *edition* of Q, because it prints such F readings and such later editorial emendations as are, in the editors' judgments, necessary to repair what may be errors and deficiencies in Q. At the same time, this edition provides readers access to the F version, in spite of our suspicions of the F text, by offering the lines and part-lines and many of the words that are to be found only in F, marking them as coming from F (see below). We want to allow readers, to the full extent possible within the bounds of a single edition, to arrive at their own judgments about the relative quality of Q and F.

Occasionally, too, F readings are *substituted* in our text for Q words. This substitution occurs under the following circumstances:

(1) Whenever a word in Q is unintelligible (i.e., is not a word) or is incorrect according to the standards of that time for acceptable grammar, rhetoric, idiom, or usage, and F provides an intelligible and acceptable

*We have also consulted the computerized texts of the First Quarto and the First Folio provided by the Text Archive of the Oxford University Computing Centre, to which we are grateful.

word (recognizing that our understanding of what was acceptable in Shakespeare's time is to some extent inevitably based on reading others' editions of *Troilus and Cressida,* but also drawing on reading of much other writing from the period).

(2) Whenever Q can reasonably be suspected to have committed its characteristic error of contextual variation, even though the Q reading is intelligible. For example, at 4.5.70, Q reads "ticklish reader," a perfectly intelligible reading, while F reads "tickling reader," which is equally acceptable. However, we choose to read with F because in the next line both texts read "sluttish," a word whose ending may well have influenced the Q reading in the line above.

In order to enable its readers to tell the difference between the Q and F versions, the present edition uses a variety of signals:

(1) All the words in this edition that are printed only in the F version but not in Q appear in pointed brackets (⟨⟩).

(2) All lines that are found only in Q and not in F are printed in square brackets ([ ]).

(3) Sometimes neither Q nor F seems to offer a satisfactory reading, and it is necessary to print a word different from what is offered by either. Such words (called "emendations" by editors) are printed within superior half-brackets (⌜ ⌝). We employ these brackets because we want our readers to be immediately aware when we have intervened. (Only when we correct an obvious typographical error in Q or F does the change not get marked.) Whenever we change the wording of Q or F, or alter their punctuation so that meaning changes, we list the change in the textual notes at the back of the book, even if all we have done is fix an obvious error. By observing these signals and by referring to the textual notes printed after the play, a reader can use this edition

to read the play as it was printed in Q, or as it was printed in F, or as it has been presented in the modern editorial tradition that usually has combined Q and F.

For the convenience of the reader, we have modernized the punctuation and the spelling of Q and F. Sometimes we go so far as to modernize certain old forms of words; for example, usually when *a* means *he,* we change it to *he;* we change *mo* to *more,* and *ye* to *you.* But it is not our practice in editing any of the plays to modernize words that sound distinctly different from modern forms. For example, when the early printed texts read *sith* or *apricocks* or *porpentine,* we have not modernized to *since, apricots, porcupine.* When the forms *an, and,* or *and if* appear instead of the modern form *if,* we have reduced *and* to *an* but have not changed any of these forms to their modern equivalent, *if.* We also modernize and, where necessary, correct passages in foreign languages, unless an error in the early printed text can be reasonably explained as a joke.

We regularize spellings of a number of the proper names, as is the usual practice in editions of the play. For example, in Q we find the following spellings of character names: Deiphobus and Diephobus, Helen and Hellen, Calchas and Calcas, Cressida and Cresseida. In this edition, we use only Deiphobus, Helen, Calchas, and Cressida. We also expand the often severely abbreviated forms of names used as speech headings in early printed texts into the full names of the characters. In addition, we regularize the speakers' names in speech headings, using only a single designation for each character, even though the early printed texts sometimes use a variety of designations. Variations in the speech headings of the early printed texts are recorded in the textual notes.

This edition differs from many earlier ones in its efforts to aid the reader in imagining the play as a performance rather than as a series of actual events. Thus stage directions are written with reference to the stage. For example, when, near the end of the play, Pandarus approaches Troilus with, according to the dialogue, "a letter from yond poor girl" Cressida, Pandarus would not bring onto the stage an actual letter. Instead, he would carry only a stage-prop piece of paper, which Troilus then acts as if he were reading and finally tears up. Thus we print *"Enter Pandarus, with a paper,"* not "a letter," thereby choosing the direction that refers more to the staging than to the story.

Whenever it is reasonably certain, in our view, that a speech is accompanied by a particular action, we provide a stage direction describing the action, setting the added direction in brackets to signal that it is not found in Q or F. (Exceptions to this rule occur when the action is so obvious that to add a stage direction would insult the reader.) Stage directions for the entrance of a character in mid-scene are, with rare exceptions, placed so that they immediately precede the character's participation in the scene, even though these entrances may appear somewhat earlier in the early printed texts. Whenever we move a stage direction, we record this change in the textual notes. Latin stage directions (e.g., *Exeunt*) are translated into English (e.g., *They exit*).

In the present edition, as well, we mark with a dash any change of address within a speech, unless a stage direction intervenes. When the **-ed** ending of a word is to be pronounced, we mark it with an accent. Like editors for the past two centuries, we print metrically linked lines in the following way:

AENEAS
In all swift haste.
TROILUS Come, go we then together.
(1.1.119–20)

However, when there are a number of short verse-lines that can be linked in more than one way, we do not, with rare exceptions, indent any of them.

The Explanatory Notes

The notes that appear on the pages facing the text are designed to provide readers with the help that they may need to enjoy the play. Whenever the meaning of a word in the text is not readily accessible in a good contemporary dictionary, we offer the meaning in a note. Sometimes we provide a note even when the relevant meaning is to be found in the dictionary but when the word has acquired since Shakespeare's time other potentially confusing meanings. In our notes, we try to offer modern synonyms for Shakespeare's words. We also try to indicate to the reader the connection between the word in the play and the modern synonym. For example, Shakespeare sometimes uses the word *head* to mean *source,* but, for modern readers, there may be no connection evident between these two words. We provide the connection by explaining Shakespeare's usage as follows: "**head:** fountainhead, source." On some occasions, a whole phrase or clause needs explanation. Then, if space allows, we rephrase in our own words the difficult passage, and add at the end synonyms for individual words in the passage. When scholars have been unable to determine the meaning of a word or phrase, we acknowledge the uncertainty. Whenever we provide a passage from the Bible to illuminate the text of the play, we use the Geneva Bible of 1560 (with spelling modernized).

However, when there are a number of short verse-lines that can be linked in more than one way, we do not, with rare exceptions, indent any of them.

The Explanatory Notes

The notes that appear on the pages facing the text are designed to provide readers with the help that they may need to enjoy the play. Whenever the meaning of a word in the text is not readily accessible in a good contemporary dictionary, we offer the meaning in a note. Sometimes we provide a note even when the relevant meaning is to be found in the dictionary but when the word has acquired since Shakespeare's time other potentially confusing meanings. In our notes, we try to offer modern synonyms for Shakespeare's words. We also try to indicate to the reader the connection between the word in the play and the modern synonym. For example, Shakespeare sometimes uses the word *head* to mean "source," but, for modern readers, there may be no connection evident between these two words. We provide the connection by explaining Shakespeare's usage as follows: "head: fountainhead, source." On some occasions, a whole phrase or clause needs explanation. Then we rephrase in our own words the difficult passage, and add at the end synonyms for individual words in the passage. When scholars have been unable to determine the meaning of a word or phrase, we acknowledge the uncertainty. Biblical quotations are from the Geneva Bible of 1560 (with spelling modernized).

TROILUS AND CRESSIDA

1. **A never writer:** i.e., one who **never** writes (perhaps the publisher of the Quarto edition) This preface appears in some copies of the play's first printing in quarto in 1609. See "An Introduction to This Text," page li.

2. **new:** i.e., newly printed (The first record of the play's existence dates from 1603, the first printing from 1609.)

2–3. **staled with the stage:** rendered stale or uninteresting through performance

3–4. **clapperclawed . . . vulgar:** applauded by a playhouse audience **clapperclawed:** thrashed, beaten (with wordplay on "to clap, applaud") **the vulgar:** ordinary persons, especially the ignorant or uneducated

4. **passing:** i.e., surpassingly, extremely, very; **the palm comical:** i.e., comic excellence (**The palm** is, literally, a palm-tree branch or leaf carried as a sign of triumph. It thus serves emblematically for excellence or supreme honor.)

5. **your:** i.e., someone's

6. **vainly:** without success; **vain:** idle

7. **changed:** i.e., exchanged; **commodities:** useful products

7–8. **of plays for pleas:** i.e., **names of plays** exchanged for legal **pleas** (lawsuits or claims)

8. **censors:** those who criticize or judge adversely

9. **style them:** i.e., call **plays; vanities:** i.e., trifles

10. **grace:** charm; **gravities:** grave or serious subjects

12. **for:** i.e., as; **of:** i.e., on

(continued)

[*A never writer to an ever reader: news.*

Eternal reader, you have here a new play, never staled with the stage, never clapperclawed with the palms of the vulgar, and yet passing full of the palm comical, for it is a birth of your brain that never undertook anything comical vainly. And were but the vain names of comedies changed for the titles of commodities, or of plays for pleas, you should see all those grand censors, that now style them such vanities, flock to them for the main grace of their gravities, especially this author's comedies, that are so framed to the life that they serve for the most common commentaries of all the actions of our lives, showing such a dexterity and power of wit that the most displeased with plays are pleased with his comedies. And all such dull and heavy-witted worldlings as were never capable of the wit of a comedy, coming by report of them to his representations, have found that wit there that they never found in themselves and have parted better witted than they came, feeling an edge of wit set upon them more than ever they dreamed they had brain to grind it on. So much and such savored salt of wit is in his comedies that they seem, for their height of pleasure, to be born in that sea that brought forth Venus. Amongst all there is none more witty than this; and had I time, I would comment upon it, though I know it needs not, for so much as will make you think your testern well bestowed, but for so much worth as even poor I know to be stuffed in it. It deserves such a labor as well as the best comedy in Terence or Plautus. And believe this, that when he is gone and his comedies out of sale, you will scramble for them and set up a new English

15–16. **heavy-witted worldlings:** i.e., worldly-minded persons of slow or dull wits

16. **capable of:** able to understand

17. **by . . . them:** i.e., through their reputations; **his representations:** performances of his plays

18. **that wit there:** wordplay on **wit** as (1) comedy in the play and (2) intelligence in the viewer

19. **parted:** gone away, departed

20–21. **feeling . . . grind it on:** wordplay on a person's **wit** being sharp (with **an edge**) or dull depending on its being ground, like an ax or knife, on a whetstone (here, the **brain**)

22. **savored salt of wit:** wordplay on **salt** as pungency of expression (which is **savored** or enjoyed) and as a seasoning (which has savor or tastiness)

24. **sea . . . Venus:** a reference to the Greek **Venus** or Aphrodite, whose name derives from a Greek word meaning "foam-born"; **Amongst all:** i.e., among **all** of **his comedies**

26–29. **for so . . . stuffed in it:** i.e., not as an indication that your money is well spent on it, but because even I know its great value **testern:** a slang term for a sixpence (a small piece of money)

30. **Terence, Plautus:** Roman comic dramatists whose surviving works, taught in Latin in schools, set the standard for comedy

31. **out of sale:** i.e., sold out

33. **Inquisition:** search, inquiry (but with wordplay on the Spanish **Inquisition,** a particularly notorious Roman Catholic tribunal for the suppression of heresy)

34. **your pleasure's loss, and judgment's:** i.e., the **loss** of pleasure and good discretion

(continued)

Inquisition. Take this for a warning, and at the peril of your pleasure's loss, and judgment's, refuse not nor like this the less for not being sullied with the smoky breath of the multitude, but thank fortune for the scape it hath made amongst you, since by the grand possessors' wills I believe you should have prayed for them rather than been prayed. And so I leave all such to be prayed for, for the states of their wits' healths, that will not praise it. *Vale.*]

35. **smoky:** steaming, reeking

36. **scape:** i.e., escape

37–38. **the grand possessors' wills:** i.e., the determination of the **grand** persons who own the playtext

38. **you . . . them:** i.e., you would have futilely had to request their comedies be published

39. **been prayed:** i.e., been requested to buy this comedy now published

41. **Vale:** farewell, goodbye (Latin)

A neuer writer, to an euer reader. Newes.

Ternall reader, you haue heere a new play, neuer stal'd with the Stage, neuer clapper-clawd with the palmes of the vulger, and yet passing full of the palme comicall; for it is a birth of your braine, that neuer under-tooke any thing commicall, vainely: And were but the vaine names of commedies changde for the titles of Commodities, or of Playes for Pleas; you should see all those grand censors, that now stile them such vanities, flock to them for the maine grace of their grauities: especially this authors Commedies, that are so fram'd to the life, that they serue for the most common Commentaries, of all the actions of our liues. shewing such a dexteritie, and power of witte, that the most displeased with Playes, are pleasd with his Commedies. And all such dull and heauy-witted worldlings, as were neuer capable of the witte of a Commedie, comming by report of them to his representations, haue found that witte there, that they neuer found in them selues, and haue parted better wittied then they came: feeling an edge of witte set vpon them, more then euer they dreamd they had braine to grinde it on. So much and such sauored salt of witte is in his Commedies, that they seeme (for their height of pleasure) to be borne in that sea that brought forth Venus. *Amongst all there is none more witty then this: And had I time I would comment vpon it, though I know it needs not, (for so*

¶ 2 *much*

From a 1609 Quarto of *Troilus and Cressida,* copy STC22332.
(From the Folger Library Collection.)

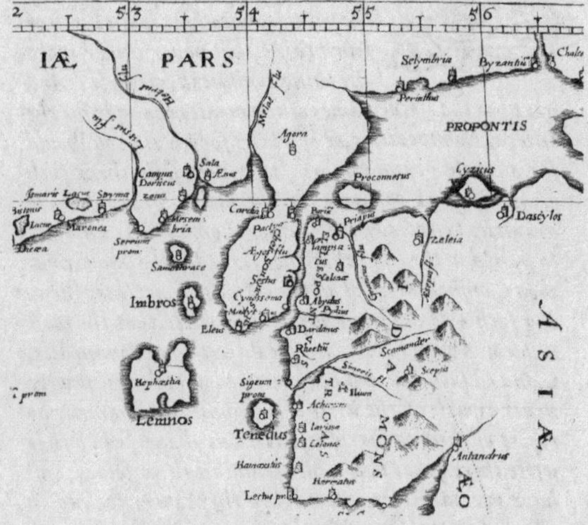

A map of the Aegean Sea, showing Tenedos and Ilium (Troy).
From Thucydides,
Eight bookes of the Peloponnesian warre . . . (1629).

Characters in the Play

(Almost all these characters are adapted from earlier literature. For background on them, see Appendix on the Characters in the Play, page 297.)

PROLOGUE

The Trojans

PRIAM, king of Troy

CASSANDRA, Priam's daughter, a soothsayer

TROILUS, HECTOR, PARIS, HELENUS, DEIPHOBUS, BASTARD — *Priam's sons*

ANDROMACHE, Hector's wife

AENEAS, ANTENOR — *Trojan leaders*

TROILUS'S BOY
TROILUS'S MAN
PARIS'S SERVINGMAN

CRESSIDA
CALCHAS, her father
PANDARUS, her uncle
ALEXANDER, her servant

The Greeks

AGAMEMNON, the general	Greek leaders
NESTOR	
ULYSSES	
DIOMEDES	
MENELAUS, brother to Agamemnon	
AJAX	
ACHILLES	

HELEN, Menelaus's wife and queen
PATROCLUS, Achilles' favorite companion
MYRMIDONS, Achilles' soldiers
THERSITES, cynical critic

DIOMEDES' SERVINGMAN

Other Trojans and Greeks, Common Soldiers of Troy and Greece, Trumpeters, Attendants, Torchbearers.

TROILUS AND CRESSIDA

ACT 1

2. **orgulous:** haughty, proud; **high:** aristocratic, noble; **chafed:** excited, heated

4. **Fraught:** laden, filled; **ministers:** agents (i.e., soldiers)

6. **crownets:** i.e., coronets

7. **Phrygia:** poetic synonym for "Troy"

8. **immures:** i.e., walls

9. **ravished:** carried off by force

10. **wanton:** lascivious; also, perhaps, rebellious

11. **Tenedos:** island near Troy in the Aegean Sea, used by the Greeks as a naval station during the Trojan War (See map, page 8.)

12. **deep-drawing barks:** i.e., heavily laden ships (Ships that draw deeply lie low in the water.)

13. **fraughtage:** freight, cargo; **Dardan:** a poetic synonym for "Trojan"

15. **brave:** splendid (See picture, page 216.)

15–19. **Priam's . . . Troy:** i.e., the walls and locked gates of **Troy** protect Troy's citizens (See longer note, page 267.)

20. **tickling:** exciting; **skittish:** excessively lively

21. **On one . . . side:** i.e., on both sides

22. **Sets . . . hazard:** i.e., puts everything at risk

23–24. **A prologue . . . voice:** i.e., a probable allusion to Ben Jonson's play *Poetaster* (1601), the **prologue** of which is **armed in** "a well erected **Confidence**" designed to counter attacks on the author by detractors (See longer note, page 267.)

24. **suited:** costumed, dressed

25. **like:** the same; **argument:** theme, subject

27. **vaunt, firstlings:** Both words mean, generally, the beginning or first part. (A *firstling* is literally a firstborn.)

(continued)

⌜*Enter the Prologue in armor.*⌝

⟨PROLOGUE

In Troy there lies the scene. From isles of Greece
The princes orgulous, their high blood chafed,
Have to the port of Athens sent their ships
Fraught with the ministers and instruments
Of cruel war. Sixty and nine, that wore
Their crownets regal, from th' Athenian bay
Put forth toward Phrygia, and their vow is made
To ransack Troy, within whose strong immures
The ravished Helen, Menelaus' queen,
With wanton Paris sleeps; and that's the quarrel.
To Tenedos they come,
And the deep-drawing ⌜barks⌝ do there disgorge
Their warlike fraughtage. Now on Dardan plains
The fresh and yet unbruisèd Greeks do pitch
Their brave pavilions. Priam's six-gated city—
Dardan and Timbria, Helias, Chetas, Troien,
And Antenorides—with massy staples
And corresponsive and fulfilling bolts,
⌜Spar⌝ up the sons of Troy.
Now expectation, tickling skittish spirits
On one and other side, Trojan and Greek,
Sets all on hazard. And hither am I come,
A prologue armed, but not in confidence
Of author's pen or actor's voice, but suited
In like conditions as our argument,
To tell you, fair beholders, that our play
Leaps o'er the vaunt and firstlings of those broils,
Beginning in the middle, starting thence away
To what may be digested in a play.
Like, or find fault; do as your pleasures are.
Now, good or bad, 'tis but the chance of war.⟩

⌜*Prologue exits.*⌝

28. **Beginning in the middle:** See longer note, page 267. **starting:** rushing, hastening

29. **digested:** (1) ordered, arranged; (2) comprehended

1.1 Troilus refuses to fight because he is too disturbed by his unrequited love for Cressida. Pandarus, her uncle, complains of Troilus's impatience and of his ingratitude for Pandarus's efforts to help. With Aeneas, Troilus goes out to fight.

---

1. **varlet:** attendant

2. **without:** outside of

5. **to field:** i.e., go to the battlefield; **hath none:** perhaps, has no **heart** that he **is master of** (line 4)

6. **gear . . . mended:** i.e., business never be improved or corrected (with possible wordplay on **gear** as clothing in need of mending)

7, 8. **to . . . to . . . to:** i.e., corresponding to, in proportion to

10. **fonder:** more foolish

12. **skilless:** ignorant; unskilled; **unpracticed:** inexperienced, inexpert

14. **meddle nor make:** i.e., concern myself, interfere

15. **tarry the grinding:** i.e., wait for **the wheat** to be ground into flour

18. **bolting:** sifting (See picture, page 36.)

⟨ACT 1⟩

⟨Scene 1⟩

Enter Pandarus and Troilus.

TROILUS
Call here my varlet; I'll unarm again.
Why should I war without the walls of Troy
That find such cruel battle here within?
Each Trojan that is master of his heart,
Let him to field; Troilus, alas, hath none.

PANDARUS Will this gear ne'er be mended?

TROILUS
The Greeks are strong and skilful to their strength,
Fierce to their skill, and to their fierceness valiant;
But I am weaker than a woman's tear,
Tamer than sleep, fonder than ignorance,
Less valiant than the virgin in the night,
And skilless as unpracticed infancy.

PANDARUS Well, I have told you enough of this. For my part, I'll not meddle nor make no farther. He that will have a cake out of the wheat must tarry the grinding.

TROILUS Have I not tarried?

PANDARUS Ay, the grinding; but you must tarry the bolting.

TROILUS Have I not tarried?

PANDARUS Ay, the bolting; but you must tarry the leavening.

27. **Patience herself:** i.e., (not even) **Patience; what goddess e'er:** i.e., whatever **goddess** (See picture below.)

28. **Doth . . . suff'rance:** i.e., shrinks or flinches less at suffering

33. **fairer:** more beautiful

36. **As:** i.e., **as** if; **wedgèd:** cut into (as if with a wedge); **rive:** split

38. **a-scorn:** perhaps, in scorn or mockery (often emended to "a storm")

42. **An:** if

43. **go to:** an expression of impatience or remonstrance

46. **but I would: but I** wish

52. **indrenched:** immersed, **drowned** (line 50)

Patience. (1.1.27)

From Cesare Ripa, *Iconologia* . . . (1603).

TROILUS Still have I tarried.

PANDARUS Ay, to the leavening; but here's yet in the word hereafter the kneading, the making of the cake, the heating the oven, and the baking. Nay, you must stay the cooling too, or you may chance burn your lips.

TROILUS
Patience herself, what goddess e'er she be,
Doth lesser blench at suff'rance than I do.
At Priam's royal table do I sit
And when fair Cressid comes into my thoughts—
So, traitor! ⌜"When⌝ she comes"? When ⌜is she⌝
thence?

PANDARUS Well, she looked yesternight fairer than ever I saw her look, or any woman else.

TROILUS
I was about to tell thee: when my heart,
As wedgèd with a sigh, would rive in twain,
Lest Hector or my father should perceive me,
I have, as when the sun doth light a-scorn,
Buried this sigh in wrinkle of a smile;
But sorrow that is couched in seeming gladness
Is like that mirth fate turns to sudden sadness.

PANDARUS An her hair were not somewhat darker than Helen's—well, go to—there were no more comparison between the women. But, for my part, she is my kinswoman; I would not, as they term it, praise her, but I would somebody had heard her talk yesterday, as I did. I will not dispraise your sister Cassandra's wit, but—

TROILUS
O, Pandarus! I tell thee, Pandarus:
When I do tell thee there my hopes lie drowned,
Reply not in how many fathoms deep
They lie indrenched. I tell thee I am mad
In Cressid's love. Thou answer'st she is fair;
Pourest in the open ulcer of my heart

56. **Handlest . . . discourse:** i.e., talk about; **that her hand:** i.e., **that hand** of hers

57. **In . . . comparison:** i.e., **in comparison** with which; **whites:** perhaps, white hands of other women (who, in line 58, write **their own reproach**); **ink:** i.e., black

58. **to . . . seizure:** i.e., in comparison **to whose soft** grasp or clasp

59. **spirit of sense:** i.e., the "sensible **spirit**" of touch (See longer note, page 268.)

61. **true:** i.e., truly

62. **oil and balm:** i.e., medicinal salves or ointments

66. **so much:** i.e., the full **truth**

67. **Faith:** a mild oath

68. **fair:** beautiful

69. **mends:** remedy

71. **my labor:** i.e., nothing but **my labor; travail:** toil, trouble (but with wordplay on *travel,* as Pandarus has **gone between and between** [lines 72–73]; the two spellings [*travail, travel*] were used interchangeably)

71–72. **ill thought on of: thought** badly **of** by

78. **o' Friday:** i.e., when fasting and dressed soberly; **on Sunday:** i.e., when dressed in her best clothes (See longer note, page 268.)

80. **'tis all one:** i.e., it's all the same

83. **stay behind her father:** Cressida's **father,** Calchas, had gone over to the Greeks, as Shakespeare's audience would have known from earlier versions of this familiar story.

Her eyes, her hair, her cheek, her gait, her voice;
Handlest in thy discourse—O—that her hand,
In whose comparison all whites are ink
Writing their own reproach, to whose soft seizure
The cygnet's down is harsh, and spirit of sense
Hard as the palm of plowman. This thou tell'st me,
As true thou tell'st me, when I say I love her.
But, saying thus, instead of oil and balm
Thou lay'st in every gash that love hath given me
The knife that made it.

PANDARUS I speak no more than truth.

TROILUS Thou dost not speak so much.

PANDARUS Faith, I'll not meddle in it. Let her be as she is. If she be fair, 'tis the better for her; an she be not, she has the mends in her own hands.

TROILUS Good Pandarus—how now, Pandarus?

PANDARUS I have had my labor for my travail, ill thought on of her, and ill thought ⟨on⟩ of you; gone between and between, but small thanks for my labor.

TROILUS What, art thou angry, Pandarus? What, with me?

PANDARUS Because she's kin to me, therefore she's not so fair as Helen; an she were ⟨not⟩ kin to me, she would be as fair o' Friday as Helen is on Sunday. But what ⟨care⟩ I? I care not an she were a blackamoor; 'tis all one to me.

TROILUS Say I she is not fair?

PANDARUS I do not care whether you do or no. She's a fool to stay behind her father. Let her to the Greeks, and so I'll tell her the next time I see her. For my part, I'll meddle nor make no more i' th' matter.

TROILUS Pandarus—

PANDARUS Not I.

TROILUS Sweet Pandarus—

PANDARUS Pray you speak no more to me. I will leave all as I found it, and there an end. *He exits.*

90 SD. **alarum:** call to arms

91. **rude:** harsh

92. **on both sides:** i.e., both Trojans and Greeks; **must needs be:** i.e., has to be

98. **tetchy:** short-tempered, irritable

99. **suit:** courtship, wooing

100. **Apollo . . . love: Apollo,** mythological god of the sun, fell in love with the maiden Daphne, who, failing to escape his pursuit, was transformed into the laurel tree. (See longer note, page 269, and picture, page 152.)

101. **what we:** i.e., **what** I am (Here and through line 106, Troilus uses the royal plural.)

102. **India:** probably the East and West Indies, synonymous with great wealth

103. **our Ilium:** i.e., the royal palace

104. **flood:** large river; or, perhaps, ocean

105. **Ourself:** i.e., myself

106. **Our . . . our . . . our:** i.e., my; **doubtful:** uncertain; **bark:** sailing vessel

107. **Wherefore:** why; **afield:** on the battlefield

108. **sorts:** fits

114. **to scorn:** i.e., worthy of scorn (But see longer note, page 269.)

115. **gored . . . horn:** Because Menelaus's wife Helen is Paris's lover, Menelaus is a cuckold, or horned man. (See longer note, page 269, and picture, page 32.)

Sound alarum.

TROILUS

Peace, you ungracious clamors! Peace, rude sounds!
Fools on both sides! Helen must needs be fair
When with your blood you daily paint her thus.
I cannot fight upon this argument;
It is too starved a subject for my sword.
But Pandarus—O gods, how do you plague me!
I cannot come to Cressid but by Pandar,
And he's as tetchy to be wooed to woo
As she is stubborn-chaste against all suit.
Tell me, Apollo, for thy Daphne's love,
What Cressid is, what Pandar, and what we.
Her bed is India; there she lies, a pearl.
Between our Ilium and where she resides,
Let it be called the wild and wand'ring flood,
Ourself the merchant, and this sailing Pandar
Our doubtful hope, our convoy, and our bark.

Alarum. Enter Aeneas.

AENEAS

How now, Prince Troilus? Wherefore not afield?

TROILUS

Because not there. This woman's answer sorts,
For womanish it is to be from thence.
What news, Aeneas, from the field today?

AENEAS

That Paris is returnèd home, and hurt.

TROILUS

By whom, Aeneas?

AENEAS

Troilus, by Menelaus.

TROILUS

Let Paris bleed. 'Tis but a scar to scorn;
Paris is gored with Menelaus' horn.

Alarum.

116. **Hark:** listen to

117. **Better at home:** i.e., the **sport** [line 116] or action would be even **better** indoors; **would I might:** i.e., I wish **I might; may:** i.e., you **may**

118. **abroad:** out of doors; **bound:** on your way

1.2 Cressida gossips with her servant Alexander, and then with Pandarus, who strives to interest her in Troilus. After Pandarus and Cressida watch the fighters return from battle, Cressida, when alone, acknowledges her attraction to Troilus.

---

0 SD. **man:** i.e., servant, attendant

7. **moved:** troubled, perturbed

8. **chid:** chided, scolded

9. **like as:** i.e., **as** if; **husbandry:** careful household management (a reference to Hector's rising so early)

10. **harnessed light:** dressed in **light** armor; or, perhaps, quickly dressed in armor

15. **noise:** rumor

Hecuba. Priam.

From [Guillaume Rouillé,] . . . *Promptuarii iconum* . . . (1553).

AENEAS
Hark what good sport is out of town today!

TROILUS
Better at home, if "would I might" were "may."
But to the sport abroad. Are you bound thither?

AENEAS
In all swift haste.

TROILUS
Come, go we then together.

They exit.

⌜Scene 2⌝

Enter Cressida and her man ⌜Alexander.⌝

CRESSIDA
Who were those went by?

ALEXANDER
Queen Hecuba and Helen.

CRESSIDA
And whither go they?

ALEXANDER
Up to the eastern tower,
Whose height commands as subject all the vale,
To see the battle. Hector, whose patience
Is as a virtue fixed, today was moved.
He chid Andromache and struck his armorer;
And, like as there were husbandry in war,
Before the sun rose he was harnessed light,
And to the field goes he, where every flower
Did as a prophet weep what it foresaw
In Hector's wrath.

CRESSIDA
What was his cause of anger?

ALEXANDER
The noise goes, this: there is among the Greeks
A lord of Trojan blood, nephew to Hector.
They call him Ajax.

CRESSIDA
Good; and what of him?

24. **additions:** i.e., distinguishing characteristics (literally, titles that distinguish a person)

26. **humors:** the bodily fluids then thought to control such characteristics as **valor** (See longer note, page 269.)

27. **crushed:** compressed with violence; **sauced:** seasoned (as with a sauce)

28. **discretion:** The proverb "the better part of **valor** is **discretion**" was popular before Shakespeare had Falstaff say it in *1 Henry IV* 5.4.122. Since the character described by Alexander lacks true **discretion** (i.e., good judgment), the word here may be Falstaff's **discretion** (i.e., cowardice).

29. **glimpse:** tinge, trace; **attaint:** touch of dishonor

31. **against the hair:** contrary to what is fitting

32. **joints:** i.e., limbs, parts

33. **Briareus:** a mythological monster with a hundred arms and **hands**

34. **purblind:** blind; **Argus:** a mythological monster with a hundred **eyes**

37. **coped:** encountered, engaged

38. **disdain:** anger

40. **waking:** i.e., lying awake

46. **morrow:** morning

47. **Cousin:** a term applied to a close kinsman, especially a nephew or niece

49. **Ilium:** See note to 1.1.103.

ALEXANDER
They say he is a very man *per se*
And stands alone.

CRESSIDA So do all men unless ⟨they⟩ are drunk, sick, or have no legs.

ALEXANDER This man, lady, hath robbed many beasts of their particular additions. He is as valiant as the lion, churlish as the bear, slow as the elephant, a man into whom nature hath so crowded humors that his valor is crushed into folly, his folly sauced with discretion. There is no man hath a virtue that he hath not a glimpse of, nor any man an attaint but he carries some stain of it. He is melancholy without cause and merry against the hair. He hath the joints of everything, but everything so out of joint that he is a gouty Briareus, many hands and no use, or purblind Argus, all eyes and no sight.

CRESSIDA But how should this man that makes me smile make Hector angry?

ALEXANDER They say he yesterday coped Hector in the battle and struck him down, the disdain and shame whereof hath ever since kept Hector fasting and waking.

⟨*Enter Pandarus.*⟩

CRESSIDA Who comes here?

ALEXANDER Madam, your Uncle Pandarus.

CRESSIDA Hector's a gallant man.

ALEXANDER As may be in the world, lady.

PANDARUS What's that? What's that?

CRESSIDA Good morrow, Uncle Pandarus.

PANDARUS Good morrow, Cousin Cressid. What do you talk of?— Good morrow, Alexander.—How do you, cousin? When were you at Ilium?

CRESSIDA This morning, uncle.

55. **E'en so:** i.e., even so, so it was

58. **he says:** Alexander **says**

60. **lay about him:** i.e., strike out violently on all sides

66. **O Jupiter:** an oath on one name of the Roman king of the gods, also called Jove (See picture below.)

68. **if you see him:** i.e., **if you see** one

73. **in some degrees:** i.e., by a considerable extent

74. **he is himself:** i.e., each **is himself**

75. **would he were:** wish **he were**

77. **Condition:** i.e., on **condition** that, with the proviso that (See longer note, page 270.)

79. **not himself:** i.e., not his normal self

80–81. **the gods . . . end:** proverbial clichés **friend:** befriend

84, 86. **Excuse me, Pardon me:** polite ways of saying "I disagree"

"Jove, the king of gods." (2.3.11)
From Vincenzo Cartari, *Le vere e noue imagini* . . . (1615).

PANDARUS What were you talking of when I came? Was Hector armed and gone ere you came to Ilium? Helen was not up, was she?

CRESSIDA Hector was gone, but Helen was not up.

PANDARUS E'en so. Hector was stirring early.

CRESSIDA That were we talking of, and of his anger.

PANDARUS Was he angry?

CRESSIDA So he says here.

PANDARUS True, he was so. I know the cause too. He'll lay about him today, I can tell them that; and there's Troilus will not come far behind him. Let them take heed of Troilus, I can tell them that too.

CRESSIDA What, is he angry too?

PANDARUS Who, Troilus? Troilus is the better man of the two.

CRESSIDA O Jupiter, there's no comparison.

PANDARUS What, not between Troilus and Hector? Do you know a man if you see him?

CRESSIDA Ay, if I ever saw him before and knew him.

PANDARUS Well, I say Troilus is Troilus.

CRESSIDA Then you say as I say, for I am sure he is not Hector.

PANDARUS No, nor Hector is not Troilus in some degrees.

CRESSIDA 'Tis just to each of them; he is himself.

PANDARUS Himself? Alas, poor Troilus, I would he were.

CRESSIDA So he is.

PANDARUS Condition I had gone barefoot to India.

CRESSIDA He is not Hector.

PANDARUS Himself? No, he's not himself. Would he were himself! Well, the gods are above. Time must friend or end. Well, Troilus, well, I would my heart were in her body. No, Hector is not a better man than Troilus.

CRESSIDA Excuse me.

PANDARUS He is elder.

CRESSIDA Pardon me, pardon me.

87. **Th' other's not come to 't:** i.e., Troilus is not yet mature (The phrase **come to 't** was used in connection with coming into possession of one's fortune at the proper time.)

88. **another tale:** i.e., a different story

89. **his wit:** i.e., Troilus's mental quickness, intellect

91. **qualities:** abilities, natural gifts

96. **for a brown favor:** i.e., for someone with a dark-complexioned face

101. **complexion:** skin color; appearance (The word also meant "temperament" and "disposition.")

104. **should have:** i.e., must **have**

105–6. **higher than his:** i.e., more vivid or intense than Paris's

107. **flaming:** bright, vivid

108. **as lief:** i.e., just as soon

109. **copper nose:** a **nose** reddened by drinking

112. **merry Greek:** wordplay on the simple meanings of the words and on the phrase itself, which means "a wanton or lascivious person"

114. **compassed window:** semicircular bay **window**

115. **past:** more than

117. **tapster's:** tavern keeper's

121. **lifter:** thief

PANDARUS Th' other's not come to 't. You shall tell me another tale when th' other's come to 't. Hector shall not have his ⌜wit⌝ this year.

CRESSIDA He shall not need it, if he have his own.

PANDARUS Nor his qualities.

CRESSIDA No matter.

PANDARUS Nor his beauty.

CRESSIDA 'Twould not become him. His own 's better.

PANDARUS You have no judgment, niece. Helen herself swore th' other day that Troilus, for a brown favor—for so 'tis, I must confess—not brown neither—

CRESSIDA No, but brown.

PANDARUS Faith, to say truth, brown and not brown.

CRESSIDA To say the truth, true and not true.

PANDARUS She praised his complexion above Paris'.

CRESSIDA Why, Paris hath color enough.

PANDARUS So he has.

CRESSIDA Then Troilus should have too much. If she praised him above, his complexion is higher than his. He having color enough, and the other higher, is too flaming a praise for a good complexion. I had as lief Helen's golden tongue had commended Troilus for a copper nose.

PANDARUS I swear to you, I think Helen loves him better than Paris.

CRESSIDA Then she's a merry Greek indeed.

PANDARUS Nay, I am sure she does. She came to him th' other day into the compassed window—and you know he has not past three or four hairs on his chin—

CRESSIDA Indeed, a tapster's arithmetic may soon bring his particulars therein to a total.

PANDARUS Why, he is very young, and yet will he within three pound ⟨lift⟩ as much as his brother Hector.

CRESSIDA Is he so young a man and so old a lifter?

123. **puts me:** i.e., **puts** (**Me** is an old form of the dative; it does not affect the meaning.) **cloven:** divided, dimpled (Cressida responds [line 125] as if **cloven** carried the meaning "split in two.")

125. **Juno:** queen of the Roman gods

131. **an 'twere:** i.e., as if it were

132. **go to:** See note to 1.1.43.

134. **stand to the proof:** i.e., meet the test (with a bawdy reference to an erection)

134–35. **you'll prove:** i.e., you want to **prove**

137. **addle:** rotten, putrid

143. **rack:** an instrument of torture used to elicit a confession (See picture below.)

144. **takes upon her:** undertakes, presumes

148. **laughed:** i.e., **laughed** so much

148–49. **her eyes . . . millstones:** A callous person proverbially wept **millstones,** not tears.

155. **Marry:** a mild oath (originally an oath on the name of the Virgin Mary)

"The rack." (1.2.143)
From Girolamo Maggi,
De tintinnabulis liber . . . (1689).

PANDARUS But to prove to you that Helen loves him: she came and puts me her white hand to his cloven chin—

CRESSIDA Juno have mercy! How came it cloven?

PANDARUS Why, you know 'tis dimpled. I think his smiling becomes him better than any man in all Phrygia.

CRESSIDA O, he smiles valiantly.

PANDARUS Does he not?

CRESSIDA O yes, an 'twere a cloud in autumn.

PANDARUS Why, go to, then. But to prove to you that Helen loves Troilus—

CRESSIDA Troilus will stand to ⌜the⌝ proof if you'll prove it so.

PANDARUS Troilus? Why, he esteems her no more than I esteem an addle egg.

CRESSIDA If you love an addle egg as well as you love an idle head, you would eat chickens i' th' shell.

PANDARUS I cannot choose but laugh to think how she tickled his chin. Indeed, she has a marvellous white hand, I must needs confess—

CRESSIDA Without the rack.

PANDARUS And she takes upon her to spy a white hair on his chin.

CRESSIDA Alas, poor chin! Many a wart is richer.

PANDARUS But there was such laughing! Queen Hecuba laughed that her eyes ran o'er—

CRESSIDA With millstones.

PANDARUS And Cassandra laughed—

CRESSIDA But there was a more temperate fire under the pot of her eyes. Did her eyes run o'er too?

PANDARUS And Hector laughed.

CRESSIDA At what was all this laughing?

PANDARUS Marry, at the white hair that Helen spied on Troilus' chin.

167–68. **his sons:** Priam reputedly had fifty **sons.**

169. **forked one:** an allusion to cuckolds as **forked** (or horned) men (See longer note to 1.1.115, page 269, and picture below.)

172. **chafed:** fumed, fretted; **passed:** exceeds description (Cressida responds as if **passed** means "went by.")

176. **Think on 't:** i.e., **think** about it

180. **an 'twere:** i.e., as if he were

180–81. **spring . . . May:** a satiric rendering of the proverb "**April** showers bring **May** flowers" **spring up:** grow **an 'twere:** i.e., as if I were **against:** in anticipation of

187. **bravely:** excellently

A cuckold. (1.1.115; 1.2.169; 3.3.66; 5.1.56)
From Bagford ballads (printed in 1878).

CRESSIDA An 't had been a green hair, I should have laughed too.

PANDARUS They laughed not so much at the hair as at his pretty answer.

CRESSIDA What was his answer?

PANDARUS Quoth she "Here's but two-and-fifty hairs on your chin, and one of them is white."

CRESSIDA This is her question.

PANDARUS That's true, make no question of that. "Two-and-fifty hairs," quoth he, "and one white. That white hair is my father, and all the rest are his sons." "Jupiter!" quoth she, "which of these hairs is Paris, my husband?" "The forked one," quoth he. "Pluck 't out, and give it him." But there was such laughing, and Helen so blushed, and Paris so chafed, and all the rest so laughed that it passed.

CRESSIDA So let it now, for it has been a great while going by.

PANDARUS Well, cousin, I told you a thing yesterday. Think on 't.

CRESSIDA So I do.

PANDARUS I'll be sworn 'tis true. He will weep you an 'twere a man born in April.

CRESSIDA And I'll spring up in his tears an 'twere a nettle against May. *Sound a retreat.*

PANDARUS Hark, they are coming from the field. Shall we stand up here and see them as they pass toward Ilium? Good niece, do, sweet niece Cressida.

CRESSIDA At your pleasure.

PANDARUS Here, here, here's an excellent place. Here we may see most bravely. I'll tell you them all by their names as they pass by, but mark Troilus above the rest.

⌜*They cross the stage; Alexander exits.*⌝

CRESSIDA Speak not so loud.

191. **brave:** fine, handsome
193. **anon:** soon
195. **shrewd:** sharp, cunning
197. **judgments:** critics, judges
198. **proper . . . person:** i.e., handsome **man** **person:** bodily frame or figure
199–203. **see him nod . . . more:** Cressida plays on **nod** and "noddy" (i.e., fool, simpleton), and on the biblical "to him who has much, more shall be given" (Matthew 25.29). **If he do . . . more:** i.e., **if** he gives you a **nod,** you who are **rich** in folly (i.e., a noddy) shall have **more** folly
205. **Go thy way:** i.e., keep it up
210. **hacks:** gashes
212. **laying on:** i.e., vigorous attacks
216. **all one:** i.e., **all** the same; **By God's lid:** i.e., **by God's** eyelid (a strong, though anachronistic, oath)

Andromache. Hector.
From [Guillaume Rouillé,] . . .
Promptuarii iconum . . . (1553).

Enter Aeneas ⌜*and crosses the stage.*⌝

PANDARUS That's Aeneas. Is not that a brave man? He's one of the flowers of Troy, I can tell you. But mark Troilus; you shall see anon.

Enter Antenor ⌜*and crosses the stage.*⌝

CRESSIDA Who's that?

PANDARUS That's Antenor. He has a shrewd wit, I can tell you, and he's ⟨a⟩ man good enough. He's one o' th' soundest judgments in Troy whosoever; and a proper man of person. When comes Troilus? I'll show you Troilus anon. If he see me, you shall see him nod at me.

CRESSIDA Will he give you the nod?

PANDARUS You shall see.

CRESSIDA If he do, the rich shall have more.

Enter Hector ⌜*and crosses the stage.*⌝

PANDARUS That's Hector, that, that, look you, that. There's a fellow!—Go thy way, Hector!—There's a brave man, niece. O brave Hector! Look how he looks. There's a countenance! Is 't not a brave man?

CRESSIDA O, a brave man!

PANDARUS Is he not? It does a ⟨man's⟩ heart good. Look you what hacks are on his helmet. Look you yonder, do you see? Look you there. There's no jesting; there's laying on, take 't off who will, as they say. There be hacks.

CRESSIDA Be those with swords?

PANDARUS Swords, anything, he cares not. An the devil come to him, it's all one. By God's lid, it does one's heart good.

Enter Paris ⌜*and crosses the stage.*⌝

Yonder comes Paris, yonder comes Paris! Look you yonder, niece. Is 't not a gallant man too? Is 't not?

226. **think he went:** i.e., **think Troilus went**

229. **indifferent:** moderately

230. **marvel:** i.e., can't imagine

232. **sneaking:** furtive

234. **Hem:** a sound to get Troilus's attention

236. **Peace:** i.e., be quiet

238. **Look you:** i.e., **look**

240. **goes:** walks

241. **never . . . twenty:** i.e., isn't even twenty-three years old

242–43. **a Grace:** i.e., one of the exquisitely beautiful mythological goddesses that bestow beauty and charm

245. **change:** i.e., make an exchange

246. **to boot:** in addition

249. **porridge:** soup; **meat:** solid food

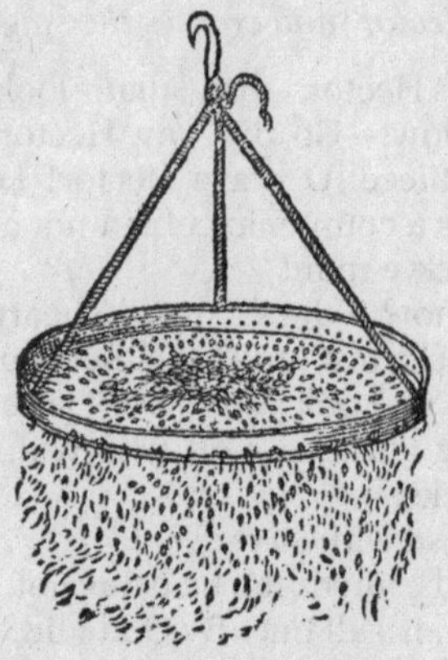

A sieve. (1.1.18, 20)
From Geoffrey Whitney, *A choice of emblemes* . . . (1586).

Why, this is brave now. Who said he came hurt home today? He's not hurt. Why, this will do Helen's heart good now, ha? Would I could see Troilus now! You shall see Troilus anon.

Enter Helenus ⌜*and crosses the stage.*⌝

CRESSIDA Who's that?

PANDARUS That's Helenus. I marvel where Troilus is. That's Helenus. I think he went not forth today. That's Helenus.

CRESSIDA Can Helenus fight, uncle?

PANDARUS Helenus? No. Yes, he'll fight indifferent well. I marvel where Troilus is. Hark, do you not hear the people cry "Troilus"? Helenus is a priest.

Enter Troilus ⌜*and crosses the stage.*⌝

CRESSIDA What sneaking fellow comes yonder?

PANDARUS Where? Yonder? That's Deiphobus. 'Tis Troilus! There's a man, niece. Hem! Brave Troilus, the prince of chivalry!

CRESSIDA Peace, for shame, peace.

PANDARUS Mark him. Note him. O brave Troilus! Look well upon him, niece. Look you how his sword is bloodied and his helm more hacked than Hector's, and how he looks, and how he goes. O admirable youth! He never saw three and twenty.—Go thy way, Troilus; go thy way!—Had I a sister were a Grace, or a daughter a goddess, he should take his choice. O admirable man! Paris? Paris is dirt to him; and I warrant Helen, to change, would give an eye to boot.

⟨*Enter Common Soldiers* ⌜*and cross the stage.*⌝⟩

CRESSIDA Here comes more.

PANDARUS Asses, fools, dolts, chaff and bran, chaff and bran, porridge after meat. I could live and die in

256. **drayman, porter, camel:** i.e., a creature capable of little more than carrying heavy loads

258. **discretion:** power of discrimination

264. **date:** i.e., dates, an ingredient in mince **pie; date is out:** To go **out** of **date** is to become obsolete.

265–66. **at what ward you lie:** i.e., the stance you take in defending yourself (technical terms from fencing, though Cressida [line 267] gives **lie** a more literal meaning)

269. **honesty:** chastity (the usual meaning of the word when applied to women); **mask:** Masks were worn by women to protect their skin from the sun.

271. **at a thousand watches:** i.e., constantly on the watch (Pandarus responds [line 272] as if she meant periods of wakefulness.) The phrase "**watch** and **ward**" referred to the duties of a watchman or sentinel.

274. **ward:** defend

276. **swell past hiding:** The sexual double meanings that begin with Pandarus's "**what ward you lie**" (line 266) surface here with this clear reference to pregnancy.

283. **doubt he be:** i.e., fear he is

the eyes of Troilus. Ne'er look, ne'er look; the eagles are gone. Crows and daws, crows and daws! I had rather be such a man as Troilus than Agamemnon and all Greece.

CRESSIDA There is amongst the Greeks Achilles, a better man than Troilus.

PANDARUS Achilles? A drayman, a porter, a very camel!

CRESSIDA Well, well.

PANDARUS "Well, well"? Why, have you any discretion? Have you any eyes? Do you know what a man is? Is not birth, beauty, good shape, discourse, manhood, learning, gentleness, virtue, youth, liberality and such-like the spice and salt that season a man?

CRESSIDA Ay, a minced man; and then to be baked with no date in the pie, for then the man's date is out.

PANDARUS You are such a woman a man knows not at what ward you lie.

CRESSIDA Upon my back to defend my belly, upon my wit to defend my wiles, upon my secrecy to defend mine honesty, my mask to defend my beauty, and you to defend all these; and at all these wards I lie, at a thousand watches.

PANDARUS Say one of your watches.

CRESSIDA Nay, I'll watch you for that, and that's one of the chiefest of them too. If I cannot ward what I would not have hit, I can watch you for telling how I took the blow—unless it swell past hiding, and then it's past watching.

PANDARUS You are such another!

Enter ⌜Troilus's⌝ Boy.

BOY Sir, my lord would instantly speak with you.

PANDARUS Where?

BOY At your own house. There he unarms him.

PANDARUS Good boy, tell him I come. ⌜*Boy exits.*⌝
I doubt he be hurt.—Fare you well, good niece.

285. **by and by:** soon

288. **bawd:** go-between, procurer

292. **glass:** looking **glass,** mirror

293. **wooing:** i.e., when men are **wooing** them

295. **That she beloved:** i.e., a woman who is loved

297. **That she was never yet that:** i.e., there has **never** been a woman who

298. **got:** achieved; **sue:** chase, pursue

299. **out of love:** i.e., from the experience (or the book) **of love**

300. **Achievement is command:** i.e., to win a woman's sexual favors is to gain the right to give her orders; **ungained, beseech:** i.e., until that moment, the man can only plead

301. **heart's content:** i.e., that which is contained in my heart; or, perhaps, **heart's** satisfaction

1.3 As the general, Agamemnon, and his councillors Nestor and Ulysses discuss the refusal of their principal warriors, Achilles and Ajax, to fight, Aeneas enters to deliver a challenge from Hector to single combat with any Greek. Ulysses and Nestor then scheme to deny Achilles the combat and give it to Ajax because, they say, Achilles is too proud already.

---

0 SD. **Sennet:** a trumpet or cornet signal for a ceremonial entry

1. **Princes:** kings; **grief:** injury, suffering; **jaundice:** perhaps, paleness (At line 18, their **cheeks** are

(continued)

CRESSIDA Adieu, uncle.
PANDARUS I will be with you, niece, by and by.
CRESSIDA To bring, uncle?
PANDARUS Ay, a token from Troilus.
CRESSIDA By the same token, you are a bawd.

⟨Pandarus exits.⟩

Words, vows, gifts, tears, and love's full sacrifice
He offers in another's enterprise;
But more in Troilus thousandfold I see
Than in the glass of Pandar's praise may be.
Yet hold I off. Women are angels, wooing;
Things won are done; joy's soul lies in the doing.
That she beloved knows naught that knows not this:
Men prize the thing ungained more than it is.
That she was never yet that ever knew
Love got so sweet as when desire did sue.
Therefore this maxim out of love I teach:
Achievement is command; ungained, beseech.
Then though my heart's content firm love doth bear,
Nothing of that shall from mine eyes appear.

She exits.

⌜Scene 3⌝

⟨Sennet.⟩ Enter Agamemnon, Nestor, Ulysses, Diomedes, Menelaus, with others.

AGAMEMNON
Princes, what grief hath set ⟨the⟩ jaundice o'er your cheeks?
The ample proposition that hope makes
In all designs begun on earth below
Fails in the promised largeness. Checks and disasters
Grow in the veins of actions highest reared,
As knots, by the conflux of meeting sap,
Infects the sound pine and diverts his grain

described as **abashed,** or stricken with a sense of shame.)

3. **proposition:** offer

5. **largeness:** magnitude; **Checks:** reverses

6. **Grow in the veins:** i.e., block the flow (of blood or sap); **reared:** elevated, exalted

7. **As:** i.e., in the same way; **conflux:** confluence

8. **Infects:** i.e., affect, influence; **his:** i.e., its

9. **Tortive:** twisted, tortuous

11. **suppose:** expectation

13. **Sith:** since

14–15. **draw . . . thwart:** i.e., pull awry and crosswise

20. **protractive:** i.e., lengthy, prolonged

21. **persistive:** i.e., steadfast

22. **fineness of which metal:** i.e., purity of men's **constancy** (with wordplay on **metal**/mettle) See longer note, page 270.

23. **In Fortune's love:** i.e., when Fortune smiles (See picture, page 138.)

24. **artist:** learned man or philosopher

26. **her:** i.e., **Fortune's** (line 23)

30. **virtue:** excellence, merit

31. **observance of:** i.e., respect for; **seat:** i.e., authority, position

32. **apply:** i.e., interpret

38. **Boreas:** in mythology, the god of the north wind or the north wind itself

39. **Thetis:** a poetic name for the sea

40. **strong-ribbed bark:** i.e., ship with a strong timber frame

(continued)

Tortive and errant from his course of growth.
Nor, princes, is it matter new to us
That we come short of our suppose so far
That after seven years' siege yet Troy walls stand,
Sith ⟨every⟩ action that hath gone before,
Whereof we have record, trial did draw
Bias and thwart, not answering the aim
And that unbodied figure of the thought
That gave 't surmisèd shape. Why then, you princes,
Do you with cheeks abashed behold our works
And call them shames, which are indeed naught else
But the protractive trials of great Jove
To find persistive constancy in men?
The fineness of which metal is not found
In Fortune's love; for then the bold and coward,
The wise and fool, the artist and unread,
The hard and soft seem all affined and kin.
But in the wind and tempest of her frown,
Distinction, with a broad and powerful fan,
Puffing at all, winnows the light away,
And what hath mass or matter by itself
Lies rich in virtue and unmingled.

NESTOR

With due observance of ⟨thy⟩ godlike seat,
Great Agamemnon, Nestor shall apply
Thy latest words. In the reproof of chance
Lies the true proof of men. The sea being smooth,
How many shallow bauble boats dare sail
Upon her ⟨patient⟩ breast, making their way
With those of nobler bulk!
But let the ruffian Boreas once enrage
The gentle Thetis, and anon behold
The strong-ribbed bark through liquid mountains cut,
Bounding between the two moist elements,
Like Perseus' horse. Where's then the saucy boat
Whose weak untimbered sides but even now

41. **two moist elements:** i.e., water and air (Of the four **elements,** air was considered hot and **moist** and water cold and **moist.**)

42. **Perseus' horse:** perhaps, the winged **horse** Pegasus (See longer note, page 270.)

44. **Corrivaled:** rivaled

45. **toast:** i.e., snack (literally, a piece of toasted bread, often served in wine or beer); **Neptune:** god of the sea

46. **show:** outward appearance

47. **ray:** radiance

48. **breese:** gadfly, a fly that bites cattle

53. **with . . . sympathize:** i.e., resembles **rage**

57. **nerves:** sinews

58. **numbers:** company; **sprite:** spirit, animating and vital principle

59. **tempers:** dispositions

60. **shut up:** i.e., enclosed, embodied

62. **The which:** i.e., **which**

62–63. **for thy place:** i.e., because of your position

68. **brass:** a symbol of the indestructible

69. **hatched in:** ornamented or inlaid with (i.e., his hair streaked with)

70. **of air:** i.e., created through his spoken words

70–71. **axletree . . . rides:** i.e., the axis around which the heavenly bodies turn

74. **expect:** expectation

75. **importless:** trivial; **burden:** theme

76. **we are confident:** perhaps, I am **confident** (See longer note, page 270.)

77. **rank:** grossly coarse, indecent; **mastic:** See longer note, page 271.

78. **oracle:** divine revelation

Corrivaled greatness? Either to harbor fled
Or made a toast for Neptune. Even so
Doth valor's show and valor's worth divide
In storms of Fortune. For in her ray and brightness
The herd hath more annoyance by the breese
Than by the tiger, but when the splitting wind
Makes flexible the knees of knotted oaks,
And flies ⌜flee⌝ under shade, why, then the thing of
  courage,
As roused with rage, with rage doth sympathize,
And with an accent tuned in selfsame key
⌜Retorts⌝ to chiding Fortune.

ULYSSES Agamemnon,
Thou great commander, nerves and bone of Greece,
Heart of our numbers, soul and only sprite,
In whom the tempers and the minds of all
Should be shut up, hear what Ulysses speaks.
Besides th' applause and approbation,
The which, (⌜*to Agamemnon*⌝) most mighty for thy
  place and sway,
(⌜*To Nestor*⌝) And thou most reverend for ⟨thy⟩
  stretched-out life,
I give to both your speeches, which were such
As Agamemnon and the hand of Greece
Should hold up high in brass; and such again
As venerable Nestor, hatched in silver,
Should with a bond of air, strong as the axletree
On which heaven rides, knit all the Greekish ears
To his experienced tongue, yet let it please both,
Thou great, and wise, to hear Ulysses speak.

⟨AGAMEMNON
Speak, Prince of Ithaca, and be 't of less expect
That matter needless, of importless burden,
Divide thy lips than we are confident
When rank Thersites opes his mastic jaws
We shall hear music, wit, and oracle.⟩

79. **his basis:** i.e., its foundation; **had been:** i.e., would have been

81. **instances:** causes

82. **specialty of rule:** "particular rights of supreme authority" (Samuel Johnson, 1765)

83–84. **And . . . factions:** i.e., there are as many unsound **factions** as there are **tents**

85–86. **hive . . . repair:** i.e., beehive to which the pollen-gathering bees return (See picture, page 94.)

87. **Degree:** relative social or official rank; **vizarded:** masked (The famous speech on **degree** that follows [lines 89–128] echoes classical writers, earlier poets, and familiar homilies on the necessity for obedience. See longer note, page 271.)

89. **this center:** i.e., the earth (See longer note, page 272, and picture, page xxxiv.)

91. **Insisture:** Editors agree that this word, used only this once, refers in some way to the motions of the heavenly bodies.

92. **Office:** function; **line:** i.e., rule, principle (literally, plumb line used for determining vertical direction)

93. **Sol:** the sun

94. **sphered:** i.e., set in its sphere (See longer note to 1.3.89, page 272.)

95. **other:** i.e., other planets; **whose:** i.e., the sun's; **med'cinable:** i.e., medicinal, having healing powers

97. **posts:** travels with speed

98. **Sans check:** without hindrance or stopping

103. **Divert:** perhaps, turn awry; **deracinate:** uproot, eradicate

104. **states:** kingdoms, governments

(continued)

ULYSSES

Troy, yet upon his ⟨basis,⟩ had been down,
And the great Hector's sword had lacked a master
But for these instances:
The specialty of rule hath been neglected,
And look how many Grecian tents do stand
Hollow upon this plain, so many hollow factions.
When that the general is not like the hive
To whom the foragers shall all repair,
What honey is expected? Degree being vizarded,
Th' unworthiest shows as fairly in the mask.
The heavens themselves, the planets, and this center
Observe degree, priority, and place,
Insisture, course, proportion, season, form,
Office, and custom, in all line of order.
And therefore is the glorious planet Sol
In noble eminence enthroned and sphered
Amidst the other, whose med'cinable eye
Corrects the influence of evil planets,
And posts, like the commandment of a king,
Sans check, to good and bad. But when the planets
In evil mixture to disorder wander,
What plagues and what portents, what mutiny,
What raging of the sea, shaking of earth,
Commotion in the winds, frights, changes, horrors
Divert and crack, rend and deracinate
The unity and married calm of states
Quite from their fixture! O, when degree is shaked,
Which is the ladder of all high designs,
The enterprise is sick. How could communities,
Degrees in schools and brotherhoods in cities,
Peaceful commerce from dividable shores,
The primogeneity and due of birth,
Prerogative of age, crowns, scepters, laurels,
But by degree stand in authentic place?
Take but degree away, untune that string,

105. **fixture:** condition of stability

106. **ladder:** By calling **degree** (line 105) a **ladder,** Ulysses plays on the original meaning of **degree** as "step or rung of a **ladder.**"

108. **Degrees:** academic ranks; **schools:** i.e., universities

109. **dividable:** i.e., divided, separated (literally, having the function of dividing)

110. **primogeneity . . . birth:** i.e., rights belonging to the firstborn son

111. **laurels:** distinctions, preeminence

115. **oppugnancy:** opposition, antagonism

116. **Should:** i.e., (without **degree**) would

117. **a sop:** literally, a piece of bread soaked in water or wine

118. **Strength . . . imbecility:** i.e., the powerful would control the weak

119. **rude:** violent, barbarous

121. **jar:** discord, dissension

123–24. **includes . . . appetite:** i.e., becomes subservient to **power,** which in turn becomes subject to **will,** which becomes dominated by **appetite** (The relation between **will** and **appetite** in the psychology of Shakespeare's day is discussed in the longer note to 2.2.67–69, page 272.)

126. **So:** thus

127. **perforce:** of necessity; **prey:** i.e., preying, violently seizing prey to devour

129. **suffocate:** suffocated, smothered

130. **the choking:** i.e., the suffocation of **degree**

131. **neglection:** neglect

132. **pace:** i.e., **step** of a ladder (line 134) (For wordplay on **degree,** see note to line 106, above.)

(continued)

And hark what discord follows. Each thing ⟨meets⟩
In mere oppugnancy. The bounded waters
Should lift their bosoms higher than the shores
And make a sop of all this solid globe;
Strength should be lord of imbecility,
And the rude son should strike his father dead;
Force should be right, or, rather, right and wrong,
Between whose endless jar justice resides,
Should lose their names, and so should justice too.
Then everything ⟨includes⟩ itself in power,
Power into will, will into appetite,
And appetite, an universal wolf,
So doubly seconded with will and power,
Must make perforce an universal prey
And last eat up himself. Great Agamemnon,
This chaos, when degree is suffocate,
Follows the choking.
And this neglection of degree it is
That by a pace goes backward, with a purpose
It hath to climb. The General's disdained
By him one step below, he by the next,
That next by him beneath; so every step,
Exampled by the first pace that is sick
Of his superior, grows to an envious fever
Of pale and bloodless emulation.
And 'tis this fever that keeps Troy on foot,
Not her own sinews. To end a tale of length,
Troy in our weakness stands, not in her strength.

NESTOR

Most wisely hath Ulysses here discovered
The fever whereof all our power is sick.

AGAMEMNON

The nature of the sickness found, Ulysses,
What is the remedy?

ULYSSES

The great Achilles, whom opinion crowns

138. **emulation:** grudge against one's **superior**

139. **this fever:** i.e., **envious fever** (line 137)

140. **sinews:** muscles

142. **discovered:** revealed, disclosed

147. **sinew:** strength; **forehand:** i.e., mainstay; **host:** army

149. **dainty:** overly scrupulous or fastidious

150. **designs:** plans, purposes

152. **scurril:** i.e., scurrilous, coarse, indecent

155. **pageants:** mimics

156. **Thy . . . puts on:** i.e., he assumes your supreme position

157. **player:** actor; **conceit:** understanding

159–60. **wooden . . . scaffollage:** i.e., the **sound** made by his strides across a **wooden** stage

161. **o'erwrested seeming:** distorted semblance

163. **chime:** apparatus for striking bells (or the bells themselves); **a-mending:** being repaired or tuned; **unsquared:** i.e., hyperbolic, exaggerated (literally, unregulated)

164. **Typhon:** terrible mythological monster from whose mouths come roars and screams

169. **play me:** i.e., **play**

170. **dressed to:** i.e., prepared or ready for

172. **Vulcan and his wife:** i.e., the crippled god of metalworking **and his wife** Venus, goddess of love and beauty (See pictures, pages 88 and 166.)

174. **right:** precisely; **play him me:** i.e., **play him**

175. **answer:** respond (to a hostile threat)

178. **palsy:** i.e., palsied; **gorget:** armor for the throat (See picture, page 74.)

182. **spleen:** the seat of laughter in the body

The sinew and the forehand of our host,
Having his ear full of his airy fame,
Grows dainty of his worth and in his tent
Lies mocking our designs. With him Patroclus,
Upon a lazy bed, the live-long day
Breaks scurril jests,
And with ridiculous and silly action,
Which, slanderer, he imitation calls,
He pageants us. Sometime, great Agamemnon,
Thy topless deputation he puts on,
And, like a strutting player whose conceit
Lies in his hamstring and doth think it rich
To hear the wooden dialogue and sound
'Twixt his stretched footing and the scaffollage,
Such to-be-pitied and o'erwrested seeming
He acts thy greatness in; and when he speaks,
'Tis like a chime a-mending, with terms ⟨unsquared⟩
Which from the tongue of roaring Typhon dropped
Would seem hyperboles. At this fusty stuff,
The large Achilles, on his pressed bed lolling,
From his deep chest laughs out a loud applause,
Cries "Excellent! 'Tis Agamemnon right.
Now play me Nestor; hem and stroke thy beard,
As he being dressed to some oration."
That's done, as near as the extremest ends
Of parallels, as like as Vulcan and his wife;
Yet god Achilles still cries "Excellent!
'Tis Nestor right. Now play him me, Patroclus,
Arming to answer in a night alarm."
And then, forsooth, the faint defects of age
Must be the scene of mirth—to cough and spit,
And, with a palsy fumbling on his gorget,
Shake in and out the rivet. And at this sport
Sir Valor dies, cries "O, enough, Patroclus,
Or give me ribs of steel! I shall split all
In pleasure of my spleen." And in this fashion,
All our abilities, gifts, natures, shapes,

184. **Severals:** particulars

186. **Excitements:** exhortations

188. **paradoxes:** i.e., absurdities (literally, statements that seem absurd)

191. **infect:** i.e., infected

193. **full:** fully

194. **keeps:** i.e., stays or remains in

197. **gall:** i.e., rancor, bitterness of spirit (literally, bile, the bitter secretion of the liver)

199. **exposure:** undefended condition

200. **rank:** thickly, densely; **rounded:** hemmed

201. **tax:** censure, blame; **policy:** sagacity, prudence

203. **Forestall:** hinder, obstruct; **prescience:** foresight

205. **contrive:** devise, plan

206. **fitness:** i.e., the proper time or circumstance

207. **enemy's weight:** force of the **enemy's** onslaught

209. **mapp'ry:** i.e., the mere making of maps; **closet war:** i.e., **war** in theory, not practice

211. **For . . . poise:** i.e., because of the **swinge** (momentum) **and rudeness** (violence) of its **poise** (weight)

212. **engine:** instrument (i.e., the battering **ram** [line 210])

214. **his execution:** i.e., its action

216. **Makes . . . sons:** is equivalent to Achilles multiplied (Achilles himself is the son of the sea nymph Thetis.)

216 SD. **Tucket:** a flourish on a **trumpet** (line 217)

Severals and generals of grace exact,
Achievements, plots, orders, preventions,
Excitements to the field, or speech for truce,
Success or loss, what is or is not, serves
As stuff for these two to make paradoxes.

NESTOR

And in the imitation of these twain,
Who, as Ulysses says, opinion crowns
With an imperial voice, many are infect:
Ajax is grown self-willed and bears his head
In such a rein, in full as proud a place
As broad Achilles; keeps his tent like him,
Makes factious feasts; rails on our state of war,
Bold as an oracle, and sets Thersites—
A slave whose gall coins slanders like a mint—
To match us in comparisons with dirt,
To weaken ⟨and⟩ discredit our exposure,
How rank soever rounded in with danger.

ULYSSES

They tax our policy and call it cowardice,
Count wisdom as no member of the war,
Forestall prescience, and esteem no act
But that of hand. The still and mental parts
That do contrive how many hands shall strike
When fitness calls them on and know by measure
Of their observant toil the enemy's weight—
Why, this hath not a finger's dignity.
They call this bed-work, mapp'ry, closet war;
So that the ram that batters down the wall,
For the great swinge and rudeness of his poise,
They place before his hand that made the engine
Or those that with the fineness of their souls
By reason guide his execution.

NESTOR

Let this be granted, and Achilles' horse
Makes many Thetis' sons. ⟨*Tucket.*⟩

223. **fair:** gentle, peaceable

224. **surety:** safety, security

227. **leave:** permission

233–34. **morning . . . Phoebus:** i.e., the **blush** of Aurora, goddess of the morn, at sunrise (**Phoebus** is a poetic name for Apollo, god of the sun. See picture, page 152.)

240. **bending:** i.e., courteous (literally, bowing)

241. **galls:** spirits to resent injuries; gall bladders (the supposed seat of rancor)

AGAMEMNON
What trumpet? Look, Menelaus.
MENELAUS From Troy.

⟨*Enter Aeneas,* ⌜*with a Trumpeter*⌝⟩

AGAMEMNON What would you 'fore our tent?
AENEAS
Is this great Agamemnon's tent, I pray you?
AGAMEMNON Even this.
AENEAS
May one that is a herald and a prince
Do a fair message to his kingly eyes?
AGAMEMNON
With surety stronger than Achilles' arm
'Fore all the Greekish ⌜host,⌝ which with one voice
Call Agamemnon head and general.
AENEAS
Fair leave and large security. How may
A stranger to those most imperial looks
Know them from eyes of other mortals?
AGAMEMNON How?
AENEAS
Ay. I ask that I might waken reverence
And bid the cheek be ready with a blush
Modest as morning when she coldly eyes
The youthful Phoebus.
Which is that god in office, guiding men?
Which is the high and mighty Agamemnon?
AGAMEMNON
This Trojan scorns us, or the men of Troy
Are ceremonious courtiers.
AENEAS
Courtiers as free, as debonair, unarmed,
As bending angels—that's their fame in peace.
But when they would seem soldiers, they have galls,

243. **Jove's accord:** i.e., Jove willing

244. **Nothing . . . heart:** i.e., no one else is as courageous

246–50. **The worthiness . . . transcends:** proverbial **distains his:** i.e., sullies its **repining:** grudging **blows:** spreads, proclaims **sole:** solely, without admixture

257. **trumpet:** trumpeter

258. **set . . . bent:** i.e., call him to attention **bent:** direction, inclination

260. **frankly:** freely

271. **resty:** restive, sluggish, inactive

Agamemnon.

From Geoffrey Whitney, *A choice of emblemes* . . . (1586).

Good arms, strong joints, true swords, and—great
Jove's accord—
Nothing so full of heart. But peace, Aeneas.
Peace, Trojan. Lay thy finger on thy lips.
The worthiness of praise distains his worth
If that the praised himself bring the praise forth.
But what the repining enemy commends,
That breath fame blows; that praise, sole pure,
transcends.

AGAMEMNON
Sir, you of Troy, call you yourself Aeneas?

AENEAS Ay, Greek, that is my name.

AGAMEMNON What's your ⟨affair,⟩ I pray you?

AENEAS
Sir, pardon. 'Tis for Agamemnon's ears.

AGAMEMNON
He hears naught privately that comes from Troy.

AENEAS
Nor I from Troy come not to whisper with him.
I bring a trumpet to awake his ear,
To set his ⟨sense⟩ on ⟨the⟩ attentive bent,
And then to speak.

AGAMEMNON Speak frankly as the wind;
It is not Agamemnon's sleeping hour.
That thou shalt know, Trojan, he is awake,
He tells thee so himself.

AENEAS Trumpet, blow ⟨loud⟩!
Send thy brass voice through all these lazy tents;
And every Greek of mettle, let him know
What Troy means fairly shall be spoke aloud.
Sound trumpet.
We have, great Agamemnon, here in Troy
A prince called Hector—Priam is his father—
Who in ⟨this⟩ dull and long-continued truce
Is resty grown. He bade me take a trumpet
And to this purpose speak: "Kings, princes, lords,

278. **truant:** idle; **to . . . loves:** i.e., **to** his beloved's **own lips**

280. **other arms:** wordplay on **arms** as armor

282. **make it good:** i.e., prove it true

284. **couple:** i.e., clasp (To **couple** is to join sexually.)

289. **retires:** withdraws (from the field)

290. **sunburnt:** i.e., blemished (Only light skin was considered beautiful.)

291. **splinter:** splintering; **Even so much:** i.e., thus **much** (I was asked to say)

300. **sucked:** fed from the breast

304. **beaver:** front piece of a helmet (See picture below.)

305. **vambrace:** defensive armor for the forearm (See picture, page 84.) **brawns:** muscles

A helmet with its beaver down. (1.3.304)
From Henry Peacham, *Minerua Britanna* . . . [1612].

If there be one among the fair'st of Greece
That holds his honor higher than his ease,
⟨That seeks⟩ his praise more than he fears his peril,
That knows his valor and knows not his fear,
That loves his mistress more than in confession
With truant vows to her own lips he loves
And dare avow her beauty and her worth
In other arms than hers—to him this challenge.
Hector, in view of Trojans and of Greeks,
Shall make it good, or do his best to do it,
He hath a lady wiser, fairer, truer
Than ever Greek did couple in his arms
And will tomorrow with his trumpet call,
Midway between your tents and walls of Troy,
To rouse a Grecian that is true in love.
If any come, Hector shall honor him;
If none, he'll say in Troy when he retires
The Grecian dames are sunburnt and not worth
The splinter of a lance." Even so much.

AGAMEMNON

This shall be told our lovers, Lord Aeneas.
If none of them have soul in such a kind,
We left them all at home. But we are soldiers,
And may that soldier a mere recreant prove
That means not, hath not, or is not in love!
If then one is, or hath, ⟨or⟩ means to be,
That one meets Hector. If none else, I am he.

NESTOR, ⌜*to Aeneas*⌝

Tell him of Nestor, one that was a man
When Hector's grandsire sucked. He is old now,
But if there be not in our Grecian host
A noble man that hath ⟨one⟩ spark of fire
To answer for his love, tell him from me
I'll hide my silver beard in a gold beaver
And in my vambrace put my withered brawns
And, meeting him, ⟨will⟩ tell him that my lady

308. **in flood:** i.e., in its prime (literally, overflowing its banks)

309. **prove this troth:** make good this pledge; **my . . . blood:** i.e., the little **blood** I have left

310. **forfend:** forbid

321. **time:** occasion, opportunity

324. **seeded:** run to seed, matured (The plant imagery continues in **blown up** [i.e., flourished], **cropped, shedding,** and **nursery.**)

326. **rank:** proud, haughty (but, applied to plants, **rank** means "of a luxuriant, gross, or coarse quality"); **or now:** i.e., either **now**

328. **overbulk:** i.e., outgrow (literally, surpass in bulk)

333–34. **substance . . . sum up:** i.e., quantity whose large size is expressed in small figures

335. **in the publication:** i.e., when it is proclaimed; **make no strain:** i.e., you may be sure that (literally, do not exert yourself to the utmost); or, **make no** strained construction or interpretation

Ulysses.
From [Guillaume Rouillé,] . . .
Promptuarii iconum . . . (1553).

Was fairer than his grandam and as chaste
As may be in the world. His youth in flood,
I'll prove this troth with my three drops of blood.

AENEAS
Now heavens forfend such scarcity of ⟨youth!⟩

ULYSSES Amen.

⟨AGAMEMNON⟩
Fair Lord Aeneas, let me touch your hand.
To our pavilion shall I lead you, sir.
Achilles shall have word of this intent;
So shall each lord of Greece from tent to tent.
Yourself shall feast with us before you go,
And find the welcome of a noble foe.
⟨All but Ulysses and Nestor exit.⟩

ULYSSES Nestor.

NESTOR What says Ulysses?

ULYSSES
I have a young conception in my brain;
Be you my time to bring it to some shape.

NESTOR What is 't?

ULYSSES ⟨This 'tis:⟩
Blunt wedges rive hard knots; the seeded pride
That hath to this maturity blown up
In rank Achilles must or now be cropped
Or, shedding, breed a nursery of like evil
To overbulk us all.

NESTOR Well, and how?

ULYSSES
This challenge that the gallant Hector sends,
However it is spread in general name,
Relates in purpose only to Achilles.

NESTOR
True. The purpose is perspicuous as substance
Whose grossness little characters sum up;
And, in the publication, make no strain
But that Achilles, were his brain as barren

337. **banks of Libya:** presumably, sandbanks in the deserts **of Libya**

341. **the answer:** i.e., acceptance of the challenge

342. **meet:** fitting, appropriate

344. **sportful:** i.e., done merely in sport

345. **opinion:** estimation, reputation

346. **repute:** reputation

348. **imputation:** reputation

349. **vile:** trivial; **success:** result, outcome

350. **particular:** pertaining to a single person; **scantling:** sample, specimen

352. **indexes:** summaries prefixed to books

352–53. **pricks . . . volumes:** minute points in comparison to the books that follow

358. **Makes . . . election:** perhaps, selects on the basis of **merit**

360. **virtues:** courage, valor, manly excellences

361–62. **a . . . themselves:** perhaps, a victorious portion to strengthen his confidence

363. **entertained:** accepted; **his:** its (i.e., strong opinion's)

364. **working:** influence, effectiveness

365. **Directive:** subject to direction

366. **Give . . . speech:** i.e., **give** me leave to speak

370. **showing:** i.e., our **showing,** our having shown

As banks of Libya—though, Apollo knows,
'Tis dry enough—will, with great speed of judgment,
Ay, with celerity, find Hector's purpose
Pointing on him.

ULYSSES And wake him to the answer, think you?

NESTOR

Why, 'tis most meet. Who may you else oppose
That can from Hector bring ⟨his honor⟩ off
If not Achilles? Though 't be a sportful combat,
Yet in the trial much opinion dwells,
For here the Trojans taste our dear'st repute
With their fin'st palate. And, trust to me, Ulysses,
Our imputation shall be oddly poised
In this vile action. For the success,
Although particular, shall give a scantling
Of good or bad unto the general;
And in such indexes, although small pricks
To their subsequent volumes, there is seen
The baby figure of the giant mass
Of things to come at large. It is supposed
He that meets Hector issues from our choice;
And choice, being mutual act of all our souls,
Makes merit her election and doth boil,
As 'twere from forth us all, a man distilled
Out of our virtues, who, miscarrying,
What heart receives from hence a conquering part
To steel a strong opinion to themselves?—
⟨Which entertained, limbs are his instruments,
In no less working than are swords and bows
Directive by the limbs.⟩

ULYSSES

Give pardon to my speech: therefore 'tis meet
Achilles meet not Hector. Let us like merchants
First show foul wares and think perchance they'll sell;
If not, the luster of the better shall exceed
By showing the worse first. Do not consent

375. **shares from:** i.e., gains at the expense of

378. **Afric:** African

379. **salt:** pungent, stinging

380. **fair:** i.e., successfully (literally, fully)

381. **main opinion:** general (or, perhaps, considerable) reputation

382. **In taint of:** i.e., in the dishonor or disgrace of

383. **device:** stratagem, trick; **blockish:** obtuse, stupid

384. **sort:** winning slip or lot

385. **Give . . . for:** i.e., allow him to be, praise him as

386. **physic . . . Myrmidon:** i.e., purge Achilles (of his pride) **Myrmidon:** the name given the warlike men led by Achilles

387. **broils:** heats up, glows

387–88. **fall / His crest:** To "let **fall** one's **crest**" is to become dispirited or humbled.

388. **Iris:** perhaps, the goddess whose sign is the rainbow; or, perhaps, the flower (For **Iris** as goddess, see picture, page 170.)

390. **voices:** reports, fame

394. **plumes:** i.e., displays of pride (literally, conspicuous feathers)

397. **straight:** straightway, immediately

399. **tar . . . on:** i.e., incite **the mastiffs**

That ever Hector and Achilles meet,
For both our honor and our shame in this
Are dogged with two strange followers.

NESTOR

I see them not with my old eyes. What are they?

ULYSSES

What glory our Achilles shares from Hector,
Were he not proud, we all should share with him;
But he already is too insolent,
And it were better parch in Afric sun
Than in the pride and salt scorn of his eyes
Should he scape Hector fair. If he were foiled,
Why then we do our main opinion crush
In taint of our best man. No, make a lott'ry,
And, by device, let blockish Ajax draw
The sort to fight with Hector. Among ourselves
Give him allowance for the better man,
For that will physic the great Myrmidon,
Who broils in loud applause, and make him fall
His crest that prouder than blue Iris bends.
If the dull brainless Ajax come safe off,
We'll dress him up in voices; if he fail,
Yet go we under our opinion still
That we have better men. But, hit or miss,
Our project's life this shape of sense assumes:
Ajax employed plucks down Achilles' plumes.

NESTOR

Now, Ulysses, I begin to relish thy advice,
And I will give a taste thereof forthwith
To Agamemnon. Go we to him straight.
Two curs shall tame each other; pride alone
Must ⟨tar⟩ the mastiffs on, as 'twere a bone.

They exit.

TROILUS AND CRESSIDA

ACT 2

2.1 Ajax beats Thersites for refusing to tell him the terms of the challenge, terms that are provided by Achilles when he and Patroclus come to Thersites' rescue.

---

3. **generally:** wordplay on (1) (almost) everywhere; (2) the general (**Agamemnon**)

5. **run:** ooze, discharge pus

5–6. **the general:** again wordplay, now on (1) Agamemnon; (2) the army in **general**

6. **run:** i.e., run away, flee; **botchy core:** (1) swollen boil; (2) rotten heart

8. **matter:** (1) pus; (2) good sense

12–13. **mongrel:** half-breed (half Greek, half Trojan)

13. **beef-witted:** beef-brained, thickheaded, stupid

14. **unsalted:** without liveliness or freshness (See also Matthew 5.13: "Ye are the salt [i.e., excellence] of the earth.") See longer note, page 272.

16. **rail . . . holiness:** i.e., make you wise and pious by abusing you verbally

17. **con:** learn, memorize

18. **without book:** from memory

19. **red . . . tricks:** i.e., plague on your ill-tempered behavior (A *jade* is a broken-down or vicious **horse** [line 17].)

20. **learn me:** inform me about

21. **sense:** (1) capacity to feel pain; (2) mental faculties

⌜ACT 2⌝

⌜Scene 1⌝

Enter Ajax and Thersites.

AJAX Thersites!

THERSITES Agamemnon—how if he had boils, full, all over, generally?

AJAX Thersites!

THERSITES And those boils did run? Say so. Did not the general run, then? Were not that a botchy core?

AJAX Dog!

THERSITES Then ⟨there⟩ would come some matter from him. I see none now.

AJAX Thou bitchwolf's son, canst thou not hear? Feel, then. *⟨Strikes him.⟩*

THERSITES The plague of Greece upon thee, thou mongrel beef-witted lord!

AJAX Speak, then, thou unsalted leaven, speak. I will beat thee into handsomeness.

THERSITES I shall sooner rail thee into wit and holiness, but I think thy horse will sooner con an oration than thou learn ⟨a⟩ prayer without book. Thou canst strike, canst thou? A red murrain o' thy jade's tricks.

AJAX Toadstool, learn me the proclamation.

THERSITES Dost thou think I have no sense, thou strikest me thus?

AJAX The proclamation!

THERSITES Thou art proclaimed ⟨a⟩ fool, I think.

25. **porpentine:** porcupine (See picture, page 102.) **My fingers itch:** i.e., I want to thrash you

28. **scab:** (1) crust that forms over a wound; (2) scoundrel

34. **Cerberus:** in mythology, the three-headed dog who guards the underworld; **Proserpina:** queen of the underworld (In some myths, Cerberus's **envy** of her **beauty** led him to attack her suitors.) See picture below and page 72.

38. **Cobloaf:** a little loaf, made with a round top

40. **biscuit:** i.e., ship **biscuit** or hardtack (proverbially hard and dry)

46. **asinego:** i.e., donkey, fool (literally, a little ass [Spanish])

49. **use to:** i.e., continue to

50. **tell:** recount; **by inches:** i.e., bit by bit

51. **bowels:** compassion, pity

55. **Mars his:** i.e., Mars's (**Mars** is the Roman god of war.) See picture, page 158.

57. **Wherefore:** why

"Proserpina's beauty." (2.1.34)
From Philippe Galle, *De deis gentium imagines* . . . (1581).

AJAX Do not, porpentine, do not. My fingers itch.

THERSITES I would thou didst itch from head to foot, and I had the scratching of thee; I would make thee the loathsomest scab in Greece. [When thou art forth in the incursions, thou strikest as slow as another.]

AJAX I say, the proclamation!

THERSITES Thou grumblest and railest every hour on Achilles, and thou art as full of envy at his greatness as Cerberus is at Proserpina's beauty, ay, that thou bark'st at him.

AJAX Mistress Thersites!

THERSITES Thou shouldst strike him—

AJAX Cobloaf!

⟨THERSITES⟩ He would pound thee into shivers with his fist as a sailor breaks a biscuit.

⟨AJAX⟩ You whoreson cur! ⌜*Strikes him.*⌝

⟨THERSITES⟩ Do, do.

AJAX Thou stool for a witch!

THERSITES Ay, do, do, thou sodden-witted lord. Thou hast no more brain than I have in mine elbows; an asinego may tutor thee, ⟨thou⟩ scurvy-valiant ass. Thou art here but to thrash Trojans, and thou art bought and sold among those of any wit, like a barbarian slave. If thou use to beat me, I will begin at thy heel and tell what thou art by inches, thou thing of no bowels, thou.

AJAX You dog!

THERSITES You scurvy lord!

AJAX You cur! ⌜*Strikes him.*⌝

THERSITES Mars his idiot! Do, rudeness, do, camel, do, do.

⟨*Enter Achilles and Patroclus.*⟩

ACHILLES Why, how now, Ajax? Wherefore do you thus?—How now, Thersites? What's the matter, man?

67. **whosomever:** i.e., whoever; **Ajax:** possibly a pun on "a jakes" (i.e., a privy or latrine)

72. **have ears thus long:** i.e., are asinine, stupid (literally, **have** the **ears** of an ass)

73. **bobbed:** (1) made a fool of; (2) pummeled

74. **I will buy:** i.e., **I** can **buy**

74–75. **pia mater:** i.e., brain

84. **stop:** block

90. **set . . . fool's:** Proverbial: "Do not **set your wit** against **a fool's.**"

92. **Good words:** i.e., don't speak so fiercely (from the Latin *bona verba*)

Cerberus. (2.1.34)
From Vincenzo Cartari, *Imagines deorum* . . . (1581).

THERSITES You see him there, do you?
ACHILLES Ay, what's the matter?
THERSITES Nay, look upon him.
ACHILLES So I do. What's the matter?
THERSITES Nay, but regard him well.
ACHILLES Well, why, so I do.
THERSITES But yet you look not well upon him, for whosomever you take him to be, he is Ajax.
ACHILLES I know that, fool.
THERSITES Ay, but that fool knows not himself.
AJAX Therefore I beat thee.
THERSITES Lo, lo, lo, lo, what modicums of wit he utters! His evasions have ears thus long. I have bobbed his brain more than he has beat my bones. ⟨I⟩ will buy nine sparrows for a penny, and his pia mater is not worth the ninth part of a sparrow. This lord, Achilles—Ajax, who wears his wit in his belly, and his guts in his head—⟨I'll⟩ tell you what I say of him.
ACHILLES What?
THERSITES I say, this Ajax— ⌜*Ajax menaces him.*⌝
ACHILLES Nay, good Ajax.
THERSITES Has not so much wit—
ACHILLES, ⌜*to Ajax*⌝ Nay, I must hold you.
THERSITES As will stop the eye of Helen's needle, for whom he comes to fight.
ACHILLES Peace, fool!
THERSITES I would have peace and quietness, but the fool will not—he there, that he. Look you there.
AJAX O, thou damned cur, I shall—
ACHILLES Will you set your wit to a fool's?
THERSITES No, I warrant you. The fool's will shame it.
PATROCLUS Good words, Thersites.
ACHILLES, ⌜*to Ajax*⌝ What's the quarrel?
AJAX I bade the vile owl go learn me the tenor of the proclamation, and he rails upon me.

97. **go to:** an expression of impatience

98. **voluntary:** voluntarily, through my own choice

99. **suff'rance:** (1) something merely allowed or tolerated; (2) pain, suffering

101. **voluntary:** one who acts of his own free will; **under an impress:** conscripted, forced into military **service** (line 99), with wordplay on **impress** as a mark stamped upon something or someone

103. **sinews:** muscles

104. **an he knock:** i.e., if he knocks

105. **were as good:** i.e., might as well

113. **good sooth:** i.e., indeed; **To:** i.e., attack, go to it (as if to warriors or **draft-oxen**)

115. **as much:** i.e., **as much** good sense or **matter**

118. **brach:** bitch hound

121. **clodpolls:** thickheads, blockheads

122. **keep:** stay, remain

123. **faction:** (1) band (literally, class or set); (2) factious quarreling

126. **by . . . sun:** i.e., during **the fifth hour** after sunrise

129. **stomach:** desire (to fight); courage

A gorget. (1.3.178)
From Louis de Gaya,
Traité des armes, des machines de guerre . . . (1678).

THERSITES I serve thee not.

AJAX Well, go to, go to.

THERSITES I serve here voluntary.

ACHILLES Your last service was suff'rance; 'twas not voluntary. No man is beaten voluntary. Ajax was here the voluntary, and you as under an impress.

THERSITES E'en so. A great deal of your wit, too, lies in your sinews, or else there be liars. Hector shall have a great catch an ⟨he⟩ knock ⟨out⟩ either of your brains; he were as good crack a fusty nut with no kernel.

ACHILLES What, with me too, Thersites?

THERSITES There's Ulysses and old Nestor—whose wit was moldy ere ⌜your⌝ grandsires had nails ⟨on their toes⟩—yoke you like draft-oxen and make you plow up the wars.

ACHILLES What? What?

THERSITES Yes, good sooth. To, Achilles! To, Ajax! To—

AJAX I shall cut out your tongue.

THERSITES 'Tis no matter. I shall speak as much as thou afterwards.

PATROCLUS No more words, Thersites. Peace.

THERSITES I will hold my peace when Achilles' ⌜brach⌝ bids me, shall I?

ACHILLES There's for you, Patroclus.

THERSITES I will see you hanged like clodpolls ere I come any more to your tents. I will keep where there is wit stirring and leave the faction of fools.

He exits.

PATROCLUS A good riddance.

ACHILLES, ⌜*to Ajax*⌝

Marry, this, sir, is proclaimed through all our host:
That Hector, by the ⟨fifth⟩ hour of the sun,
Will with a trumpet 'twixt our tents and Troy
Tomorrow morning call some knight to arms
That hath a stomach, and such a one that dare
Maintain—I know not what; 'tis trash. Farewell.

131. **answer him:** meet his challenge

2.2 The Trojan leaders discuss whether to keep Helen and thereby continue the war. They decide to do so in spite of Cassandra's prophecies of Troy's destruction.

---

4. **travel:** includes the meaning of "travail" (labor)

6. **cormorant:** i.e., insatiably ravenous (literally, a voracious seabird)

7. **struck off:** canceled

9. **my particular:** my own case

11. **of more softer bowels:** i.e., **more** sensitive to the tender emotions

12. **fear:** apprehension of future catastrophe

14. **wound . . . surety:** i.e., **peace** is most easily lost through overconfidence (Proverbial: "He that is secure [i.e., too self-confident] is not safe.")

15. **modest doubt:** i.e., caution, prudence (literally, moderate fear)

16. **tent:** probe

19–20. **Every . . . ours:** Hector argues that the war has claimed one out of every ten Trojan lives, each as valuable as Helen. **tithe:** tenth **dismes:** tenths

23. **one ten:** perhaps, **one** of every **ten** men lost in the war

AJAX Farewell. Who shall answer him?

ACHILLES

I know not. 'Tis put to lott'ry. Otherwise,
He knew his man. ⌜*Achilles and Patroclus exit.*⌝

AJAX O, meaning you? I will go learn more of it.
⟨*He exits.*⟩

⌜Scene 2⌝

Enter Priam, Hector, Troilus, Paris and Helenus.

PRIAM

After so many hours, lives, speeches spent,
Thus once again says Nestor from the Greeks:
"Deliver Helen, and all damage else—
As honor, loss of time, travel, expense,
Wounds, friends, and what else dear that is consumed
In hot digestion of this cormorant war—
Shall be struck off."—Hector, what say you to 't?

HECTOR

Though no man lesser fears the Greeks than I
As far as toucheth my particular,
Yet, dread Priam,
There is no lady of more softer bowels,
More spongy to suck in the sense of fear,
More ready to cry out "Who knows what follows?"
Than Hector is. The wound of peace is ⟨surety,
Surety⟩ secure; but modest doubt is called
The beacon of the wise, the tent that searches
To th' bottom of the worst. Let Helen go.
Since the first sword was drawn about this question,
Every tithe soul, 'mongst many thousand dismes,
Hath been as dear as Helen; I mean, of ours.
If we have lost so many tenths of ours
To guard a thing not ours—nor worth to us,
Had it our name, the value of one ten—

24. **reason:** argument

29. **counters:** tokens used for adding and subtracting

30. **past-proportion:** immeasurableness, immensity; **infinite:** i.e., infinite being

31. **fathomless:** immeasurable, ungraspable

32. **spans:** i.e., handbreadths

36. **reason:** sanity, rational thought (introducing wordplay on **reason** as "thought" and as "argument" [See, e.g., lines 24, 39–40.])

37. **none:** i.e., no **reasons**

38. **brother priest:** In Homer's *Iliad,* **Helenus,** son of Priam, is soothsayer to the Trojans.

43. **object:** image

47. **Mercury:** As messenger to the gods, **Mercury** had **wings** on **his heels** (line 46). He was **chidden** by **Jove** for stealing Apollo's cattle.

48. **star disorbed:** i.e., shooting **star** **disorbed:** removed from its sphere (See longer note to 1.3.89, page 272, and picture, page 126.)

50. **Should:** i.e., would; **hare:** i.e., timid; **would . . . fat:** i.e., if they merely fattened

52. **crammed:** overfed; **respect:** consideration

53. **Make . . . pale:** It was believed that fear turned the liver white. **lustihood:** vigor, robustness; **deject:** downcast, dispirited

55. **The keeping:** i.e., in defending or taking care of her

56. **What's . . . valued:** proverbial

What merit's in that reason which denies
The yielding of her up?

TROILUS Fie, fie, my brother,
Weigh you the worth and honor of a king
So great as our dread father's in a scale
Of common ounces? Will you with counters sum
The past-proportion of his infinite,
And buckle in a waist most fathomless
With spans and inches so diminutive
As fears and reasons? Fie, for godly shame!

HELENUS
No marvel though you bite so sharp ⟨at⟩ reasons,
You are so empty of them. Should not our father
Bear the great sway of his affairs with reason,
Because your speech hath none that tell him so?

TROILUS
You are for dreams and slumbers, brother priest.
You fur your gloves with reason. Here are your
reasons:
You know an enemy intends you harm;
You know a sword employed is perilous,
And reason flies the object of all harm.
Who marvels, then, when Helenus beholds
A Grecian and his sword, if he do set
The very wings of reason to his heels
And fly like chidden Mercury from Jove
Or like a star disorbed? Nay, if we talk of reason,
⟨Let's⟩ shut our gates and sleep. Manhood and honor
Should have hare hearts, would they but fat their
thoughts
With this crammed reason. Reason and respect
Make livers pale and lustihood deject.

HECTOR
Brother, she is not worth what she doth cost
The keeping.

TROILUS What's aught but as 'tis valued?

57. **particular will:** i.e., the **will** of a given individual

58. **his estimate:** its reputation

61. **the service:** i.e., that which is offered up

62–64. **And . . . merit:** i.e., it is foolish to confer value on something that does not appear to have any **dotes:** loves foolishly **is attributive:** i.e., attributes **infectiously:** contagiously **affects:** fancies, loves **affected:** sought after; desired; loved **merit:** claim or title to excellence, worth

65. **I . . . wife:** This statement is Troilus's hypothesis, chosen for the sake of argument. (See longer note, page 272.) **election:** act of deliberate choice

66. **in the conduct of:** i.e., guided by, led by

67–69. **My will . . . judgment:** In Troilus's account, the **will** is inflamed by **eyes and ears,** which then negotiate between **will and judgment.** (See longer note, page 272.) **traded:** skilled, experienced

69. **avoid:** dismiss, send away

70. **elected:** picked out

71. **evasion:** means

72. **blench:** swerve, deviate; **from this:** presumably, **from** standing by one's choice of **wife** (line 71)

73. **turn . . . upon:** i.e., do not return pieces of silk fabric to

74–75. **remainder viands:** i.e., leftover food

76. **unrespective sieve:** i.e., scrap basket **unrespective:** undiscriminating **sieve:** strainer or basket

77. **meet:** appropriate, fitting

79. **bellied:** swelled

80. **old wranglers:** i.e., longtime enemies (literally, quarrelers)

(continued)

HECTOR
But value dwells not in particular will;
It holds his estimate and dignity
As well wherein 'tis precious of itself
As in the prizer. 'Tis mad idolatry
To make the service greater than the god;
And the will dotes that is attributive
To what infectiously itself affects
Without some image of th' affected merit.

TROILUS
I take today a wife, and my election
Is led on in the conduct of my will—
My will enkindled by mine eyes and ears,
Two traded pilots 'twixt the dangerous ⟨shores⟩
Of will and judgment. How may I avoid,
Although my will distaste what it elected,
The wife I choose? There can be no evasion
To blench from this and to stand firm by honor.
We turn not back the silks upon the merchant
When we have soiled them, nor the remainder viands
We do not throw in unrespective sieve
Because we now are full. It was thought meet
Paris should do some vengeance on the Greeks.
Your breath with full consent bellied his sails;
The seas and winds, old wranglers, took a truce
And did him service. He touched the ports desired,
And for an old aunt whom the Greeks held captive,
He brought a Grecian queen, whose youth and freshness
Wrinkles Apollo's and makes pale the morning.
Why keep we her? The Grecians keep our aunt.
Is she worth keeping? Why, she is a pearl
Whose price hath launched above a thousand ships
And turned crowned kings to merchants.
If you'll avouch 'twas wisdom Paris went—

81. **did him service:** i.e., served him; **touched:** arrived at

82. **aunt:** i.e., Priam's sister Hesione, married to a Greek and, in some sources, the mother of Ajax

85. **Wrinkles . . . morning:** i.e., **makes** the radiant Apollo, god of the sun, look old, and **makes the** rosy **morning** look **pale** (See picture, page 152.)

87. **Is she worth:** i.e., **is** Helen **worth**

88. **Whose . . . ships:** See longer note, page 273. **price:** value, worth **above:** more than

91. **must needs:** i.e., necessarily **must**

95. **issue:** outcome; **proper:** own; **rate:** chide, reprove

97. **Beggar:** i.e., devalue (literally, impoverish); **estimation:** i.e., treasure (literally, something which one values); **prized:** reckoned, accounted

100. **But thieves:** i.e., **but** we are **thieves**

102. **warrant:** sanction

103 SD. **within:** i.e., offstage

105. **mad sister:** Cassandra was under the curse that her hearers would never believe her prophecies, but would instead consider her **mad.**

112. **canst:** i.e., can do

113. **betimes:** forthwith, at once

114. **moiety:** portion

115. **Practice . . . tears:** i.e., make **your eyes** accustomed to (or skilled in) weeping

116. **goodly:** beautiful

117. **firebrand brother:** an allusion to Virgil's *Aeneid,* which mentions the "night that—pregnant with a **firebrand**— . . . Hecuba bore **Paris**" (10.704–5; see also 7.316–20)

As you must needs, for you all cried "Go, go"—
If you'll confess ⟨he⟩ brought home worthy prize—
As you must needs, for you all clapped your hands
And cried "Inestimable"—why do you now
The issue of your proper wisdoms rate
And do a deed that never Fortune did,
Beggar the estimation which you prized
Richer than sea and land? O, theft most base,
That we have stol'n what we do fear to keep!
But thieves unworthy of a thing so stol'n,
That in their country did them that disgrace
We fear to warrant in our native place.

CASSANDRA, ⌜*within*⌝
Cry, Trojans, cry!

PRIAM What noise? What shriek is this?

TROILUS
'Tis our mad sister. I do know her voice.

CASSANDRA, ⌜*within*⌝ Cry, Trojans!

HECTOR It is Cassandra.

Enter Cassandra raving.

CASSANDRA
Cry, Trojans, cry! Lend me ten thousand eyes,
And I will fill them with prophetic tears.

HECTOR Peace, sister, peace!

CASSANDRA
Virgins and boys, mid-age and wrinkled elders,
Soft infancy, that nothing canst but cry,
Add to my clamors. Let us pay betimes
A moiety of that mass of moan to come.
Cry, Trojans, cry! Practice your eyes with tears.
Troy must not be, nor goodly Ilium stand.
Our firebrand brother Paris burns us all.
Cry, Trojans, cry! A Helen and a woe!
Cry, cry! Troy burns, or else let Helen go. *She exits.*

120. **strains:** i.e., speeches (literally, passages of song or poetry)

123. **discourse of reason:** i.e., rational **discourse**

124. **success:** outcome

129. **deject:** overthrow

131. **distaste:** spoil the savor of

132. **several:** individual

133. **gracious:** acceptable, worthy of favor

136. **spleen:** i.e., person ruled by his **spleen,** an organ of the body connoting courage (but also caprice and melancholy)

138. **Else:** otherwise; **convince:** convict

140. **attest the gods:** call **the gods** to witness

141. **propension:** inclination

142. **attending on:** accompanying

143. **can . . . arms:** i.e., **can my arms** alone accomplish

144. **propugnation:** defense, protection

145. **stand the push:** withstand the attack

147. **pass:** undergo, experience

150. **pursuit:** endeavor

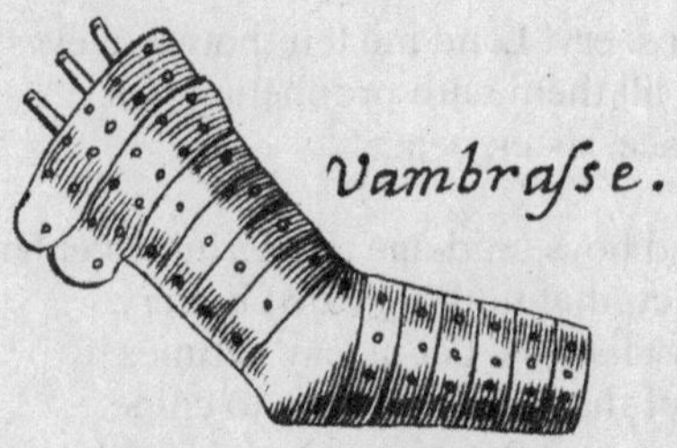

A vambrace. (1.3.305)
From Louis de Gaya, *A treatise of the arms* . . . (1678).

HECTOR

Now, youthful Troilus, do not these high strains
Of divination in our sister work
Some touches of remorse? Or is your blood
So madly hot that no discourse of reason
Nor fear of bad success in a bad cause
Can qualify the same?

TROILUS Why, brother Hector,
We may not think the justness of each act
Such and no other than event doth form it,
Nor once deject the courage of our minds
Because Cassandra's mad. Her brainsick raptures
Cannot distaste the goodness of a quarrel
Which hath our several honors all engaged
To make it gracious. For my private part,
I am no more touched than all Priam's sons;
And Jove forbid there should be done amongst us
Such things as might offend the weakest spleen
To fight for and maintain!

PARIS

Else might the world convince of levity
As well my undertakings as your counsels.
But I attest the gods, your full consent
Gave wings to my propension and cut off
All fears attending on so dire a project.
For what, alas, can these my single arms?
What propugnation is in one man's valor
To stand the push and enmity of those
This quarrel would excite? Yet, I protest,
Were I alone to pass the difficulties
And had as ample power as I have will,
Paris should ne'er retract what he hath done
Nor faint in the pursuit.

PRIAM Paris, you speak
Like one besotted on your sweet delights.
You have the honey still, but these the gall.
So to be valiant is no praise at all.

157. **her fair rape:** i.e., the abduction of **her** (who is so **fair**)

159. **ransacked queen:** i.e., **queen** stolen as plunder

161. **her possession:** i.e., the **possession** of **her**

162. **base:** ignoble

165. **meanest:** most ignobly born

171. **parallel:** find or furnish a match for

174. **glozed:** commented

176. **hear:** learn; **moral philosophy:** ethics

177–78. **conduce / To:** promote

178. **distempered:** disordered, diseased

181. **more deaf than adders:** Proverbial: "**Deaf** as an adder."

183. **All . . . owners:** Proverbial: "Give everyone his due."

186. **affection:** lust

187. **And that:** i.e., and if

187–88. **of . . . / To:** i.e., through biased gratification of

Helen.

Paris.

From [Guillaume Rouillé,] . . . *Promptuarii iconum* . . . (1553).

PARIS

Sir, I propose not merely to myself
The pleasures such a beauty brings with it,
But I would have the soil of her fair rape
Wiped off in honorable keeping her.
What treason were it to the ransacked queen,
Disgrace to your great worths, and shame to me,
Now to deliver her possession up
On terms of base compulsion? Can it be
That so degenerate a strain as this
Should once set footing in your generous bosoms?
There's not the meanest spirit on our party
Without a heart to dare or sword to draw
When Helen is defended, nor none so noble
Whose life were ill bestowed or death unfamed
Where Helen is the subject. Then I say,
Well may we fight for her whom, we know well,
The world's large spaces cannot parallel.

HECTOR

Paris and Troilus, you have both said well,
And on the cause and question now in hand
Have glozed—but superficially, not much
Unlike young men, whom Aristotle thought
Unfit to hear moral philosophy.
The reasons you allege do more conduce
To the hot passion of distempered blood
Than to make up a free determination
'Twixt right and wrong, for pleasure and revenge
Have ears more deaf than adders to the voice
Of any true decision. Nature craves
All dues be rendered to their owners. Now,
What nearer debt in all humanity
Than wife is to the husband? If this law
Of nature be corrupted through affection,
And that great minds, of partial indulgence
To their benumbèd wills, resist the same,

193. **moral laws:** requirements determining right or virtuous actions

196. **doing wrong:** breaking the law; acting unjustly; **extenuates not wrong:** does **not** extenuate injury

198. **in way of truth:** i.e., in abstract principle; or, as a general principle

199. **sprightly:** lively; **propend:** incline

201. **no . . . dependence:** i.e., **no** small effect **dependence:** connection, relation

203. **touched:** hit upon, represented accurately; **life:** animating principle, soul

204. **affected:** loved, sought

205. **spleens:** peevish tempers; high spirits

214. **forehead:** forefront, front part

215. **revenue:** accent on second syllable

218. **roisting:** blustering, boisterous

221. **advertised:** informed (accent on second syllable)

222. **emulation:** contention, rivalrous ill will

Vulcan. (1.3.172; 5.2.200)
From Johann Basilius Herold, *Heydenweldt* . . . [1554].

There is a law in each well-ordered nation
To curb those raging appetites that are
Most disobedient and refractory.
If Helen, then, be wife to Sparta's king,
As it is known she is, these moral laws
Of nature and of nations speak aloud
To have her back returned. Thus to persist
In doing wrong extenuates not wrong,
But makes it much more heavy. Hector's opinion
Is this in way of truth; yet, ne'ertheless,
My sprightly brethren, I propend to you
In resolution to keep Helen still,
For 'tis a cause that hath no mean dependence
Upon our joint and several dignities.

TROILUS

Why, there you touched the life of our design!
Were it not glory that we more affected
Than the performance of our heaving spleens,
I would not wish a drop of Trojan blood
Spent more in her defense. But, worthy Hector,
She is a theme of honor and renown,
A spur to valiant and magnanimous deeds,
Whose present courage may beat down our foes,
And fame in time to come canonize us;
For I presume brave Hector would not lose
So rich advantage of a promised glory
As smiles upon the forehead of this action
For the wide world's revenue.

HECTOR

I am yours,
You valiant offspring of great Priamus.
I have a roisting challenge sent amongst
The dull and factious nobles of the Greeks
Will ⟨strike⟩ amazement to their drowsy spirits.
I was advertised their great general slept,
Whilst emulation in the army crept.
This, I presume, will wake him.

They exit.

2.3 Thersites rails against Achilles and Ajax, and then, joined by Achilles and Patroclus, ridicules them to their faces. As Agamemnon and his councillors approach, Achilles goes inside his tent and refuses to meet them. The Greek leaders then heap praise on Ajax to prepare him to take up Hector's challenge.

2–3. **carry it:** i.e., win the day, gain the advantage

5. **'Sfoot:** an oath, "by God's foot"

5–6. **I'll learn . . . devils but I'll see:** i.e., even if I have to **learn . . . devils I'll see**

6. **issue of:** results from

8. **enginer:** (1) maker of military devices; (2) layer of snares and plots

9. **fall of:** i.e., **fall** by

10. **thunder-darter:** wielder of thunderbolts (i.e., bolts of lightning conceived of as hot solid bodies thrown by **Jove** [line 11]) See picture, page 26.

10–11. **Olympus:** a mountain in Greece where, in mythology, the greater gods lived

12. **Mercury:** a Roman divinity, messenger of the gods and wielder of the **caduceus** (line 13), a winged staff with two serpents twined around it (hence the word **serpentine**) See picture, page 96.

16. **circumvention:** crafty expedience, guile

17. **irons:** swords

19–20. **Neapolitan bone-ache:** a common name for syphilis

20. **methinks:** it seems to me

20–21. **depending on:** belonging to

(continued)

⌜Scene 3⌝

Enter Thersites, alone.

⌜THERSITES⌝ How now, Thersites? What, lost in the labyrinth of thy fury? Shall the elephant Ajax carry it thus? He beats me, and I rail at him. O, worthy satisfaction! Would it were otherwise, that I could beat him whilst he railed at me. 'Sfoot, I'll learn to conjure and raise devils but I'll see some issue of my spiteful execrations. Then there's Achilles, a rare enginer! If Troy be not taken till these two undermine it, the walls will stand till they fall of themselves. O thou great thunder-darter of Olympus, forget that thou art Jove, the king of gods; and, Mercury, lose all the serpentine craft of thy caduceus, if you take not that little, little, less than little wit from them that they have, which short-armed ignorance itself knows is so abundant scarce it will not in circumvention deliver a fly from a spider without drawing their massy irons and cutting the web. After this, the vengeance on the whole camp! Or rather, the Neapolitan bone-ache! For that, methinks, is the curse depending on those that war for a placket. I have said my prayers, and devil Envy say "Amen."—What ho, my lord Achilles!

PATROCLUS, ⌜*within*⌝ Who's there? Thersites? Good Thersites, come in and rail.

THERSITES If I could 'a remembered a gilt counterfeit, thou couldst not have slipped out of my contemplation. But it is no matter. Thyself upon thyself! The common curse of mankind, folly and ignorance, be thine in great revenue! Heaven bless thee from a tutor, and discipline come not near thee! Let thy blood be thy direction till thy death; then if she that lays thee out says thou art a fair corse, I'll be

21. **placket:** i.e., woman (literally, petticoat or apron)

22. **Envy:** malice, malignant hostility

27–28. **thou . . . contemplation:** i.e., I would not have forgotten to curse you **slipped:** wordplay on **a gilt counterfeit** (coin [line 26]), also called a "slip"

28. **Thyself upon thyself:** perhaps, "you are a sufficient curse against yourself"

30. **in great revenue:** i.e., in abundance

31. **discipline:** learning, education

32. **blood:** sensual appetite; **direction:** i.e., guide

33. **lays thee out:** prepares your **corse** (corpse) for burial (See picture, page 104.) **fair:** handsome

35. **lazars:** lepers (See picture, page 164.)

38. **prayer:** Patroclus presumably alludes to the word **Amen** (line 35).

44. **cheese:** Proverbially, **cheese,** eaten at the end of **meals** (line 46), aids **digestion** (line 45). (Thersites acts as Achilles' Fool or entertainer, cheering him up and thus improving his health.)

55. **decline:** recite formally; **question:** subject under consideration

60. **a privileged man:** i.e., one who, as a Fool, is allowed to do or say as he pleases (See picture, page 118.)

65. **Derive:** i.e., explain, support (literally, trace the derivation of)

sworn and sworn upon 't she never shrouded any but lazars. Amen.

⟨*Enter Patroclus.*⟩

Where's Achilles?

PATROCLUS What, art thou devout? Wast thou in prayer?

THERSITES Ay. The heavens hear me!

[PATROCLUS Amen.]

ACHILLES, ⌜*within*⌝ Who's there?

PATROCLUS Thersites, my lord.

ACHILLES, ⌜*within*⌝ Where? Where? O, where?

Enter Achilles.

⌜*To Thersites.*⌝ Art thou come? Why, my cheese, my digestion, why hast thou not served thyself in to my table so many meals? Come, what's Agamemnon?

THERSITES Thy commander, Achilles.—Then, tell me, Patroclus, what's Achilles?

PATROCLUS Thy lord, Thersites. Then, tell me, I pray thee, what's Thersites?

THERSITES Thy knower, Patroclus. Then, tell me, Patroclus, what art thou?

PATROCLUS Thou must tell that knowest.

ACHILLES O tell, tell.

THERSITES I'll decline the whole question. Agamemnon commands Achilles, Achilles is my lord, I am Patroclus' knower, and Patroclus is a fool.

⟨PATROCLUS You rascal!

THERSITES Peace, fool. I have not done.

ACHILLES, ⌜*to Patroclus*⌝ He is a privileged man.—Proceed, Thersites.

THERSITES Agamemnon is a fool, Achilles is a fool, Thersites is a fool, and, as aforesaid, Patroclus is a fool.⟩

ACHILLES Derive this. Come.

66. **offer:** attempt, endeavor

69. **positive:** absolute, unconditional

76. **patchery:** roguery; **juggling:** trickery

77. **argument:** (1) subject of contention; (2) debate

78. **draw:** bring together; **emulous:** rivalrous

79. **serpigo:** spreading skin disease; ringworm

80. **subject:** topic, theme; **confound:** destroy

82. **ill-disposed:** unwell (with possible wordplay on "unfavorably inclined")

84. **shent:** reviled; **we:** i.e., I (See longer note to 1.3.76, page 270.)

85. **Our appertainments:** i.e., those rights and privileges that properly belong to me

87. **move:** bring forward, propose; **place:** (superior) position

92. **lion-sick:** The **lion,** as "king of beasts," is associated with pride.

93. **favor the man:** i.e., treat **the man** kindly

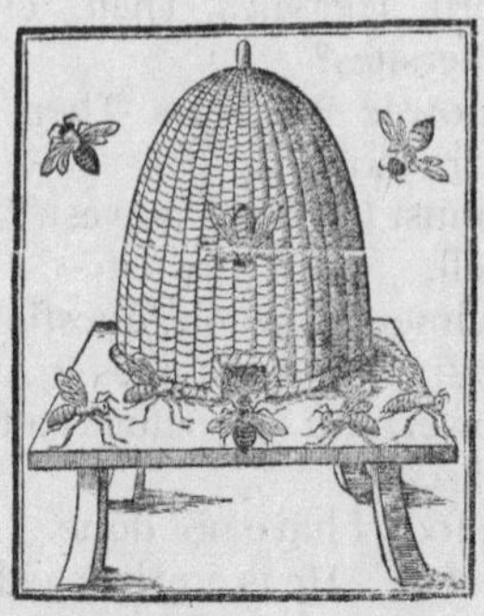

A beehive. (1.3.85)
From Thomas Moffet, *Insectorum* . . . (1634).

THERSITES Agamemnon is a fool to offer to command Achilles, Achilles is a fool to be commanded ⟨of Agamemnon,⟩ Thersites is a fool to serve such a fool, and this Patroclus is a fool positive.

PATROCLUS Why am I a fool?

THERSITES Make that demand of the ⟨creator.⟩ It suffices me thou art.

Enter ⌜at a distance⌝ Agamemnon, Ulysses, Nestor, Diomedes, Ajax, and Calchas.

Look you, who comes here?

ACHILLES Patroclus, I'll speak with nobody.—Come in with me, Thersites. ⟨*He exits.*⟩

THERSITES Here is such patchery, such juggling, and such knavery. All the argument is a whore and a cuckold, a good quarrel to draw emulous factions and bleed to death upon. ⟨Now the dry serpigo on the subject, and war and lechery confound all!⟩

⌜*He exits.*⌝

AGAMEMNON, ⌜*to Patroclus*⌝ Where is Achilles?

PATROCLUS
Within his tent, but ill-disposed, my lord.

AGAMEMNON
Let it be known to him that we are here.
He ⌜shent⌝ our messengers, and we lay by
Our ⟨appertainments,⟩ visiting of him.
Let him be told so, lest perchance he think
We dare not move the question of our place
Or know not what we are.

PATROCLUS I shall say so to him. ⌜*He exits.*⌝

ULYSSES
We saw him at the opening of his tent.
He is not sick.

AJAX Yes, lion-sick, sick of proud heart. You may call it melancholy if you will favor the man, but, by my

100. **lack matter:** i.e., have nothing to say
101. **argument:** theme, subject
104. **fraction:** dissension, breakup
105. **composure:** fabric, structure
112. **his legs:** i.e., its **legs**
114. **sport:** amusement, entertainment
115. **state:** i.e., group of dignitaries
118. **breath:** i.e., walk, constitutional
122. **apprehensions:** conceptions, ideas
123. **attribute:** honor, distinguished reputation
124. **virtues:** abilities, merits
125. **beheld:** perhaps, observed, regarded

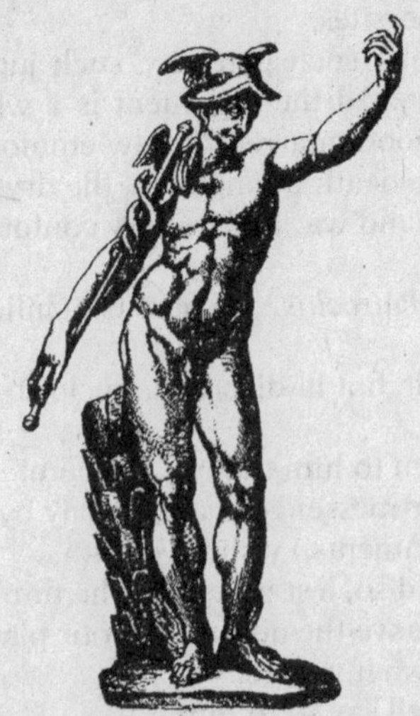

Mercury bearing his caduceus. (2.3.12–13)
From Giovanni Battista Cavalleriis,
Antiquarum statuarum . . . (1585–94).

head, 'tis pride. But, why, why? Let him show us a cause.—⟨A word, my lord.⟩

⌜*He and Agamemnon walk aside.*⌝

NESTOR What moves Ajax thus to bay at him?

ULYSSES Achilles hath inveigled his fool from him.

NESTOR Who, Thersites?

ULYSSES He.

NESTOR Then will Ajax lack matter, if he have lost his argument.

ULYSSES No. You see, he is his argument that has his argument: Achilles.

NESTOR All the better. Their fraction is more our wish than their faction. But it was a strong composure a fool could disunite.

ULYSSES The amity that wisdom knits not, folly may easily untie.

⟨*Enter Patroclus.*⟩

Here comes Patroclus.

NESTOR No Achilles with him.

ULYSSES The elephant hath joints, but none for courtesy; his legs are legs for necessity, not for flexure.

PATROCLUS, ⌜*to Agamemnon*⌝

Achilles bids me say he is much sorry
If anything more than your sport and pleasure
Did move your greatness and this noble state
To call upon him. He hopes it is no other
But for your health and your digestion sake,
An after-dinner's breath.

AGAMEMNON Hear you, Patroclus:
We are too well acquainted with these answers,
But his evasion, winged thus swift with scorn,
Cannot outfly our apprehensions.
Much attribute he hath, and much the reason
Why we ascribe it to him. Yet all his virtues,
Not virtuously on his own part beheld,

127. **fair:** sound, unblemished

128. **like:** likely

131. **self-assumption:** arrogance

132. **note:** distinguishing mark; **judgment:** wisdom; **and worthier:** i.e., **and** men who are **worthier**

134. **tend:** attend to; wait upon; **strangeness:** coldness, aloofness

136. **underwrite:** support; **observing:** obsequious, compliant

137. **humorous:** capricious (For **humorous predominance,** see longer note, page 274.)

138–40. **course . . . tide:** an image of Achilles' moods or behaviors as tides that determine the general's decisions **course:** flow; direction of flow **passage:** progress **carriage:** conduct **Rode:** moved, floated

141. **overhold:** hold at too high a rate, overestimate; **price:** worth

142. **We'll none of:** i.e., we want no part of; **engine:** military machine

143. **lie under:** be subject to; **report:** reputation

145. **stirring:** active, energetic, busy; **allowance:** approval, approbation

146. **Before:** in preference to

147. **presently:** immediately

148. **In . . . satisfied:** i.e., **his answer** (line 147) **in** someone else's **voice** will **not** satisfy me

155. **subscribe:** support, concur in

Do in our eyes begin to lose their gloss,
Yea, ⟨and⟩ like fair fruit in an unwholesome dish,
Are like to rot untasted. Go and tell him
We come to speak with him; and you shall not sin
If you do say we think him overproud
And underhonest, in self-assumption greater
Than in the note of judgment; and worthier than
himself
Here tend the savage strangeness he puts on,
Disguise the holy strength of their command,
And underwrite in an observing kind
His humorous predominance—yea, watch
His course and time, his ebbs and flows, ⟨as⟩ if
The passage and whole ⟨carriage of this action⟩
Rode on his tide. Go tell him this, and add
That, if he overhold his price so much,
We'll none of him. But let him, like an engine
Not portable, lie under this report:
"Bring action hither; this cannot go to war."
A stirring dwarf we do allowance give
Before a sleeping giant. Tell him so.

PATROCLUS
I shall, and bring his answer presently.

AGAMEMNON
In second voice we'll not be satisfied;
We come to speak with him.—Ulysses, ⟨enter you.⟩
⟨*Ulysses exits,* ⌜*with Patroclus.*⌝⟩

AJAX What is he more than another?

AGAMEMNON No more than what he thinks he is.

AJAX Is he so much? Do you not think he thinks himself a better man than I am?

AGAMEMNON No question.

AJAX Will you subscribe his thought and say he is?

AGAMEMNON No, noble Ajax. You are as strong, as valiant, as wise, no less noble, much more gentle, and altogether more tractable.

162. **fairer:** i.e., better, purer

163. **his own glass:** i.e., its **own** mirror (See picture, page 136.)

164–65. **but in the deed:** i.e., except in the performance

172. **carries on:** maintains; **dispose:** frame of mind

174. **will peculiar:** i.e., his own individual **will; self-admission:** i.e., trusting only himself

177. **for . . . only:** merely because they are requested

178. **Possessed . . . greatness:** i.e., it is as if he is controlled by a demon of **greatness**

180. **quarrels at:** finds fault with, objects to; **self-breath:** i.e., speech he directs **to himself**

180–84. **Imagined . . . himself:** See longer note, page 274. **Kingdomed:** constituted as a kingdom **commotion:** mental perturbation

185. **plaguy:** i.e., plaguily, terribly (with wordplay on the word *plague,* a disease signaled by pustules as **death-tokens** or signs of death)

Achilles.
From [Guillaume Rouillé,] . . .
Promptuarii iconum . . . (1553).

AJAX Why should a man be proud? How doth pride grow? I know not what pride is.

AGAMEMNON Your mind is the clearer, ⟨Ajax,⟩ and your virtues the fairer. He that is proud eats up himself. Pride is his own glass, his own trumpet, his own chronicle; and whatever praises itself but in the deed devours the deed in the praise.

AJAX I do hate a proud man as I hate the engendering of toads.

NESTOR, ⌜*aside*⌝
And yet he loves himself. Is 't not strange?

Enter Ulysses.

ULYSSES
Achilles will not to the field tomorrow.

AGAMEMNON
What's his excuse?

ULYSSES He doth rely on none,
But carries on the stream of his dispose,
Without observance or respect of any,
In will peculiar and in self-admission.

AGAMEMNON
Why, will he not, upon our fair request,
Untent his person and share th' air with us?

ULYSSES
Things small as nothing, for request's sake only,
He makes important. Possessed he is with greatness
And speaks not to himself but with a pride
That quarrels at self-breath. Imagined worth
Holds in his blood such swoll'n and hot discourse
That 'twixt his mental and his active parts
Kingdomed Achilles in commotion rages
And batters down himself. What should I say?
He is so plaguy proud that the death-tokens of it
Cry "No recovery."

AGAMEMNON Let Ajax go to him.—

193. **go from:** i.e., **go** away **from**

194. **seam:** fat, grease

195–96. **suffers . . . Enter:** i.e., allows . . . to **enter**

196. **revolve:** ponder, meditate upon

197. **ruminate:** consider

198. **Of that:** i.e., by him whom

200. **stale his palm:** i.e., depreciate his honorable reputation through excessive familiarity **palm:** an emblem of triumph or supreme honor

201. **assubjugate:** reduce to subjugation

204. **enlard:** fill with lard or fat

205–6. **add . . . Hyperion:** i.e., **add** fuel to the summer heat (**Cancer** is the zodiacal sign that the sun enters at the summer equinox. **Hyperion** is a Titan who, in some accounts, drives the sun's chariot.)

209. **the vein of him:** i.e., Ajax's desire; or, his feeling, mood

212. **pash:** strike so as to smash

214. **An:** if; **feeze:** fix, take care of

A porcupine. (2.1.25)
From Edward Topsell,
The historie of foure-footed beastes . . . (1607).

Dear lord, go you and greet him in his tent.
'Tis said he holds you well and will be led
At your request a little from himself.

ULYSSES

O Agamemnon, let it not be so!
We'll consecrate the steps that Ajax makes
When they go from Achilles. Shall the proud lord
That bastes his arrogance with his own seam
And never suffers matter of the world
Enter his thoughts, save such as doth revolve
And ruminate himself—shall he be worshipped
Of that we hold an idol more than he?
No. This thrice-worthy and right valiant lord
Shall not so stale his palm, nobly acquired,
Nor, by my will, assubjugate his merit,
As amply ⟨titled⟩ as Achilles is,
By going to Achilles.
That were to enlard his fat-already pride
And add more coals to Cancer when he burns
With entertaining great Hyperion.
This lord go to him? Jupiter forbid
And say in thunder "Achilles, go to him."

NESTOR, ⌜*aside to Diomedes*⌝

O, this is well; he rubs the vein of him.

DIOMEDES, ⌜*aside to Nestor*⌝

And how his silence drinks up ⟨this⟩ applause!

AJAX

If I go to him, with my armèd fist
I'll ⟨pash⟩ him o'er the face.

AGAMEMNON O, no, you shall not go.

AJAX

An he be proud with me, I'll feeze his pride.
Let me go to him.

ULYSSES

Not for the worth that hangs upon our quarrel.

AJAX A paltry, insolent fellow.

221. **let . . . blood:** i.e., open a vein to allow **his** peevish **blood** to flow out (a medical treatment)

225. **Wit:** mental quickness, intellectual ability

226. **bear it:** i.e., carry the day; **eat swords:** i.e., be stabbed

227. **carry it:** be victorious

229. **ten shares:** perhaps, all of it

231. **through:** i.e., thoroughly; **Force:** i.e., farce, stuff

232. **dry:** thirsty

233. **dislike:** discord, disagreement (referring presumably to their disagreement with Achilles)

236. **naming of him:** i.e., talking about Achilles

239. **Wherefore:** why

240. **emulous:** greedy for praise or power

241. **Know . . . world:** i.e., let **the whole world know**

242. **palter:** deal evasively, play fast and loose

247. **surly borne:** i.e., if he bore himself in a **surly** manner

248. **strange:** noncompliant, cold in demeanor; **self-affected:** attached or partial to himself

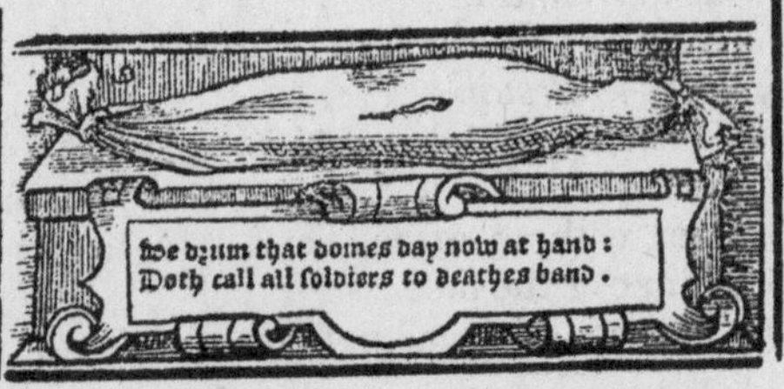

A body shrouded for burial. (2.3.34)
From [Richard Day,]
A booke of christian prayers . . . (1578).

NESTOR, ⌜*aside*⌝ How he describes himself!
AJAX Can he not be sociable?
ULYSSES, ⌜*aside*⌝ The raven chides blackness.
AJAX I'll ⟨let⟩ his humorous blood.
AGAMEMNON, ⌜*aside*⌝ He will be the physician that should be the patient.
AJAX An all men were of my mind—
ULYSSES, ⌜*aside*⌝ Wit would be out of fashion.
AJAX —he should not bear it so; he should eat swords first. Shall pride carry it?
NESTOR, ⌜*aside*⌝ An 'twould, you'd carry half.
⟨ULYSSES,⟩ ⌜*aside*⌝ He would have ten shares.
AJAX I will knead him; I'll make him supple.
⌜NESTOR,⌝ ⌜*aside*⌝ He's not yet through warm. Force him with ⟨praises.⟩ Pour in, pour ⟨in;⟩ his ambition is dry.
ULYSSES, ⌜*to Agamemnon*⌝
My lord, you feed too much on this dislike.
NESTOR, ⌜*to Agamemnon*⌝
Our noble general, do not do so.
DIOMEDES, ⌜*to Agamemnon*⌝
You must prepare to fight without Achilles.
ULYSSES
Why, 'tis this naming of him does him harm.
Here is a man—but 'tis before his face;
I will be silent.
NESTOR Wherefore should you so?
He is not emulous, as Achilles is.
ULYSSES
Know the whole world, he is as valiant—
AJAX A whoreson dog, that shall palter with us thus! Would he were a Trojan!
NESTOR What a vice were it in Ajax now—
ULYSSES If he were proud—
DIOMEDES Or covetous of praise—
ULYSSES Ay, or surly borne—
DIOMEDES Or strange, or self-affected—

250. **composure:** temperament

251. **gat:** i.e., begot; **gave thee suck:** i.e., nursed you as a baby

252. **parts of nature:** natural gifts

254. **disciplined:** drilled, trained

257. **Bull-bearing Milo:** a Greek athlete of immense strength, reputed to have carried a bull on his shoulders, killed it with a blow of his fist, and eaten it, all in a single day; **addition:** title

258. **sinewy:** brawny, muscular

259. **bourn:** bound, limit; **pale:** fence, palisade; **confines:** secures, keeps in place

260. **spacious:** ample; **dilated:** expanded, distended; **parts:** gifts

261. **antiquary:** ancient

264. **green:** youthful (though perhaps with wordplay on "immature" or "gullible"); **tempered:** composed

265. **have the eminence of:** i.e., have mastery over, be superior to

271. **Keeps thicket:** i.e., stays hidden (literally, remains in the **thicket**); **Please it:** a polite phrase of request

272. **state:** council

274. **all our main of power:** utmost strength of our armed forces

276. **cull their flower:** i.e., select their best; **cope:** engage in battle, strike

278. **hulks:** cargo vessels; **draw deep:** i.e., lie low in the water (thus needing **deep** water in which to sail)

ULYSSES, ⌜*to Ajax*⌝
Thank the heavens, lord, thou art of sweet
composure.
Praise him that gat thee, she that gave thee suck;
Famed be thy tutor, and thy parts of nature
Thrice famed beyond, ⟨beyond⟩ thy erudition;
But he that disciplined thine arms to fight,
Let Mars divide eternity in twain
And give him half; and for thy vigor,
Bull-bearing Milo his addition yield
To sinewy Ajax. I will not praise thy wisdom,
Which like a ⟨bourn,⟩ a pale, a shore confines
⟨Thy⟩ spacious and dilated parts. Here's Nestor,
Instructed by the antiquary times;
He must, he is, he cannot but be wise.—
But pardon, father Nestor, were your days
As green as Ajax' and your brain so tempered,
You should not have the eminence of him,
But be as Ajax.

AJAX Shall I call you father?

NESTOR
Ay, my good son.

DIOMEDES Be ruled by him, Lord Ajax.

ULYSSES
There is no tarrying here; the hart Achilles
Keeps thicket. Please it our great general
To call together all his state of war.
Fresh kings are come to Troy. Tomorrow
We must with all our main of power stand fast.
And here's a lord—come knights from east to west
And ⟨cull⟩ their flower, Ajax shall cope the best.

AGAMEMNON
Go we to council. Let Achilles sleep.
Light boats sail swift, though greater hulks draw deep.
They exit.

TROILUS AND CRESSIDA

ACT 3

3.1 Pandarus asks Paris to make excuses for Troilus's absence from his father Priam's supper table that night. At Helen's insistence, Pandarus sings about love.

---

0 SD. **within:** i.e., offstage

1. **pray you:** i.e., please

4. **depend upon:** i.e., belong to him as his servant (with wordplay on the meaning "rely upon" in line 5)

7. **must needs:** of necessity

10. **Faith:** a mild oath

11. **know me better:** i.e., become **better** acquainted with **me**

15. **state of grace:** i.e., the condition of one sanctified by God

16. **Grace:** a courtesy title given to kings, dukes, and archbishops

18. **in parts:** i.e., having several instruments or voices playing together, each with its own part in the harmony (See picture, page 114.)

23. **pleasure:** desire, will, discretion (with wordplay on "enjoyment" in line 24)

⌜ACT 3⌝

⌜Scene 1⌝

⟨*Music sounds within.*⟩ *Enter Pandarus* ⌜*and Paris's Servingman.*⌝

PANDARUS Friend, you, pray you, a word. Do you not follow the young Lord Paris?

MAN Ay, sir, when he goes before me.

PANDARUS You depend upon him, I mean.

MAN Sir, I do depend upon the Lord.

PANDARUS You depend upon a notable gentleman. I must needs praise him.

MAN The Lord be praised!

PANDARUS You know me, do you not?

MAN Faith, sir, superficially.

PANDARUS Friend, know me better. I am the Lord Pandarus.

MAN I hope I shall know your Honor better.

PANDARUS I do desire it.

MAN You are in the state of grace?

PANDARUS Grace? Not so, friend. "Honor" and "Lordship" are my titles. What music is this?

MAN I do but partly know, sir. It is music in parts.

PANDARUS Know you the musicians?

MAN Wholly, sir.

PANDARUS Who play they to?

MAN To the hearers, sir.

PANDARUS At whose pleasure, friend?

25. **Command:** i.e., **at whose command**

30. **to 't:** i.e., to the point; **Marry:** a mild oath

32. **Venus:** See note to 1.3.172 and picture, page 166.

39–40. **complimental assault:** perhaps, an attack of flattery and compliments

40. **seethes:** is in a state of turmoil (The words **Sodden** and **stewed** [line 41] play on **seethes** as "boils, soaks in a liquid.")

42. **Fair be to:** i.e., good wishes to (Pandarus goes on to use **fair** as a term of courteous address and also with such meanings as "handsome, elegant, propitious, peaceable, unblemished.")

48. **broken music:** i.e., **music** in parts (See note to line 18, above.) Pandarus may allude to the offstage **music** discussed at lines 17–24, or the musicians may enter with Paris and Helen.

49. **broke:** interrupted (with wordplay on "ruptured"); **cousin:** used here as a term of friendship

55. **Rude:** discordant, harsh; **in sooth:** a very mild oath

56. **in fits:** wordplay on (1) in strains of music; (2) in sudden bursts of speech

MAN At mine, sir, and theirs that love music.

PANDARUS Command, I mean, ⟨friend.⟩

MAN Who shall I command, sir?

PANDARUS Friend, we understand not one another. I am too courtly and thou ⟨art⟩ too cunning. At whose request do these men play?

MAN That's to 't indeed, sir. Marry, sir, at the request of Paris my lord, who is there in person; with him the mortal Venus, the heart blood of beauty, love's ⌜visible⌝ soul.

PANDARUS Who, my cousin Cressida?

MAN No, sir, Helen. Could not you find out that by her attributes?

PANDARUS It should seem, fellow, ⟨that⟩ thou hast not seen the Lady Cressid. I come to speak with Paris from the Prince Troilus. I will make a complimental assault upon him, for my business seethes.

MAN Sodden business! There's a stewed phrase indeed.

Enter Paris and Helen ⌜with Attendants.⌝

PANDARUS Fair be to you, my lord, and to all this fair company! Fair desires in all fair measure fairly guide them!—Especially to you, fair queen, fair thoughts be your fair pillow!

HELEN Dear lord, you are full of fair words.

PANDARUS You speak your fair pleasure, sweet queen.—Fair prince, here is good broken music.

PARIS You have broke it, cousin, and, by my life, you shall make it whole again; you shall piece it out with a piece of your performance.

HELEN He is full of harmony.

PANDARUS Truly, lady, no.

HELEN O, sir—

PANDARUS Rude, in sooth; in good sooth, very rude.

PARIS Well said, my lord; well, you say so in fits.

59. **hedge us out:** shut or keep me **out** (Helen, as Menelaus's queen, uses the royal plural, here and at lines 154–57.)

65. **Go to:** an expression of remonstrance

67. **bob:** cheat

72. **serve your turn:** suit, answer, avail

80. **in hand:** in process, going on

82. **My cousin:** i.e., Paris (See note to **cousin,** line 49, above.)

84. **You must not know:** i.e., Pandarus doesn't want you to **know**

85. **disposer:** a word of uncertain meaning in this context

86. **wide:** i.e., far from the right answer

88. **make 's:** i.e., **make** his

91. **spy:** i.e., observe, see

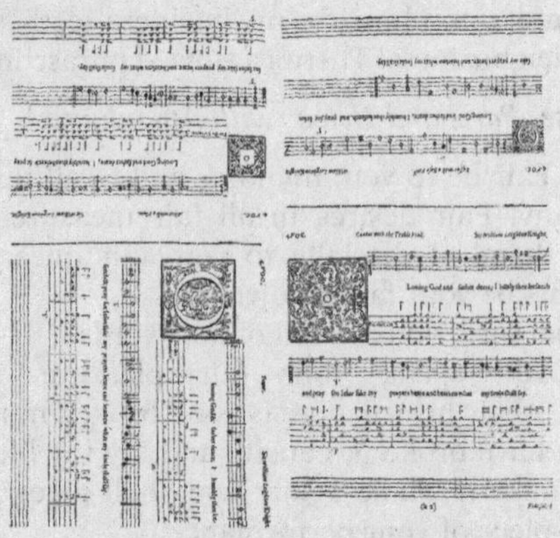

"It is music in parts." (3.1.18)
From Sir William Leighton,
The teares of lamentacions . . . (1614).

PANDARUS I have business to my lord, dear queen.— My lord, will you vouchsafe me a word?

HELEN Nay, this shall not hedge us out. We'll hear you sing, certainly.

PANDARUS Well, sweet queen, you are pleasant with me.—But, marry, thus, my lord: my dear lord and most esteemed friend, your brother Troilus—

HELEN My Lord Pandarus, honey-sweet lord—

PANDARUS Go to, sweet queen, go to—commends himself most affectionately to you—

HELEN You shall not bob us out of our melody. If you do, our melancholy upon your head!

PANDARUS Sweet queen, sweet queen, that's a sweet queen, i' faith—

HELEN And to make a sweet lady sad is a sour offence.

PANDARUS Nay, that shall not serve your turn, that shall it not, in truth, la. Nay, I care not for such words, no, no.—And, my lord, he desires you that if the King call for him at supper, you will make his excuse.

HELEN My Lord Pandarus—

PANDARUS What says my sweet queen, my very, very sweet queen?

PARIS What exploit's in hand? Where sups he tonight?

HELEN Nay, but, my lord—

PANDARUS What says my sweet queen? My cousin will fall out with you.

HELEN, ⌜*to Paris*⌝ You must not know where he sups.

PARIS I'll lay my life, with my disposer Cressida.

PANDARUS No, no, no such matter; you are wide. Come, your disposer is sick.

PARIS Well, I'll make 's excuse.

PANDARUS Ay, good my lord. Why should you say Cressida? No, your ⟨poor⟩ disposer's sick.

PARIS I spy.

101. **twain:** parted asunder, estranged

106. **prithee:** i.e., I pray thee, please; **by my troth:** a mild oath (See also **i' faith** [lines 111, 126] and **In good troth** [line 113].)

109. **undo:** ruin, destroy

110. **Cupid:** Roman god of love (See picture, page 206.)

112. **good now:** an interjection, here noting entreaty

115–16. **love's . . . doe:** i.e., Cupid's **bow shoots** males and females

117–25. **The shaft . . . Hey ho:** These lines represent the sex act as an arrow entering a wound, with wordplay on the word **die** to mean "experience a sexual orgasm" and imitating sounds made during intercourse. (Many editors change "**O ho**" to "O! O!" to make this meaning clearer.) **confounds:** destroys **tickles:** excites, gratifies **sore:** wound (but with wordplay on the name for a four-year-old **buck**)

An orchard. (3.2.15)
From Octavio Boldoni,
Theatrum temporaneum . . . (1636).

PANDARUS You spy? What do you spy?—Come, give me an instrument. ⌜*An Attendant gives him an instrument.*⌝ Now, sweet queen.

HELEN Why, this is kindly done.

PANDARUS My niece is horribly in love with a thing you have, sweet queen.

HELEN She shall have it, my lord, if it be not my Lord Paris.

PANDARUS He? No, she'll none of him. They two are twain.

HELEN Falling in after falling out may make them three.

PANDARUS Come, come, I'll hear no more of this. I'll sing you a song now.

HELEN Ay, ay, prithee. Now, by my troth, sweet ⟨lord,⟩ thou hast a fine forehead.

PANDARUS Ay, you may, you may.

HELEN Let thy song be love. "This love will undo us all." O Cupid, Cupid, Cupid!

PANDARUS Love? Ay, that it shall, i' faith.

PARIS Ay, good now, "Love, love, nothing but love."

PANDARUS ⟨In good troth, it begins so.⟩

Love, love, nothing but love, still love, still more!
For, O, love's bow
Shoots buck and doe.
The ⟨shaft confounds⟩
Not that it wounds
But tickles still the sore.

These lovers cry "O ho!" they die,
Yet that which seems the wound to kill
Doth turn "O ho!" to "Ha ha he!"
So dying love lives still.
"O ho!" awhile, but "Ha ha ha!"
"O ho!" groans out for "ha ha ha!"—Hey ho!

127. **doves:** associated with Venus and her chariot

130. **generation:** genealogy, line of descent

132. **a generation of vipers:** an offspring of **vipers** (playing on the phrase used by Jesus and John the Baptist to attack nonbelievers as a "**generation** [i.e., breed, set, family; offspring] **of vipers**" [See, e.g., Matthew 3.7, 12.34, 23.33; Luke 3.7.])

135. **gallantry:** i.e., gallants, fine gentlemen; **fain:** gladly

136. **my Nell:** i.e., Helen

138. **hangs the lip at:** i.e., sulks about

141. **sped:** succeeded, fared

152. **sinews:** muscles

153. **island kings:** i.e., the **kings** from the **isles of Greece** (Prologue, line 1)

154–57. **'Twill . . . ourself:** For **us, we,** and **ourself,** see note to line 59, above. **palm:** honor **overshines:** surpasses, outshines

An Elizabethan fool. (2.3.60)
From August Casimir Redel,
Apophtegmata symbolica . . . [n.d.].

HELEN In love, i' faith, to the very tip of the nose.

PARIS He eats nothing but doves, love, and that breeds hot blood, and hot blood begets hot thoughts, and hot thoughts beget hot deeds, and hot deeds is love.

PANDARUS Is this the generation of love? Hot blood, hot thoughts, and hot deeds? Why, they are vipers. Is love a generation of vipers? Sweet lord, who's afield today?

PARIS Hector, Deiphobus, Helenus, Antenor, and all the gallantry of Troy. I would fain have armed today, but my Nell would not have it so. How chance my brother Troilus went not?

HELEN He hangs the lip at something.—You know all, Lord Pandarus.

PANDARUS Not I, honey sweet queen. I long to hear how they sped today.—You'll remember your brother's excuse?

PARIS To a hair.

PANDARUS Farewell, sweet queen.

HELEN Commend me to your niece.

PANDARUS I will, sweet queen. ⌜*He exits.*⌝

Sound a retreat.

PARIS
⟨They're⟩ come from the field. Let us to Priam's hall
To greet the warriors. Sweet Helen, I must woo you
To help unarm our Hector. His stubborn buckles,
With ⟨these⟩ your white enchanting fingers touched,
Shall more obey than to the edge of steel
Or force of Greekish sinews. You shall do more
Than all the island kings: disarm great Hector.

HELEN
'Twill make us proud to be his servant, Paris.
Yea, what he shall receive of us in duty
Gives us more palm in beauty than we have,
Yea, overshines ourself.

PARIS Sweet, above thought I love ⟨thee.⟩

They exit.

3.2 Pandarus brings together Troilus and a seemingly reluctant Cressida, who finally acknowledges her love for Troilus.

---

1. **How now:** a greeting meaning "**how** is it **now**"

3. **stays:** waits

5. **Sirrah:** a term of address to, e.g., a servingman

8–9. **strange soul . . . waftage:** The image is of the **soul** of someone recently dead, **staying** (waiting) on the **banks** of the river Styx in the classical underworld, impatient for **waftage** (conveyance by boat) across the river.

9. **Charon:** ferryman who transports the souls of the dead across the Styx (See picture, page 128.)

10. **transportance:** transport, conveyance; **fields:** i.e., the Elysian **fields,** the abode of the blessed in the underworld

12. **Proposed:** i.e., set as an expectation; **the deserver:** i.e., one who deserves well

15. **orchard:** garden (See picture, page 116.)

16. **straight:** straightway, immediately

18. **relish:** taste, flavor

20. **wat'ry:** i.e., salivating

21. **thrice-repurèd:** i.e., three-times purified

22. **fine:** absolute, perfect

23. **tuned . . . sweetness:** The metaphor shifts here to music, though **sweetness** echoes the metaphor of eating. **sharp:** penetrating or high-pitched **sweetness:** melodiousness; sweet sound or tone

24. **ruder:** more unrefined; **powers:** faculties

(continued)

⌜Scene 2⌝

Enter Pandarus ⟨and⟩ Troilus's Man, ⌜meeting.⌝

PANDARUS How now? Where's thy master? At my cousin Cressida's?

MAN No, sir, ⟨he⟩ stays for you to conduct him thither.

⟨Enter Troilus.⟩

PANDARUS O, here he comes.—How now, how now?

TROILUS, ⌜*to his Man*⌝ Sirrah, walk off. ⌜*Man exits.*⌝

PANDARUS Have you seen my cousin?

TROILUS

No, Pandarus. I stalk about her door
Like a strange soul upon the Stygian banks
Staying for waftage. O, be thou my Charon,
And give me swift transportance to ⟨those⟩ fields
Where I may wallow in the lily beds
Proposed for the deserver! O, gentle Pandar,
From Cupid's shoulder pluck his painted wings
And fly with me to Cressid!

PANDARUS Walk here i' th' orchard. I'll bring her straight.

⟨Pandarus exits.⟩

TROILUS

I am giddy; expectation whirls me round.
Th' imaginary relish is so sweet
That it enchants my sense. What will it be
When that the wat'ry ⌜palate⌝ taste indeed
Love's thrice-repurèd nectar? Death, I fear me,
Swooning destruction, or some joy too fine,
Too subtle-potent, tuned too sharp in sweetness
For the capacity of my ruder powers.
I fear it much; and I do fear besides
That I shall lose distinction in my joys,
As doth a battle when they charge on heaps
The enemy flying.

26. **distinction in:** i.e., ability to distinguish

27. **battle:** i.e., body of troops, battalion; **on heaps:** in a mass

29. **making her:** i.e., **making** herself

31. **fetches . . . short:** i.e., breathes **so** rapidly; **frayed with:** i.e., frightened by

32. **spirit:** ghost; **villain:** here, a term of affection

33. **new-ta'en:** i.e., newly caught

35. **thicker:** more quickly

36. **bestowing:** i.e., function (literally, employment, occupation)

37. **vassalage:** i.e., vassals; **at unawares:** suddenly

43. **watched:** forced to remain awake (as were hawks to make them **tame**)

44. **Come your ways:** i.e., **come** along; **An:** if

45. **thills:** shafts of a cart or wagon

49. **close:** come together, unite

49–50. **rub . . . mistress:** wordplay on language from the game of bowls, in which to **rub** is to encounter an impediment and **kiss the mistress** is to have one ball touch the master ball or jack

51. **in fee-farm:** i.e., in perpetuity (literally, land held with a perpetual fixed rent)

53. **The falcon . . . tercel:** i.e., the female and the male are equally matched

53–54. **for . . . river:** i.e., I'll bet **all the ducks** in the **river**

56. **Words . . . debts:** proverbial; **deeds:** (1) acts; (2) legal documents (See lines 59–60.)

57. **bereave:** deprive (playing on **bereft** in line 55)

58. **activity:** i.e., virility (literally, vigorous action); **billing:** i.e., kissing

⟨*Enter Pandarus.*⟩

PANDARUS She's making her ready; she'll come straight. You must be witty now. She does so blush and fetches her wind so short as if she were frayed with a spirit. I'll fetch her. It is the prettiest villain. She fetches her breath as short as a new-ta'en sparrow.

⟨*Pandarus exits.*⟩

TROILUS
Even such a passion doth embrace my bosom.
My heart beats thicker than a feverous pulse,
And all my powers do their bestowing lose,
Like vassalage at ⟨unawares⟩ encount'ring
The eye of majesty.

Enter Pandarus, and Cressida ⌜*veiled.*⌝

PANDARUS, ⌜*to Cressida*⌝ Come, come, what need you blush? Shame's a baby.—Here she is now. Swear the oaths now to her that you have sworn to me. ⌜*Cressida offers to leave.*⌝ What, are you gone again? You must be watched ere you be made tame, must you? Come your ways; come your ways. An you draw backward, we'll put you i' th' ⌜thills.⌝—Why do you not speak to her?—Come, draw this curtain and let's see your picture. ⌜*He draws back her veil.*⌝ Alas the day, how loath you are to offend daylight! An 'twere dark, you'd close sooner.—So, so, rub on, and kiss the mistress. (⌜*They kiss.*⌝) How now? A kiss in fee-farm? Build there, carpenter; the air is sweet. Nay, you shall fight your hearts out ere I part you. The falcon as the tercel, for all the ducks i' th' river. Go to, go to.

TROILUS You have bereft me of all words, lady.

PANDARUS Words pay no debts; give her deeds. But she'll bereave you o' th' deeds too, if she call your activity in question. (⌜*They kiss.*⌝) What, billing

59–60. **In witness . . . interchangeably:** a common legal formula used in indentures (contracts executed between two or more parties) **interchangeably:** reciprocally

60. **get a fire:** i.e., have **a fire** lit in the bedroom

66. **abruption:** interruption; **too-curious:** hidden; abstruse (This word may refer to Cressida's way of looking—too inquisitively—rather than to what she sees.) **dreg:** corrupt or defiling matter

67. **fountain:** spring of water, source

68. **dregs:** sediment

69. **cherubins:** angelic beings

73. **To fear . . . worse:** proverbial

74. **apprehend:** feel

74–75. **In . . . monster:** i.e., there is nothing frightening about romantic love (See longer note, page 274.)

77. **undertakings:** i.e., (monstrous) promises we vow to fulfill (to prove our love)

79–80. **imposition:** commands, duties

81. **monstruosity:** monstrosity (referring to **monster** [line 75] as a grotesque being made up of two conjoined forms)

82–83. **the will . . . limit:** See longer note, page 275. **limit:** limitations

85. **yet reserve:** i.e., continue to keep in reserve

89. **monsters:** See note to line 81, above.

90. **are not we:** i.e., am not I; or, perhaps, **are not** lovers such as I

91. **tasted:** tested; **allow:** commend, praise; approve of; **prove:** show ourselves to be

(continued)

again? Here's "In witness whereof the parties interchangeably—." Come in, come in. I'll go get a fire.

⌜*Pandarus exits.*⌝

CRESSIDA Will you walk in, my lord?

TROILUS O Cressid, how often have I wished me thus!

CRESSIDA "Wished," my lord? The gods grant—O, my lord!

TROILUS What should they grant? What makes this pretty abruption? What too-curious dreg espies my sweet lady in the fountain of our love?

CRESSIDA More dregs than water, if my ⌜fears⌝ have eyes.

TROILUS Fears make devils of cherubins; they never see truly.

CRESSIDA Blind fear, that seeing reason leads, finds safer footing than blind reason, stumbling without fear. To fear the worst oft cures the worse.

TROILUS O, let my lady apprehend no fear. In all Cupid's pageant there is presented no monster.

CRESSIDA Nor nothing monstrous neither?

TROILUS Nothing but our undertakings, when we vow to weep seas, live in fire, eat rocks, tame tigers, thinking it harder for our mistress to devise imposition enough than for us to undergo any difficulty imposed. This ⟨is⟩ the monstruosity in love, lady, that the will is infinite and the execution confined, that the desire is boundless and the act a slave to limit.

CRESSIDA They say all lovers swear more performance than they are able and yet reserve an ability that they never perform, vowing more than the perfection of ten and discharging less than the tenth part of one. They that have the voice of lions and the act of hares, are they not monsters?

TROILUS Are there such? Such are not we. Praise us as we are tasted, allow us as we prove; our head shall go bare till merit ⟨crown it. No perfection⟩ in reversion shall have a praise in present. We will not

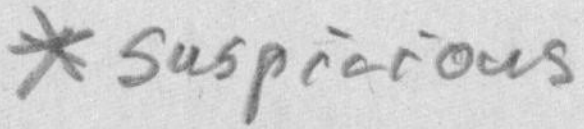

91–92. **our . . . bare:** i.e., I will keep my head uncovered (as a sign of deference) See longer note, page 275.

92–93. **reversion:** i.e., (mere) expectation

93. **in present:** now, at the present time

94. **desert:** excellence, worth; **his:** its

95. **addition:** title; **Few . . . faith:** Proverbial: "Where many **words** are, the truth goes by."

96–97. **what . . . worst:** i.e., malice's **worst** accusation

97. **a mock for:** i.e., something to be derided by; **truth:** faithfulness, constancy

98. **truth:** truthfulness, honesty; **truer:** more faithful

102. **folly:** (1) unwise action; (2) lewd or unchaste action

104–5. **get . . . you:** i.e., beget **a boy** on **you**

105. **give him me:** i.e., **give me** the **boy**

106. **flinch:** draw back; sneak off

107. **hostages:** i.e., pledges of security

108. **faith:** promise

110. **be long:** i.e., take a **long** time

113. **heart:** courage

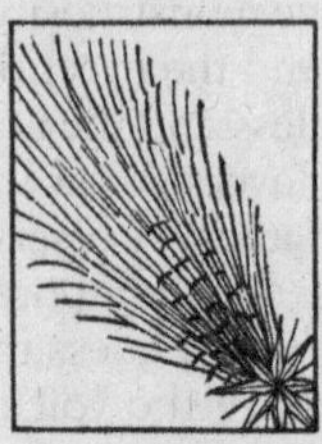

"A star disorbed." (2.2.48)
From Hartmann Schedel, *Liber chronicorum* [1493].

name desert before his birth, and, being born, his addition shall be humble. Few words to fair faith. Troilus shall be such to Cressid as what envy can say worst shall be a mock for his truth, and what truth can speak truest not truer than Troilus.

CRESSIDA Will you walk in, my lord?

⟨*Enter Pandarus.*⟩

PANDARUS What, blushing still? Have you not done talking yet?

CRESSIDA Well, uncle, what folly I commit I dedicate to you.

PANDARUS I thank you for that. If my lord get a boy of you, you'll give him me. Be true to my lord. If he flinch, chide me for it.

TROILUS, ⌜*to Cressida*⌝ You know now your hostages: your uncle's word and my firm faith.

PANDARUS Nay, I'll give my word for her too. Our kindred, though they be long ere they be wooed, they are constant being won. They are burrs, I can tell you; they'll stick where they are thrown.

CRESSIDA
Boldness comes to me now and brings me heart.
Prince Troilus, I have loved you night and day
For many weary months.

TROILUS
Why was my Cressid then so hard to win?

CRESSIDA
Hard to seem won; but I was won, my lord,
With the first glance that ever—pardon me;
If I confess much, you will play the tyrant.
I love you now, but till now not so much
But I might master it. In faith, I lie;
My thoughts were like unbridled children grown
Too headstrong for their mother. See, we fools!
Why have I blabbed? Who shall be true to us

125. **unsecret:** untrustworthy
132. **dumbness:** muteness
133. **My . . . counsel:** i.e., the **very** heart of **my** secret; **Stop my mouth:** i.e., **stop** me from speaking
134. **albeit:** although
139. **take my leave:** depart; bid farewell
141. **An:** if
143. **Pray . . . you:** i.e., please be content or satisfied
149. **an unkind self:** i.e., (it is) **an** unnatural **self**
150. **To . . . fool:** i.e., (in order) **to be another's** dupe
151. **wit:** mind, brain
153. **craft:** cunning, guile
154. **roundly:** outspokenly, bluntly
155. **wise:** perhaps, (too) clever (to reveal **your thoughts**)

Charon. (3.2.9)
From Vincenzo Cartari, *Le vere e noue imagini* . . . (1615).

When we are so unsecret to ourselves?
But though I loved you well, I wooed you not;
And yet, good faith, I wished myself a man;
Or that we women had men's privilege
Of speaking first. Sweet, bid me hold my tongue,
For in this rapture I shall surely speak
The thing I shall repent. See, see, your silence,
⌜Cunning⌝ in dumbness, from my weakness draws
My very soul of counsel! Stop my mouth.

TROILUS
And shall, albeit sweet music issues thence.
⌜*They kiss.*⌝

PANDARUS Pretty, i' faith!

CRESSIDA, ⌜*to Troilus*⌝
My lord, I do beseech you pardon me.
'Twas not my purpose thus to beg a kiss.
I am ashamed. O heavens, what have I done!
For this time will I take my leave, my lord.

TROILUS Your leave, sweet Cressid?

PANDARUS Leave? An you take leave till tomorrow morning—

CRESSIDA Pray you, content you.

TROILUS What offends you, lady?

CRESSIDA Sir, mine own company.

TROILUS You cannot shun yourself.

CRESSIDA Let me go and try.
I have a kind of self resides with you,
But an unkind self that itself will leave
To be another's fool. I would be gone.
Where is my wit? I know not what I speak.

TROILUS
Well know they what they speak that speak so wisely.

CRESSIDA
Perchance, my lord, I show more craft than love
And fell so roundly to a large confession
To angle for your thoughts. But you are wise,

156. **else:** instead

156–57. **to be . . . might:** proverbial (Here, **wise** means "sagacious, discerning.")

159. **presume:** i.e., **presume** it is

160. **To . . . love:** The image is of **love** as the **flames of** a **lamp** burning forever (as at a monument). **feed:** supply with fuel **for aye:** forever

161. **in plight and youth:** i.e., healthy and vigorous **plight:** good condition, health

163. **blood decays:** (1) **blood** deteriorates with age; (2) passion fails

165. **truth:** loyalty, faithfulness

166. **affronted:** set face to face

166–67. **the match . . . Of:** i.e., that which exactly equals (in strength and substance)

168. **How . . . uplifted:** i.e., **how** elated **I** would be

170. **simpler:** more innocent

174. **swains in love:** i.e., lovers; **world to come:** i.e., future

175. **Approve:** corroborate, confirm

176. **big compare:** boastful comparisons

177. **Wants:** lacks; **tired:** hackneyed, trite

178. **plantage:** plants, vegetation

179. **turtle:** turtledove (famed for its constancy) See picture, page 162.

180. **adamant:** i.e., loadstone, magnet; **th' center:** i.e., its **center**

182. **author:** authority

183. **crown up:** i.e., complete, add the finishing touch to

184. **numbers:** verses

186. **false:** inconstant; **truth:** constancy

Or else you love not; for to be wise and love
Exceeds man's might. That dwells with gods above.

TROILUS

O, that I thought it could be in a woman—
As, if it can, I will presume in you—
To feed for ⟨aye⟩ her lamp and flames of love,
To keep her constancy in plight and youth,
Outliving beauty's outward, with a mind
That doth renew swifter than blood decays!
Or that persuasion could but thus convince me
That my integrity and truth to you
Might be affronted with the match and weight
Of such a winnowed purity in love;
How were I then uplifted! But, alas,
I am as true as truth's simplicity
And simpler than the infancy of truth.

CRESSIDA

In that I'll war with you.

TROILUS

O virtuous fight,
When right with right wars who shall be most right!
True swains in love shall in the world to come
Approve their truth by Troilus. When their rhymes,
Full of protest, of oath and big compare,
Wants similes, truth tired with iteration—
"As true as steel, as plantage to the moon,
As sun to day, as turtle to her mate,
As iron to adamant, as earth to th' center"—
⟨Yet,⟩ after all comparisons of truth,
As truth's authentic author to be cited,
"As true as Troilus" shall crown up the verse
And sanctify the numbers.

CRESSIDA

Prophet may you be!
If I be false or swerve a hair from truth,
When time is old ⟨and⟩ hath forgot itself,
When water drops have worn the stones of Troy
And blind oblivion swallowed cities up,

190. **characterless:** perhaps, unrecorded (See longer note, page 276.) **grated:** pulverized

192. **From false:** i.e., from inconstancy, treachery; **false . . . love:** i.e., unfaithful young women

193–94. **as false . . . earth:** In these **similes** (line 177), **false** means untrustworthy, insecure, deceptive. **sandy earth:** i.e., sand

195–96. **As fox . . . son:** In these **similes, false** means treacherous. **Pard:** panther **hind:** female deer **stepdame:** stepmother

197. **stick:** transfix, pierce

199. **Go to:** come, come

203. **pitiful:** compassionate (but suggesting also "deplorable")

206. **brokers-between:** i.e., matchmakers (also, procurers, pimps)

211. **press . . . death:** wordplay on pressing **to death** as a form of execution for a felon who refuses to **speak** (See picture, page 224.)

213. **maidens here:** i.e., virgins (of either sex) in this audience

214. **gear:** apparatus (i.e., **bed** and **chamber**)

3.3 Calchas asks the Greek leaders to demand his daughter Cressida from the Trojans in exchange for Antenor, whom the Greeks have captured. The leaders agree and dispatch Diomedes to conduct the exchange of prisoners. The Greek leaders shun Achilles. After Ulysses and Achilles discuss the briefness of fame, and Ulysses attacks Achilles for loving

(continued)

And mighty states characterless are grated
To dusty nothing, yet let memory,
From false to false, among false maids in love,
Upbraid my falsehood! When they've said "as false
As air, as water, wind or sandy earth,
As fox to lamb, or wolf to heifer's calf,
Pard to the hind, or stepdame to her son,"
Yea, let them say, to stick the heart of falsehood,
"As false as Cressid."

PANDARUS Go to, a bargain made. Seal it, seal it. I'll be the witness. Here I hold your hand, here my cousin's. If ever you prove false one to another, since I have taken such ⟨pains⟩ to bring you together, let all pitiful goers-between be called to the world's end after my name: call them all panders. Let all constant men be Troiluses, all false women Cressids, and all brokers-between panders. Say "Amen."

TROILUS Amen.

CRESSIDA Amen.

PANDARUS Amen. Whereupon I will show you a chamber ⌜with a bed,⌝ which bed, because it shall not speak of your pretty encounters, press it to death. Away. *⌜Troilus and Cressida⌝ exit.*

And Cupid grant all tongue-tied maidens here
Bed, chamber, pander to provide this gear.

He exits.

⌜Scene 3⌝

⟨Flourish.⟩ Enter Ulysses, Diomedes, Nestor, Agamemnon, Calchas, ⟨Menelaus,⟩ ⌜and Ajax.⌝

CALCHAS

Now, princes, for the service I have done ⟨you,⟩
Th' advantage of the time prompts me aloud
To call for recompense. Appear it to ⟨your⟩ mind

the Trojan Polyxena, Achilles watches as Thersites and Patroclus perform an impromptu playlet mocking Ajax.

---

0 SD. **Flourish:** fanfare of trumpets

2. **advantage:** favorable occasion, opportunity

3. **Appear it:** i.e., let **it appear**

4. **sight . . . come:** i.e., my ability to foresee the future

8. **doubtful:** uncertain; **sequest'ring:** separating

10. **tame:** ordinary, customary, usual

12. **As . . . world:** i.e., **as** if newly created; **strange:** foreign, alien

13. **in . . . taste:** i.e., a foretaste of what's to come

14. **benefit:** favor, gift

17. **make demand:** claim

19. **holds . . . dear:** i.e., values him highly

21. **Desired:** requested, asked for

22. **still:** always

23. **wrest:** tuning key (an implement for tightening or loosening the strings of such musical instruments as the harp or spinet)

24. **slack:** go more slowly, fall off (also, loosen, with reference to **wrest** [line 23])

25. **Wanting his manage:** i.e., lacking his direction or control

27. **change of:** i.e., exchange for

29. **strike off:** cancel (your obligation for)

30. **most accepted pain:** i.e., in hardships gladly **accepted** (by me and by you)

31. **him:** i.e., **Antenor** (line 22)

(continued)

That, through the sight I bear in things to ⌜come,⌝
I have abandoned Troy, left my ⌜possessions,⌝
Incurred a traitor's name, exposed myself,
From certain and possessed conveniences,
To doubtful fortunes, sequest'ring from me all
That time, acquaintance, custom, and condition
Made tame and most familiar to my nature,
And here, to do you service, am become
As new into the world, strange, unacquainted.
I do beseech you, as in way of taste,
To give me now a little benefit
Out of those many regist'red in promise,
Which you say live to come in my behalf.

AGAMEMNON
What wouldst thou of us, Trojan, make demand?

CALCHAS
You have a Trojan prisoner called Antenor
Yesterday took. Troy holds him very dear.
Oft have you—often have you thanks therefor—
Desired my Cressid in right great exchange,
Whom Troy hath still denied; but this Antenor,
I know, is such a wrest in their affairs
That their negotiations all must slack,
Wanting his manage; and they will almost
Give us a prince of blood, a son of Priam,
In change of him. Let him be sent, great princes,
And he shall buy my daughter; and her presence
Shall quite strike off all service I have done
In most accepted pain.

AGAMEMNON Let Diomedes bear him,
And bring us Cressid hither. Calchas shall have
What he requests of us. Good Diomed,
Furnish you fairly for this interchange.
Withal, bring word if Hector will tomorrow
Be answered in his challenge. Ajax is ready.

34. **Furnish you fairly:** i.e., equip yourself properly; **interchange:** exchange

35. **Withal:** in addition; **will:** wishes to

36. **Be answered in:** i.e., meet the one who is answering

40. **strangely:** coldly, distantly

42. **loose:** careless, vague

43. **like:** likely

44. **unplausive:** i.e., disapproving

46. **medicinable:** medicinal, having healing properties

47. **strangeness:** coldness, aloofness

49. **glass:** looking **glass,** mirror (See picture below.)

50. **show itself:** i.e., reveal **itself; supple knees:** i.e., **knees** bent in obsequious bows

51. **the . . . fees:** i.e., (no more than) what **the proud** man expects as his due from inferiors

52. **put on:** assume

Pride with her looking glass. (2.3.159–65)
From Johann Theodor de Bry,
Proscenium vitae humanae . . . (1627).

DIOMEDES
This shall I undertake, and 'tis a burden
Which I am proud to bear. *He exits ⌜with Calchas.⌝*

Achilles and Patroclus stand in their tent.

ULYSSES
Achilles stands i' th' entrance of his tent.
Please it our General pass strangely by him
As if he were forgot, and, princes all,
Lay negligent and loose regard upon him.
I will come last. 'Tis like he'll question me
Why such unplausive eyes are bent, why turned on him.
If so, I have derision medicinable
To use between your strangeness and his pride,
Which his own will shall have desire to drink.
It may do good; pride hath no other glass
To show itself but pride, for supple knees
Feed arrogance and are the proud man's fees.

AGAMEMNON
We'll execute your purpose and put on
A form of strangeness as we pass along;
So do each lord, and either greet him not
Or else disdainfully, which shall shake him more
Than if not looked on. I will lead the way.

⌜They pass before Achilles and Patroclus. Ulysses remains in place, reading.⌝

ACHILLES
What, comes the General to speak with me?
You know my mind: I'll fight no more 'gainst Troy.

AGAMEMNON, *⌜to Nestor⌝*
What says Achilles? Would he aught with us?

NESTOR, *⌜to Achilles⌝*
Would you, my lord, aught with the General?

ACHILLES No.

66. **cuckold:** See note to 1.1.115.

73. **used:** accustomed

75. **use to:** i.e., customarily

78. **fall'n out:** i.e., having quarreled

79. **the declined:** i.e., the person who has declined in fortune

82. **mealy:** i.e., powdery (literally, as if covered with fine powder)

84. **but:** except

85. **without:** i.e., outside of; **as place:** i.e., such **as** position, office

86. **Prizes:** rewards; **accident:** fortune, chance

87. **slippery:** unreliable; **standers:** supports

92. **At ample point:** i.e., abundantly

93. **methinks:** i.e., it seems to me

94. **not . . . me:** i.e., **in me not** worthy of; **beholding:** consideration, regard

Fortune. (1.3.22-30, 46-47; 3.3.78-79, 91, 139–40)
From Giovanni Boccaccio,
A treatise . . . shewing . . . the falles of . . . princes . . . (1554).

NESTOR Nothing, my lord.
AGAMEMNON The better. ⌜*Agamemnon and Nestor exit.*⌝
ACHILLES, ⌜*to Menelaus*⌝ Good day, good day.
MENELAUS How do you? How do you? ⌜*He exits.*⌝
ACHILLES What, does the cuckold scorn me?
AJAX How now, Patroclus?
ACHILLES Good morrow, Ajax.
AJAX Ha?
ACHILLES Good morrow.
AJAX Ay, and good next day too. ⌜*He exits.*⌝
ACHILLES
What mean these fellows? Know they not Achilles?
PATROCLUS
They pass by strangely. They were used to bend,
To send their smiles before them to Achilles,
To come as humbly as they ⌜use⌝ to creep
To holy altars.
ACHILLES What, am I poor of late?
'Tis certain, greatness, once fall'n out with Fortune,
Must fall out with men too. What the declined is
He shall as soon read in the eyes of others
As feel in his own fall, for men, like butterflies,
Show not their mealy wings but to the summer,
And not a man, for being simply man,
Hath any honor, but honor for those honors
That are without him—as place, riches, and favor,
Prizes of accident as oft as merit,
Which, when they fall, as being slippery standers,
The love that leaned on them, as slippery too,
Doth one pluck down another and together
Die in the fall. But 'tis not so with me.
Fortune and I are friends. I do enjoy,
At ample point, all that I did possess,
Save these men's looks, who do, methinks, find out
Something not worth in me such rich beholding

97. **Thetis' son:** See note to 1.3.216.

100. **Writes me:** i.e., **writes; how . . . parted:** i.e., however richly talented or gifted

101. **having:** wealth, possessions; **or without:** either externally; **in:** within

103. **owes:** owns

105. **retort:** reflect

109. **but:** i.e., unless it

111. **That . . . sense:** i.e., the purest of the five senses

112. **Not . . . itself:** i.e., since it cannot go out of **itself**

113. **Salutes . . . form:** i.e., see themselves in **each other's** eyes

114. **speculation:** sight, vision; **turns not to:** (1) does **not** return **to;** (2) does **not** direct **itself** toward

117. **do not strain at:** i.e., have no difficulty accepting

118. **drift:** intention, aim, purpose

119. **circumstance:** detailed narration

121. **in . . . consisting:** i.e., he and his deeds constitute a great deal

122. **parts:** gifts, talents

125. **Where they're extended:** i.e., of those to whom they are directed

127. **Fronting:** facing

128. **His . . . heat:** i.e., its image **and** its **heat; rapt in:** intent upon

129. **apprehended:** recognized

As they have often given. Here is Ulysses.
I'll interrupt his reading.—How now, Ulysses?
ULYSSES Now, great Thetis' son—
ACHILLES What are you reading?
ULYSSES A strange fellow here
Writes me that man, how dearly ever parted,
How much in having, or without or in,
Cannot make boast to have that which he hath,
Nor feels not what he owes, but by reflection;
As when his virtues, ⟨shining⟩ upon others,
Heat them, and they retort that heat again
To the first ⟨giver.⟩
ACHILLES This is not strange, Ulysses.
The beauty that is borne here in the face
The bearer knows not, but commends itself
[To others' eyes; nor doth the eye itself,
That most pure spirit of sense, behold itself,]
Not going from itself, but eye to eye opposed
Salutes each other with each other's form.
For speculation turns not to itself
Till it hath traveled and is ⌜mirrored⌝ there
Where it may see itself. This is not strange at all.
ULYSSES
I do not strain at the position—
It is familiar—but at the author's drift,
Who in his circumstance expressly proves
That no man is the lord of anything—
Though in and of him there be much consisting—
Till he communicate his parts to others;
Nor doth he of himself know them for aught
Till he behold them formed in the applause
Where they're extended; who, like an arch, reverb'rate
The voice again or, like a gate of steel
Fronting the sun, receives and renders back
His figure and his heat. I was much rapt in this
And apprehended here immediately

130. **unknown:** i.e., not renowned or famous

133. **abject:** lowly; **dear:** valuable

138. **leave to do:** neglect doing

139. **creep in:** advance slowly into; **skittish:** fickle, inconstant

141. **pride:** honor, glory

142. **wantonness:** arrogance

144. **lubber:** lout; clumsy, stupid fellow

150. **wallet:** a bag such as a knapsack or beggar's pack

151. **oblivion:** (1) the state or condition of being forgotten; (2) the act of forgetting, forgetfulness (See Shakespeare's *Lucrece,* 939–47: "Time's glory is . . . To feed **oblivion** with decay of things.")

153. **scraps:** bits of food given as **alms** to **oblivion** (line 151)

155. **Perseverance:** accent on second syllable

157–58. **mail . . . mock'ry:** i.e., coat of armor hung on a tomb, an empty reminder of past glory

158. **Take . . . way:** perhaps, act without hesitation; or, perhaps, choose the most immediate path or course of action

159. **strait:** lane or passage

160. **but goes abreast:** i.e., must go single file

161. **Emulation:** the personification of ambitious rivalry for honor

162. **give way:** i.e., make **way,** yield

163. **forthright:** straight course or path

Th' unknown Ajax. Heavens, what a man is there!
A very horse, that has he knows not what!
Nature, what things there are
Most ⟨abject⟩ in regard, and dear in use,
What things again most dear in the esteem
And poor in worth! Now shall we see tomorrow—
An act that very chance doth throw upon him—
Ajax renowned. O, heavens, what some men do
While some men leave to do!
How some men creep in skittish Fortune's hall,
Whiles others play the idiots in her eyes!
How one man eats into another's pride,
While pride is fasting in his wantonness!
To see these Grecian lords—why, even already
They clap the lubber Ajax on the shoulder
As if his foot were on brave Hector's breast
And great Troy shrieking.

ACHILLES

I do believe it, for they passed by me
As misers do by beggars, neither gave to me
Good word nor look. What, are my deeds forgot?

ULYSSES

Time hath, my lord, a wallet at his back
Wherein he puts alms for oblivion,
A great-sized monster of ingratitudes.
Those scraps are good deeds past, which are devoured
As fast as they are made, forgot as soon
As done. Perseverance, dear my lord,
Keeps honor bright. To have done is to hang
Quite out of fashion like a rusty ⌜mail⌝
In monumental mock'ry. Take the instant way,
For honor travels in a strait so narrow
Where one but goes abreast. Keep, then, the path,
For Emulation hath a thousand sons
That one by one pursue. If you give way
Or turn aside from the direct forthright,

166. **in first rank:** i.e., at the head of the line

167. **for pavement to:** i.e., like a paved surface for; **abject:** lowly regarded

172. **slightly:** carelessly, indifferently

173. **as he:** i.e., **as** if **he**

174. **comer:** i.e., one just arriving

175. **virtue:** excellence, merit, distinction

180. **envious:** malicious, spiteful; **calumniating:** slandering

182. **gauds:** toys, ornaments

184. **dust:** i.e., that which is worthless; **gilt:** overlaid with a thin coating of gold

185. **laud:** praise; **gilt:** gold; **o'erdusted:** covered in **dust**

187. **complete:** perfect, consummate

190. **cry:** loud and excited speech

191. **still:** now as formerly; **yet:** in the future

194. **Whose:** i.e., you **whose; but . . . late:** i.e., only recently on these battlefields

195–96. **Made . . . faction:** i.e., caused **the gods** to descend to help one side or the other, driving even the god of war to take sides (These incidents occur in Homer's *Iliad,* books 5 and 20.) **emulous:** desirous of rivaling or imitating **missions:** actions or acts of sending

197. **privacy:** seclusion

Like to an entered tide they all rush by
And leave you ⟨hindmost;
Or, like a gallant horse fall'n in first rank,
Lie there for pavement to the abject ⌜rear,⌝
O'errun and trampled on.⟩ Then what they do in
present,
Though less than yours in ⟨past,⟩ must o'ertop yours;
For Time is like a fashionable host
That slightly shakes his parting guest by th' hand
And, with his arms outstretched as he would fly,
Grasps in the comer. Welcome ever smiles,
And Farewell goes out sighing. Let not virtue seek
Remuneration for the thing it was,
For beauty, wit,
High birth, vigor of bone, desert in service,
Love, friendship, charity are subjects all
To envious and calumniating Time.
One touch of nature makes the whole world kin,
That all, with one consent, praise newborn gauds,
Though they are made and molded of things past,
And ⌜give⌝ to dust that is a little gilt
More laud than gilt o'erdusted.
The present eye praises the present object.
Then marvel not, thou great and complete man,
That all the Greeks begin to worship Ajax,
Since things in motion sooner catch the eye
⟨Than⟩ what stirs not. The cry went once on thee,
And still it might, and yet it may again,
If thou wouldst not entomb thyself alive
And case thy reputation in thy tent,
Whose glorious deeds but in these fields of late
Made emulous missions 'mongst the gods themselves
And drave great Mars to faction.

ACHILLES Of this my privacy,
I have strong reasons.

ULYSSES But 'gainst your privacy

205. **providence:** foresight, prudence; **state:** government, sphere of supreme political power

206. **Pluto's gold:** i.e., Plutus's **gold** (Plutus, god of wealth and the personification of riches, was often confused in Shakespeare's day with Pluto, god of the underworld.) See picture, page 220.

207. **uncomprehensive:** incomprehensible, unfathomable; **deep:** ocean

208. **Keeps place with:** perhaps, adheres to (See longer note, page 276.)

209. **Do . . . cradles:** i.e., reveals **thoughts** that are yet unformed **dumb:** silent, mute

210. **whom:** i.e., which; **relation:** report

211. **Durst:** dares

213. **expressure:** expression

214. **commerce:** dealings

215. **As . . . yours:** i.e., we know **as** well **as** you do

216. **fit:** become, befit

217. **throw down:** wordplay on (1) overcome (**Hector**); (2) sexually overpower (**Polyxena**)

218. **Pyrrhus:** son of Achilles (He later comes to Troy and is the slayer of Priam.)

219. **trump:** trumpet (See picture, page 238.)

220. **tripping:** capering, dancing

222. **him:** i.e., Hector

223. **lover:** friend, one who cares about your welfare

224. **should:** would certainly (This puzzling line may play with the phrase "to **break the ice**"—i.e., to be the first to make a beginning in some enterprise.)

225. **moved:** tried to persuade

227. **effeminate:** feeble, self-indulgent

228. **for this:** i.e., for your behavior

(continued)

The reasons are more potent and heroical.
'Tis known, Achilles, that you are in love
With one of Priam's daughters.

ACHILLES Ha? Known?

ULYSSES Is that a wonder?
The providence that's in a watchful state
Knows almost every ⟨grain of Pluto's gold,⟩
Finds bottom in the uncomprehensive ⌜deep,⌝
Keeps place with thought and almost, like the gods,
Do thoughts unveil in their dumb cradles.
There is a mystery—with whom relation
Durst never meddle—in the soul of state,
Which hath an operation more divine
Than breath or pen can give expressure to.
All the commerce that you have had with Troy
As perfectly is ours as yours, my lord;
And better would it fit Achilles much
To throw down Hector than Polyxena.
But it must grieve young Pyrrhus now at home
When Fame shall in our islands sound her trump,
And all the Greekish girls shall tripping sing
"Great Hector's sister did Achilles win,
But our great Ajax bravely beat down him."
Farewell, my lord. I as your lover speak.
The fool slides o'er the ice that you should break.

⌜*He exits.*⌝

PATROCLUS
To this effect, Achilles, have I moved you.
A woman impudent and mannish grown
Is not more loathed than an effeminate man
In time of action. I stand condemned for this.
They think my little stomach to the war,
And your great love to me, restrains you thus.
Sweet, rouse yourself, and the weak wanton Cupid
Shall from your neck unloose his amorous fold

229. **stomach:** inclination

231. **Cupid:** here, Achilles' love for **Polyxena** (line 217)

232. **fold:** clasp, embrace

235. **Shall Ajax fight:** i.e., is **Ajax** to **fight**

238. **shrewdly gored:** severely wounded

240. **ill:** badly, with difficulty

242. **Seals . . . danger:** i.e., gives **danger** unlimited power **Seals a commission:** places a seal of authority on a warrant **blank:** a blank space in a document to be filled in (here, by **danger** itself)

243. **ague:** sickness characterized by chills and fever; **taints:** infects, putrefies

246. **desire:** ask, request

248. **unarmed:** i.e., not wearing a suit of armor; **a woman's longing:** i.e., an intense desire

249. **withal:** with

250. **weeds of peace:** nonmilitary clothing

251. **visage:** face (which, on the battlefield, would be covered with the face guard of the helmet)

252. **my full of view:** i.e., the utmost extent of **my view** or sight

257. **himself:** possible wordplay on **Ajax** and "a jakes" (i.e., a toilet)

261. **in saying nothing:** i.e., even though he says **nothing**

And, like ⟨a⟩ dewdrop from the lion's mane,
Be shook to air.

ACHILLES Shall Ajax fight with Hector?

PATROCLUS
Ay, and perhaps receive much honor by him.

ACHILLES
I see my reputation is at stake;
My fame is shrewdly gored.

PATROCLUS O, then, beware!
Those wounds heal ill that men do give themselves.
Omission to do what is necessary
Seals a commission to a blank of danger,
And danger, like an ague, subtly taints
Even then when they sit idly in the sun.

ACHILLES
Go call Thersites hither, sweet Patroclus.
I'll send the fool to Ajax and desire him
T' invite the Trojan lords after the combat
To see us here unarmed. I have a woman's longing,
An appetite that I am sick withal,
To see great Hector in his weeds of peace,
To talk with him, and to behold his visage,
Even to my full of view.

Enter Thersites.

A labor saved.

THERSITES A wonder!

ACHILLES What?

THERSITES Ajax goes up and down the field, asking for himself.

ACHILLES How so?

THERSITES He must fight singly tomorrow with Hector and is so prophetically proud of an heroical cudgeling that he raves in saying nothing.

ACHILLES How can that be?

264. **stand:** halt

264–66. **an hostess . . . reckoning:** The image is of a tavern **hostess** adding up a customer's **reckoning** (bill) in her head. **arithmetic:** art of computation

266–67. **politic regard:** sagacious air

267. **as who should say:** i.e., **as** one **who** would **say; wit:** intelligence

268. **an 'twould out:** i.e., if it would come out

269–70. **as coldly . . . knocking:** wordplay on **knocking** (i.e., striking) a piece of **flint** to create a spark of **fire** and **knocking** (i.e., hitting) Ajax's **head** in order to let out the **wit**

270. **undone:** destroyed, ruined

275–76. **grown . . . land-fish:** i.e., become an unnatural creature (like a fish on land)

276. **A plague of:** i.e., curses on

277. **opinion:** favorable estimate of oneself

277–78. **may . . . jerkin:** i.e., **opinion,** like a tight-fitting **leather** jacket, is reversible and can be worn as self-confidence or as arrogance

281–82. **professes not answering:** i.e., makes a profession of **not answering**

283. **arms:** weapons

283–84. **put on his presence:** i.e., pretend to be him

THERSITES Why, he stalks up and down like a peacock—a stride and a stand; ruminates like an hostess that hath no arithmetic but her brain to set down her reckoning; bites his lip with a politic regard, as who should say "There were wit in this head an 'twould out"—and so there is, but it lies as coldly in him as fire in a flint, which will not show without knocking. The man's undone forever, for if Hector break not his neck i' th' combat, he'll break 't himself in vainglory. He knows not me. I said "Good morrow, Ajax," and he replies "Thanks, Agamemnon." What think you of this man that takes me for the General? He's grown a very land-fish, languageless, a monster. A plague of opinion! A man may wear it on both sides, like a leather jerkin.

ACHILLES Thou must be my ambassador ⟨to him,⟩ Thersites.

THERSITES Who, I? Why, he'll answer nobody. He professes not answering; speaking is for beggars; he wears his tongue in 's arms. I will put on his presence. Let Patroclus make ⟨his⟩ demands to me. You shall see the pageant of Ajax.

ACHILLES To him, Patroclus. Tell him I humbly desire the valiant Ajax to invite the ⟨most⟩ valorous Hector to come unarmed to my tent, and to procure safe-conduct for his person of the magnanimous and most illustrious, six-or-seven-times-honored captain general of the ⟨Grecian⟩ army, Agamemnon, ⟨*et cetera.*⟩ Do this.

PATROCLUS, ⌜*to Thersites, who is playing Ajax*⌝ Jove bless great Ajax.

THERSITES Hum!

PATROCLUS I come from the worthy Achilles—

THERSITES Ha?

307. **God b' wi' you:** i.e., goodbye

310. **it:** i.e., the combat; **Howsoever:** i.e., in any case; nevertheless

313 SD. **He . . . exit:** In performance, Thersites may bow and Achilles may applaud to signal the end of this **pageant** (line 285).

314. **tune:** mood, disposition (with wordplay in **out of tune** [not in order or harmony] in line 315)

315–18. **What music . . . catlings on:** Thersites continues the wordplay on **tune** as **music** by suggesting that **Apollo,** god of **music,** might use Ajax's muscles as catgut for the smallest size lutestrings. (See picture below.)

320. **straight:** straightway, immediately

322. **capable:** intelligent, competent

323. **fountain:** spring of water; **stirred:** agitated (and therefore cloudy or muddy)

327. **such . . . ignorance:** i.e., **be** so valiantly ignorant

Apollo. (1.1.100; 1.3.234; 2.2.85; 3.3.318)
From Giulio Cesare Capaccio, *Gli apologi* . . . (1619).

PATROCLUS Who most humbly desires you to invite Hector to his tent—

THERSITES Hum!

PATROCLUS And to procure safe-conduct from Agamemnon.

THERSITES Agamemnon?

PATROCLUS Ay, my lord.

THERSITES Ha!

PATROCLUS What say you to 't?

THERSITES God b' wi' you, with all my heart.

PATROCLUS Your answer, sir.

THERSITES If tomorrow be a fair day, by eleven of the clock it will go one way or other. Howsoever, he shall pay for me ere he has me.

PATROCLUS Your answer, sir.

THERSITES Fare you well with all my heart.

⌜*He pretends to exit.*⌝

ACHILLES Why, but he is not in this tune, is he?

THERSITES No, but ⟨he's⟩ out of tune thus. What music will be in him when Hector has knocked out his brains I know not. But I am sure none, unless the fiddler Apollo get his sinews to make catlings on.

ACHILLES Come, thou shalt bear a letter to him straight.

THERSITES Let me bear another to his horse, for that's the more capable creature.

ACHILLES

My mind is troubled, like a fountain stirred,
And I myself see not the bottom of it.

⌜*Achilles and Patroclus exit.*⌝

THERSITES Would the fountain of your mind were clear again, that I might water an ass at it. I had rather be a tick in a sheep than such a valiant ignorance.

⌜*He exits.*⌝

TROILUS AND CRESSIDA

ACT 4

4.1 Aeneas, summoned to Priam's palace, meets Paris and a deputation from the Greek camp bringing Antenor to be exchanged for Cressida. Paris sends Aeneas to warn Troilus of their approach.

---

0 SD. **torches:** These indicate to the audience that the action takes place at night.

3. **the Prince:** i.e., Paris

9. **Witness . . . speech:** i.e., your **speech** testified (to his worth) **process:** tenor, gist

10. **a whole . . . days:** i.e., every day for **a week**

12. **Health to you:** i.e., I wish you good **health**

13. **During . . . truce:** i.e., while talks continue during this time **of truce** **question:** talk, discourse **gentle:** courteous, polite; or, mild, nonviolent

14. **as black:** i.e., I wish **as black**

16. **The one and other:** i.e., **health** (line 12) **and defiance** (line 14)

17. **so long:** i.e., as **long** as this continues

18. **occasion:** opportunity of attacking

Aeneas.
From [Guillaume Rouillé,] . . .
Promptuarii iconum . . . (1553).

⌜ACT 4⌝

⌜Scene 1⌝

Enter at one door Aeneas ⌜with a Torchbearer,⌝ at another Paris, Deiphobus, Antenor, Diomedes ⌜and Grecians⌝ with torches.

PARIS See, ho! Who is that there?

DEIPHOBUS It is the Lord Aeneas.

AENEAS Is the Prince there in person?—
Had I so good occasion to lie long
As ⟨you,⟩ Prince Paris, nothing but heavenly business
Should rob my bedmate of my company.

DIOMEDES
That's my mind too.—Good morrow, Lord Aeneas.

PARIS
A valiant Greek, Aeneas; take his hand.
Witness the process of your speech, wherein
You told how Diomed a whole week by days
Did haunt you in the field.

AENEAS Health to you, valiant sir,
During all question of the gentle truce;
But when I meet you armed, as black defiance
As heart can think or courage execute.

DIOMEDES
The one and other Diomed embraces.
Our bloods are now in calm, and, so long, health;
⟨But⟩ when contention and occasion meet,

20. **pursuit:** action of chasing with the intent to kill; **policy:** cunning, craftiness

22. **With . . . backward:** i.e., facing its foe

23–24. **by Anchises' life . . . By Venus' hand:** Aeneas swears by Anchises, his father, and by Venus, his mother.

25. **sort:** way

27. **sympathize:** i.e., agree, are alike (in this)

28. **fate:** death

30. **in . . . honor:** i.e., with regard to my ambitious or rivalrous pursuit of **honor**

34. **despiteful gentle:** cruel polite

37. **the King:** i.e., Priam

39. **Calchas' house:** i.e., the **house** where Cressida lives in her father's absence; **render him:** i.e., give him in return

40. **enfreed:** freed, released

42. **constantly:** firmly, assuredly

44. **certain knowledge:** i.e., certainty

47. **quality:** cause, occasion; **whereof:** why

Mars. (2.1.55; 4.5.219, 281)
From Vincenzo Cartari,
Le imagini de i dei de gli antichi . . . (1587).

By Jove, I'll play the hunter for thy life
With all my force, pursuit, and policy.

AENEAS
And thou shalt hunt a lion that will fly
With his face backward. In human gentleness,
Welcome to Troy. Now, by Anchises' life,
Welcome indeed. By Venus' hand I swear
No man alive can love in such a sort
The thing he means to kill more excellently.

DIOMEDES
We sympathize. Jove, let Aeneas live,
If to my sword his fate be not the glory,
A thousand complete courses of the sun!
But in mine emulous honor let him die
With every joint a wound and that tomorrow.

AENEAS We know each other well.

DIOMEDES
We do, and long to know each other worse.

PARIS
This is the most despiteful gentle greeting,
The noblest hateful love, that e'er I heard of.
⌜*To Aeneas.*⌝ What business, lord, so early?

AENEAS
I was sent for to the King, but why I know not.

PARIS
His purpose meets you. 'Twas to bring this Greek
To Calchas' house, and there to render him,
For the enfreed Antenor, the fair Cressid.
Let's have your company, or, if you please,
Haste there before us. (⌜*Aside to Aeneas*⌝) I constantly
believe—
Or, rather, call my thought a certain knowledge—
My brother Troilus lodges there tonight.
Rouse him, and give him note of our approach,
With the whole quality ⟨whereof.⟩ I fear
We shall be much unwelcome.

57. **soul:** principle

61. **He:** i.e., **Menelaus**

62. **Not making . . . of:** i.e., **not** hesitating because **of; soilure:** sullying, staining

63. **world:** vast quantity; **charge:** (1) trouble; (2) expense

65. **palating:** i.e., perceiving on your palate

67. **puling:** sickly, ailing

68. **flat tamèd piece:** i.e., an already broached (and therefore stale) keg of wine (with possible wordplay on **a piece** as a woman)

70. **breed out:** i.e., engender, create, with probable wordplay on the phrase's primary meaning, "exhaust the breed"

71. **poised:** weighed; **nor less:** i.e., neither **less**

72. **he as he:** i.e., **he** the same **as he; heavier:** weightier, sadder, stupider, more weighed down

73. **bitter:** hostile, harsh

74. **She's bitter:** i.e., **she's** injurious, cruel

75. **false:** treacherous; inconstant

76. **scruple:** i.e., tiny portion (literally, a unit of apothecary weight of 20 grains)

A scale. (2.2.28)

From Silvestro Pietrasanta, . . . *Symbola heroica* . . . (1682).

AENEAS, ⌜*aside to Paris*⌝ That I assure you.
Troilus had rather Troy were borne to Greece
Than Cressid borne from Troy.

PARIS, ⌜*aside to Aeneas*⌝ There is no help.
The bitter disposition of the time
Will have it so.—On, lord, we'll follow you.

AENEAS Good morrow, all.

⟨*Aeneas exits* ⌜*with the Torchbearer.*⌝⟩

PARIS
And tell me, noble Diomed, faith, tell me true,
Even in ⟨the⟩ soul of sound good-fellowship,
Who, in your thoughts, deserves fair Helen best,
Myself or Menelaus?

DIOMEDES Both alike.
He merits well to have her that doth seek her,
Not making any scruple of her ⟨soilure,⟩
With such a hell of pain and world of charge;
And you as well to keep her that defend her,
Not palating the taste of her dishonor,
With such a costly loss of wealth and friends.
He, like a puling cuckold, would drink up
The lees and dregs of a flat tamèd piece;
You, like a lecher, out of whorish loins
Are pleased to breed out your inheritors.
Both merits poised, each weighs nor less nor more;
But he as he, the heavier for a whore.

PARIS
You are too bitter to your countrywoman.

DIOMEDES
She's bitter to her country. Hear me, Paris:
For every false drop in her bawdy veins
A Grecian's life hath sunk; for every scruple
Of her contaminated carrion weight
A Trojan hath been slain. Since she could speak,
She hath not given so many good words breath
As for her Greeks and Trojans suffered death.

81. **chapmen:** traders, merchants
84. **that not:** i.e., who do **not**

4.2 As morning breaks after Troilus and Cressida's night of lovemaking, Troilus, Pandarus, and Cressida each learn in turn that Cressida must leave Troy immediately.

---

6. **attachment:** i.e., confinement, arrest
12. **ribald:** offensively foulmouthed
16. **Beshrew the witch:** i.e., curses on **Night** (called a **witch** perhaps because of its cruelty and its magical ability to stay with some and fly from others); **venomous wights:** pernicious or injurious persons
18. **more . . . thought:** Proverbial: "As swift as **thought.**"

A turtledove. (3.2.179)
From Konrad Gesner, . . .
Historiae animalium . . . (1585-1604).

PARIS
Fair Diomed, you do as chapmen do,
Dispraise the thing that they desire to buy.
But we in silence hold this virtue well:
We'll not commend ⌜that not⌝ intend to sell.
Here lies our way.

They exit.

⌜Scene 2⌝

Enter Troilus and Cressida.

TROILUS
Dear, trouble not yourself. The morn is cold.

CRESSIDA
Then, sweet my lord, I'll call mine uncle down.
He shall unbolt the gates.

TROILUS Trouble him not.
To bed, to bed! Sleep kill those pretty eyes
And give as soft attachment to thy senses
As infants' empty of all thought!

CRESSIDA
Good morrow, then.

TROILUS I prithee now, to bed.

CRESSIDA Are you aweary of me?

TROILUS
O Cressida! But that the busy day,
Waked by the lark, hath roused the ribald crows,
And dreaming night will hide our joys no longer,
I would not from thee.

CRESSIDA Night hath been too brief.

TROILUS
Beshrew the witch! With venomous wights she stays
As tediously as hell, but flies the grasps of love
With wings more momentary-swift than thought.
You will catch cold and curse me.

20. **tarry:** remain, stay

23. **What's:** i.e., why are

27. **How go:** i.e., at what price can one buy

28. **maid:** girl, young woman (**Maid** also meant "virgin.")

29. **naughty:** wicked

30. **flout:** mock

34. **suffer others:** i.e., allow **others** (to **be good**)

35–36. **capocchia:** simpleton (Italian)

36. **Has 't:** i.e., have you (literally, **has** it, a kind of talk used with babies and small children)

37. **let it sleep:** See note to line 36, above. **bugbear:** an imaginary creature invoked to frighten children

41. **naughtily:** i.e., something naughty or improper

A leper. (2.3.35; 5.1.67)
From [Gillaume Guéroult,]
Figures de la Bible . . . (1565–70).

CRESSIDA
Prithee, tarry. You men will never tarry.
O foolish Cressid! I might have still held off,
And then you would have tarried. Hark, there's one up.

PANDARUS, ⟨*within*⟩ What's all the doors open here?

TROILUS It is your uncle.

CRESSIDA
A pestilence on him! Now will he be mocking.
I shall have such a life!

⟨*Enter Pandarus.*⟩

PANDARUS How now, how now? How go maidenheads? Here, you maid! Where's my Cousin Cressid?

CRESSIDA
Go hang yourself, you naughty mocking uncle.
You bring me to do—and then you flout me too.

PANDARUS To do what, to do what?—Let her say what.—What have I brought you to do?

CRESSIDA
Come, come, beshrew your heart! You'll ne'er be good
Nor suffer others.

PANDARUS Ha, ha! Alas, poor wretch! Ah, poor *capocchia!* Has 't not slept tonight? Would he not—a naughty man—let it sleep? A bugbear take him!

CRESSIDA, ⌜*to Troilus*⌝
Did not I tell you? Would he were knocked i' th' head!

One knocks.

Who's that at door?—Good uncle, go and see.—
My lord, come you again into my chamber.
You smile and mock me, as if I meant naughtily.

TROILUS Ha, ha!

CRESSIDA
Come, you are deceived. I think of no such thing.

Knock.

How earnestly they knock! Pray you, come in.
I would not for half Troy have you seen here.

⌜*Troilus and Cressida*⌝ *exit.*

53. **should he do:** i.e., would he be doing

55. **doth import him much:** i.e., is of great importance to him

60. **ware:** aware

60–61. **to be false:** i.e., as **to be** treacherous

61. **Do . . . of him:** i.e., remain ignorant of his presence (if you like)

64. **salute:** properly greet

65. **rash:** pressing, urgent; **at hand:** close by

68. **for him:** i.e., in exchange **for him**

69. **first sacrifice:** presumably, the **first** daily ritual **sacrifice** to the gods

74. **They:** i.e., the party named above (lines 66–67)

Venus. (1.3.172; 3.1.32)
From Vincenzo Cartari, *Le vere e noue imagini* . . . (1615).

PANDARUS Who's there? What's the matter? Will you beat down the door?

⌜Enter Aeneas.⌝

How now? What's the matter?

AENEAS Good morrow, lord, good morrow.

PANDARUS Who's there? My Lord Aeneas? By my troth, I knew you not. What news with you so early?

AENEAS Is not Prince Troilus here?

PANDARUS Here? What should he do here?

AENEAS
Come, he is here, my lord. Do not deny him.
It doth import him much to speak with me.

PANDARUS Is he here, say you? It's more than I know, I'll be sworn. For my own part, I came in late. What should he do here?

AENEAS ⌜Ho,⌝ nay, then! Come, come, you'll do him wrong ere you are ware. You'll be so true to him to be false to him. Do not you know of him, but yet go fetch him hither. Go.

⟨Enter Troilus.⟩

TROILUS How now? What's the matter?

AENEAS
My lord, I scarce have leisure to salute you,
My matter is so rash. There is at hand
Paris your brother and Deiphobus,
The Grecian Diomed, and our Antenor
Delivered to ⟨us;⟩ and ⟨for him⟩ forthwith,
Ere the first sacrifice, within this hour,
We must give up to Diomedes' hand
The Lady Cressida.

TROILUS Is it so concluded?

AENEAS
By Priam and the general state of Troy.
They are at hand and ready to effect it.

82. **would:** i.e., wish

96. **wench:** here, a familiar term of address to a kinswoman

97. **changed:** exchanged; **must to:** i.e., **must** go **to**

99. **his bane:** that which destroys his life

A fly caught in a spider's web. (2.3.16–18)
From John Heywood, *The spider and the flie* . . . (1556).

TROILUS How my achievements mock me!
I will go meet them. And, my Lord Aeneas,
We met by chance; you did not find me here.

AENEAS
Good, good, my lord; the secrets of ⟨nature⟩
Have not more gift in taciturnity.

⌜Troilus and Aeneas⌝ exit.

PANDARUS Is 't possible? No sooner got but lost? The devil take Antenor! The young prince will go mad. A plague upon Antenor! I would they had broke 's neck!

Enter Cressida.

⟨CRESSIDA⟩
How now? What's the matter? Who was here?

PANDARUS Ah, ah!

CRESSIDA
Why sigh you so profoundly? Where's my lord?
Gone? Tell me, sweet uncle, what's the matter?

PANDARUS Would I were as deep under the earth as I am above!

CRESSIDA O the gods! What's the matter?

PANDARUS Pray thee, get thee in. Would thou hadst ne'er been born! I knew thou wouldst be his death. O, poor gentleman! A plague upon Antenor!

CRESSIDA Good uncle, I beseech you, on my knees ⟨I beseech you,⟩ what's the matter?

PANDARUS Thou must be gone, wench; thou must be gone. Thou art changed for Antenor. Thou must to thy father and be gone from Troilus. 'Twill be his death; 'twill be his bane. He cannot bear it.

CRESSIDA
O you immortal gods! I will not go.

PANDARUS Thou must.

CRESSIDA
I will not, uncle. I have forgot my father.

104. **blood:** blood relationship, family

106. **falsehood:** faithlessness, inconstancy

107. **force:** violence, physical coercion

108. **extremes:** hardships

111. **Drawing . . . it:** It was believed that the **center of the earth** (line 110) drew everything on **earth** toward **it.**

4.3 Paris sends Troilus to bring Cressida to Diomedes.

1–10. **It is . . . heart:** This dialogue, or parts of it, may well be spoken by Paris and Troilus in asides to each other as they stand apart from the others onstage. Paris's speech, lines 11–12, seems also to be spoken as an aside. **great morning:** i.e., broad daylight (from the French *grand jour*) **prefixed:** appointed **And haste her:** i.e., and to make haste **to the purpose:** i.e., getting ready (literally, so as to secure the result desired)

12. **would:** wish

Iris. (1.3.388)
From Natale Conti, *Mythologiae* . . . (1616).

I know no touch of consanguinity,
No kin, no love, no blood, no soul so near me
As the sweet Troilus. O you gods divine,
Make Cressid's name the very crown of falsehood
If ever she leave Troilus! Time, force, and death
Do to this body what extremes you can,
But the strong base and building of my love
Is as the very center of the earth,
Drawing all things to it. I'll go in and weep—

PANDARUS Do, do.

CRESSIDA
Tear my bright hair, and scratch my praisèd cheeks,
Crack my clear voice with sobs, and break my heart
With sounding "Troilus." I will not go from Troy.

⟨They exit.⟩

⌜Scene 3⌝

Enter Paris, Troilus, Aeneas, Deiphobus, Antenor, ⟨and⟩ Diomedes.

PARIS
It is great morning, and the hour prefixed
For her delivery to this valiant Greek
Comes fast upon. Good my brother Troilus,
Tell you the lady what she is to do
And haste her to the purpose.

TROILUS Walk into her house.
I'll bring her to the Grecian presently;
And to his hand when I deliver her,
Think it an altar and thy brother Troilus
A priest there off'ring to it his own heart. *⌜He exits.⌝*

PARIS I know what 'tis to love,
And would, as I shall pity, I could help.—
Please you walk in, my lords?

They exit.

4.4 As Troilus and Cressida part, he urges her to be faithful to him, and he promises to visit her in the Greek camp. In introducing her to Diomedes, Troilus first requests, then commands, that Diomedes treat Cressida well. Diomedes dismisses Troilus's words and addresses Cressida in the language of courtly love.

---

3. **fine:** pure

4. **violenteth:** rages with violence; or, perhaps, compels (me) through violence

6. **temporize:** effect a compromise; **affection:** (1) love; (2) inclination

7. **palate:** sense of taste

8. **like allayment:** i.e., same mitigation or moderation

9. **admits:** allows, permits; **qualifying:** moderating; **dross:** foreign matter

14. **spectacles:** sights, shows

15. **goodly:** proper or appropriate; **saying:** i.e., song (literally, proverb)

18. **he answers again:** i.e., the **heart answers** in return

19. **smart:** grief, suffering

20. **By friendship:** i.e., through mere **friendship**

23. **We see it:** i.e., experience shows this (to be true)

24. **strained:** purified, refined

25. **as:** i.e., **as** though; **fancy:** love, inclination

26. **More bright:** i.e., which is **more** glorious

(continued)

⌜Scene 4⌝

Enter Pandarus and Cressida, ⌜weeping.⌝

PANDARUS Be moderate, be moderate.

CRESSIDA
Why tell you me of moderation?
The grief is fine, full, perfect that I taste,
And violenteth in a sense as strong
As that which causeth it. How can I moderate it?
If I could temporize with my ⟨affection⟩
Or brew it to a weak and colder palate,
The like allayment could I give my grief.
My love admits no qualifying dross;
No more my grief in such a precious loss.

Enter Troilus.

PANDARUS Here, here, here he comes. ⌜Ah,⌝ sweet ducks!

CRESSIDA, ⌜*embracing Troilus*⌝ O Troilus, Troilus!

PANDARUS What a pair of spectacles is here! Let me embrace too. "O heart," as the goodly saying is,
O heart, heavy heart,
Why sigh'st thou without breaking?
where he answers again,
Because thou canst not ease thy smart
By friendship nor by speaking.
There was never a truer rhyme. Let us cast away nothing, for we may live to have need of such a verse. We see it, we see it. How now, lambs?

TROILUS
Cressid, I love thee in so strained a purity
That the blest gods, as angry with my fancy—
More bright in zeal than the devotion which
Cold lips blow to their deities—take thee from me.

CRESSIDA Have the gods envy?

PANDARUS Ay, ay, ay, ay, 'tis too plain a case.

27. **Cold . . . blow:** i.e., chaste **lips** utter or vow (probably a reference to virgins who dedicate their lives to the classical **deities**)

28. **envy:** (1) jealousy; (2) malice

35. **suddenly:** without warning or preparation; **injury of chance:** i.e., the wrongful action of fortune or luck

36. **Puts back:** rejects

37. **beguiles:** deprives

38. **all rejoindure:** i.e., any possible reunion

39. **embrasures:** embraces

39–40. **strangles . . . breath:** The image is of **vows** as infants strangled at **birth. laboring:** (1) striving or struggling; (2) suffering the pangs of childbirth

43. **rude:** violent, rough; **discharge:** wordplay on (1) exhalation; (2) payment; **one:** i.e., a single sigh

45. **thiev'ry:** stolen property; **he . . . how:** i.e., in a very careless way

47. **With . . . breath:** i.e., each **with** its own **breath; and . . . them:** i.e., **and with kisses** given in trust (**consigned**) **to them**

48. **He fumbles up:** i.e., **Time** (line 44) wraps **up** clumsily

49. **scants us with:** i.e., limits us to

50. **Distasted:** rendered distasteful

52. **the genius:** In classical thought, **the genius** or attendant spirit guides a person through life and conducts **him** out of the world.

54. **anon:** soon

55. **Rain . . . wind:** i.e., (send me) tears (**rain**) to cause these sighs (**this wind**) to subside

CRESSIDA
And is it true that I must go from Troy?
TROILUS
A hateful truth.
CRESSIDA What, and from Troilus too?
TROILUS From Troy and Troilus.
CRESSIDA Is 't possible?
TROILUS
And suddenly, where injury of chance
Puts back leave-taking, jostles roughly by
All time of pause, rudely beguiles our lips
Of all rejoindure, forcibly prevents
Our locked embrasures, strangles our dear vows
Even in the birth of our own laboring breath.
We two, that with so many thousand sighs
Did buy each other, must poorly sell ourselves
With the rude brevity and discharge of one.
Injurious Time now with a robber's haste
Crams his rich thiev'ry up, he knows not how.
As many farewells as be stars in heaven,
With distinct breath and consigned kisses to them,
He fumbles up into a loose adieu
And scants us with a single famished kiss,
Distasted with the salt of broken tears.
AENEAS, *within* My lord, is the lady ready?
TROILUS
Hark, you are called. Some say the genius
Cries so to him that instantly must die.—
Bid them have patience. She shall come anon.
PANDARUS Where are my tears? Rain, to lay this wind,
or my heart will be blown up by ⟨the root.⟩
⌜*He exits.*⌝
CRESSIDA
I must, then, to the Grecians?
TROILUS No remedy.

59. **merry Greeks:** See note to 1.2.112.
60. **see:** meet
62. **deem:** judgment, opinion
63–64. **we . . . us:** i.e., let us be gentle in reproving each other, since soon we will have no chance to reprove (The image is of **expostulation** [reproof, protest] as a guest who is departing and who should be treated **kindly.**)
65. **fearing:** doubting, distrusting
66. **throw . . . to:** i.e., challenge
67. **maculation:** (moral) stain or spot
68. **fashion in:** i.e., introduce (literally, contrive)
69. **sequent:** subsequent, following
70. **see:** meet
73. **sleeve:** a detachable piece of clothing, often worn as a favor or token, as is the **glove** (line 74)
75. **corrupt:** bribe
76. **give . . . visitation:** i.e., visit you at night
80. **quality:** natural gifts
81. **loving:** i.e., wooing, lovemaking
83. **arts:** learning; **exercise:** skill
84. **move:** persuade; **parts with person:** i.e., talents combined with (handsome) bodily frame or figure
85. **godly jealousy:** For the biblical echo here, see longer note, page 276.
87. **afeard:** frightened, afraid

CRESSIDA
A woeful Cressid 'mongst the merry Greeks.
When shall we see again?
TROILUS
Hear me, ⟨my⟩ love. Be thou but true of heart—
CRESSIDA
I true? How now, what wicked deem is this?
TROILUS
Nay, we must use expostulation kindly,
For it is parting from us.
I speak not "Be thou true" as fearing thee,
For I will throw my glove to Death himself
That there is no maculation in thy heart;
But "Be thou true," say I, to fashion in
My sequent protestation: "Be thou true,
And I will see thee."
CRESSIDA
O, you shall be exposed, my lord, to dangers
As infinite as imminent! But I'll be true.
TROILUS
And I'll grow friend with danger. Wear this sleeve.
CRESSIDA And you this glove. When shall I see you?
⌜*They exchange love-tokens.*⌝
TROILUS
I will corrupt the Grecian sentinels,
To give thee nightly visitation.
But yet, be true.
CRESSIDA O heavens! "Be true" again?
TROILUS Hear why I speak it, love.
The Grecian youths are full of quality,
⟨Their loving well composed, with gift of nature
⌜flowing,⌝⟩
And swelling o'er with arts and exercise.
How novelty may move, and parts with ⟨person,⟩
Alas, a kind of godly jealousy—
Which I beseech you call a virtuous sin—
Makes me afeard.

89. **Die I:** i.e., let me **die**

91. **mainly:** strongly, vehemently

92. **heel:** i.e., dance; **lavolt:** i.e., lavolta, a lively bounding dance

93. **virtues:** accomplishments

94. **prompt, pregnant:** inclined or disposed

95. **can tell:** perceive, am able to state; **grace:** charm, pleasing quality

96. **dumb-discursive:** perhaps, mute but speaking

100. **we will not:** i.e., **we** do **not** choose to have **done**

102. **tempt:** make trial of, put to the test (with wordplay on the familiar meaning of the word)

103. **Presuming . . . potency:** i.e., (imprudently) relying on their **potency,** which is variable, inconstant

111. **with craft:** i.e., using skill or cunning (**craft**) as bait; **opinion:** reputation

112. **simplicity:** i.e., (a reputation for) obtuseness, stupidity; or, straightforwardness

114. **wear mine bare:** i.e., go with my head uncovered (wordplay on *crown* as the human head)

115. **moral:** i.e., statement that summarizes the meaning; **wit:** wisdom, judgment

116. **reach:** extent

CRESSIDA O heavens, you love me not!
TROILUS Die I a villain then!
In this I do not call your faith in question
So mainly as my merit. I cannot sing,
Nor heel the high lavolt, nor sweeten talk,
Nor play at subtle games—fair virtues all,
To which the Grecians are most prompt and pregnant.
But I can tell that in each grace of these
There lurks a still and dumb-discursive devil
That tempts most cunningly. But be not tempted.
CRESSIDA Do you think I will?
TROILUS No.
But something may be done that we will not,
And sometimes we are devils to ourselves
When we will tempt the frailty of our powers,
Presuming on their changeful potency.
AENEAS, *within*
Nay, good my lord—
TROILUS Come, kiss, and let us part.
⌜*They kiss.*⌝
PARIS, *within*
Brother Troilus!
TROILUS, ⌜*calling*⌝ Good brother, come you hither,
And bring Aeneas and the Grecian with you.
CRESSIDA My lord, will you be true?
TROILUS
Who, I? Alas, it is my vice, my fault.
Whiles others fish with craft for great opinion,
I with great truth catch mere simplicity.
Whilst some with cunning gild their copper crowns,
With truth and plainness I do wear mine bare.
Fear not my truth. The moral of my wit
Is "plain and true"; there's all the reach of it.

⟨*Enter* ⌜*Aeneas, Paris, Antenor, Deiphobus, and Diomedes.*⌝⟩

119. **port:** city gate

120. **by the way:** i.e., as we walk; **possess thee:** inform you, acquaint you with

121. **Entreat her fair:** i.e., treat her well

122. **at mercy of:** wholly within the power of

126. **So please you:** a polite phrase of request

128. **Pleads . . . usage:** i.e., urge your good treatment

129. **mistress:** a term used in the courtly love tradition for the woman who has command over the man's heart

131. **petition:** formal request

134. **servant:** the courtly love term for the man devoted to the service of a lady

135. **charge thee:** order you to; **even . . . charge:** i.e., just because of my command

136. **by . . . Pluto:** an oath on the god of the underworld (See picture, page 220.)

137. **great bulk:** massive body

139. **moved:** angry

140–41. **Let . . . free:** an allusion to Diomedes' diplomatic mission, which allows him the privilege of speaking freely

142. **answer . . . lust:** i.e., respond (to your words) as I please **lust:** pleasure

143. **on charge:** i.e., at someone's command

144. **prized:** valued, rated

147. **brave:** bravado, defiance

Welcome, Sir Diomed. Here is the lady
Which for Antenor we deliver you.
At the port, lord, I'll give her to thy hand
And by the way possess thee what she is.
Entreat her fair and, by my soul, fair Greek,
If e'er thou stand at mercy of my sword,
Name Cressid, and thy life shall be as safe
As Priam is in Ilium.

DIOMEDES Fair Lady Cressid,
So please you, save the thanks this prince expects.
The luster in your eye, heaven in your cheek,
Pleads your fair usage, and to Diomed
You shall be mistress and command him wholly.

TROILUS
Grecian, thou dost not use me courteously,
To shame the ⌜zeal⌝ of my petition to thee
In praising her. I tell thee, lord of Greece,
She is as far high-soaring o'er thy praises
As thou unworthy to be called her servant.
I charge thee use her well, even for my charge,
For, by the dreadful Pluto, if thou dost not,
Though the great bulk Achilles be thy guard,
I'll cut thy throat.

DIOMEDES O, be not moved, Prince Troilus.
Let me be privileged by my place and message
To be a speaker free. When I am hence,
I'll answer to my lust, and know you, lord,
I'll nothing do on charge. To her own worth
She shall be prized; but that you say "Be 't so,"
I speak it in my spirit and honor: "no."

TROILUS
Come, to the port. I'll tell thee, Diomed,
This brave shall oft make thee to hide thy head.—
Lady, give me your hand, and, as we walk,
To our own selves bend we our needful talk.

⌜Cressida, Diomedes, and Troilus exit.⌝

153. **The Prince:** i.e., Hector

154. **him:** i.e., Hector

156–60. **Let . . . chivalry:** At least one editor points out that these closing lines, omitted from the Quarto, are unusually weak; he is inclined to credit Shakespeare with cutting them. (See longer note, page 276.) **straight:** immediately **single chivalry:** i.e., **single** combat; feat of knightly arms carried out by him alone

4.5 The Greek leaders, Menelaus and Ulysses excepted, kiss Cressida as Diomedes brings her to the Greek camp. After Hector and Ajax fight their bloodless and inconclusive single combat, Hector is introduced to the Greek leaders, including Achilles, who boasts that he will kill Hector. The Greeks invite Hector, joined by Troilus, to feast with them.

---

1. **appointment:** equipment, outfit

2. **starting:** bounding

4. **dreadful:** awe-inspiring

5. **head:** i.e., ear

6. **hale:** haul, drag

7. **trumpet:** i.e., trumpeter

8. **brazen pipe:** i.e., **trumpet** (line 3) See longer note, page 277.

9. **villain:** a standard form of address to a social inferior

9–10. **thy . . . Aquilon:** The image here of the trumpeter's cheeks puffed out as he blows recalls the round-cheeked wind blowers pictured on

(continued)

⟨*Sound trumpet* ⌜*within.*⌝⟩

PARIS
Hark, Hector's trumpet.
AENEAS How have we spent this morning!
The Prince must think me tardy and remiss
That swore to ride before him to the field.

PARIS
'Tis Troilus' fault. Come, come to field with him.

⟨DEIPHOBUS Let us make ready straight.

AENEAS
Yea, with a bridegroom's fresh alacrity
Let us address to tend on Hector's heels.
The glory of our Troy doth this day lie
On his fair worth and single chivalry.⟩

They exit.

⌜Scene 5⌝

Enter Ajax, armed, Achilles, Patroclus, Agamemnon, Menelaus, Ulysses, Nestor, etc. ⌜*and Trumpeter.*⌝

AGAMEMNON, ⌜*to Ajax*⌝
Here art thou in appointment fresh and fair,
Anticipating time with starting courage.
Give with thy trumpet a loud note to Troy,
Thou dreadful Ajax, that the appallèd air
May pierce the head of the great combatant
And hale him hither.

AJAX Thou, trumpet, there's my purse.

⌜*He gives money to Trumpeter.*⌝

Now crack thy lungs and split thy brazen pipe.
Blow, villain, till thy spherèd bias cheek
Outswell the colic of puffed Aquilon.
Come, stretch thy chest, and let thy eyes spout blood.
Thou blowest for Hector. ⌜*Sound trumpet.*⌝

Renaissance maps. (See picture below.) For the metaphors in **bias, colic,** and **Aquilon,** see longer note, page 277.

14. **early days:** i.e., **early** for us to expect him

15. **yond:** yonder, over there

16. **ken:** recognize

18. **aspiration:** steadfast desire for something above one

23. **but particular:** i.e., merely individual, not **general** (playing on **general** in line 22, and setting up wordplay for line 24)

26. **So much:** i.e., thus **much**

27. **that winter:** i.e., the cold left by old Nestor's lips

29. **argument:** reason

31. **hardiment:** boldness, daring

32. **argument:** i.e., Helen, Menelaus's **argument** (theme, subject) for kissing (playing on **argument** in lines 29–30)

Wind blowers. (4.5.9–10)
From Giulio Cesare Capaccio,
Delle imprese trattato . . . (1592).

ULYSSES
No trumpet answers.
ACHILLES
'Tis but early days.

⌜*Enter Cressida and Diomedes.*⌝

AGAMEMNON
Is not yond Diomed with Calchas' daughter?
ULYSSES
'Tis he. I ken the manner of his gait.
He rises on the toe; that spirit of his
In aspiration lifts him from the earth.
AGAMEMNON
Is this the Lady Cressid?
DIOMEDES
Even she.
AGAMEMNON
Most dearly welcome to the Greeks, sweet lady.
⌜*He kisses her.*⌝
NESTOR
Our general doth salute you with a kiss.
ULYSSES
Yet is the kindness but particular.
'Twere better she were kissed in general.
NESTOR
And very courtly counsel. I'll begin. ⌜*He kisses her.*⌝
So much for Nestor.
ACHILLES
I'll take that winter from your lips, fair lady.
Achilles bids you welcome. ⌜*He kisses her.*⌝
MENELAUS
I had good argument for kissing once.
PATROCLUS, ⌜*stepping between Menelaus and Cressida*⌝
But that's no argument for kissing now,
For thus popped Paris in his hardiment
[And parted thus you and your argument.]
⌜*He kisses her.*⌝

33. **gall:** bitterness; **our scorns:** i.e., (1) our mockery of ourselves, and (2) ourselves as the butt of others' mockery

34. **gild his horns:** i.e., cover his cuckold's **horns** with a thin layer of gold (alluding to the superficial splendor of the war being fought for him and to its enormous cost)

37. **trim:** fine, nice (ironic)

38. **Paris and I kiss:** i.e., **Paris** (kisses Helen) **and I kiss** (you)

39. **by your leave:** a polite phrase of request

40. **render:** give

42. **make . . . live:** perhaps, wager my life (The phrase "a **match**" was used to signal an agreement to wager.)

45. **boot:** odds; something in addition

46–49. **odd, even:** Wordplay on these opposites include such meanings of **odd** as (1) a person left over after others have paired off; (2) a number that is not **even** (divisible by two); (3) single, solitary; (4) unique **is even with:** i.e., has settled accounts with

50. **fillip . . . head:** i.e., hit me on a sensitive spot **fillip:** flick with one's fingernail **o' th' head:** i.e., on my cuckold's horns

52. **match:** contest; **nail:** fingernail

55. **desire:** (1) request; (2) want

ULYSSES
O deadly gall and theme of all our scorns,
For which we lose our heads to gild his horns!

PATROCLUS
The first was Menelaus' kiss; this mine.
Patroclus kisses you. ⌜*He kisses her again.*⌝

MENELAUS O, this is trim!

PATROCLUS
Paris and I kiss evermore for him.

MENELAUS
I'll have my kiss, sir.—Lady, by your leave.

CRESSIDA
In kissing, do you render or receive?

⌜MENELAUS⌝
Both take and give.

CRESSIDA I'll make my match to live,
The kiss you take is better than you give.
Therefore no kiss.

MENELAUS
I'll give you boot: I'll give you three for one.

CRESSIDA
You are an odd man. Give even, or give none.

MENELAUS
An odd man, lady? Every man is odd.

CRESSIDA
No, Paris is ⟨not,⟩ for you know 'tis true
That you are odd, and he is even with you.

MENELAUS
You fillip me o' th' head.

CRESSIDA No, I'll be sworn.

ULYSSES
It were no match, your nail against his horn.
May I, sweet lady, beg a kiss of you?

CRESSIDA
You may.

ULYSSES I do desire it.

58. **maid:** virgin; **his:** i.e., Menelaus's

59. **when 'tis due:** referring perhaps to the terms given in line 58

62. **quick sense:** lively perceptions

63. **Fie:** an exclamation of disgust

64–66. **There's . . . body:** For echoes of biblical and early Christian writers here, see longer note, page 278. **motive:** moving limb or organ

67. **encounterers:** i.e., flirts

68. **accosting:** The verb *accost* means "make up to, approach."

69. **wide . . . thoughts:** i.e., spread open their minds (See longer note, page 278.)

70. **tickling:** eager (with the sense of impatient or "itching" desire)

70–71. **Set them down / For:** i.e., put them on record as being

71–72. **sluttish . . . game:** i.e., prostitutes

73. **The Trojan's:** i.e., Hector's

75. **state:** counsel, dignitaries

75–76. **What . . . commands:** i.e., **what** is the reward for the **victor** (line 77) See longer note, page 278.

76–77. **do . . . known:** i.e., **do you** intend (**purpose**) that **a victor be** declared

77–79. **Will . . . other:** i.e., do you wish **the knights** to fight to the death (See line 105, below.)

CRESSIDA Why, beg ⌜two.⌝

ULYSSES

Why, then, for Venus' sake, give me a kiss
When Helen is a maid again and his.

CRESSIDA

I am your debtor; claim it when 'tis due.

ULYSSES

Never's my day, and then a kiss of you.

DIOMEDES

Lady, a word. I'll bring you to your father.

⌜Diomedes and Cressida talk aside.⌝

NESTOR

A woman of quick sense.

ULYSSES Fie, fie upon her!

There's language in her eye, her cheek, her lip;
Nay, her foot speaks. Her wanton spirits look out
At every joint and motive of her body.
O, these encounterers, so glib of tongue,
That give ⌜accosting⌝ welcome ere it comes
And wide unclasp the tables of their thoughts
To every ⟨tickling⟩ reader! Set them down
For sluttish spoils of opportunity
And daughters of the game.

⟨⌜Diomedes and Cressida⌝ exit.⟩
Flourish.

ALL

The Trojan's trumpet.

Enter all of Troy: ⟨Hector, ⌜armed,⌝ Paris, Aeneas, Helenus, ⌜Troilus,⌝ and Attendants.⟩

AGAMEMNON Yonder comes the troop.

AENEAS

Hail, all the state of Greece! What shall be done
To him that victory commands? Or do you purpose
A victor shall be known? Will you the knights
Shall to the edge of all extremity

79. **divided:** separated (before there is a fatality)

80. **By . . . field:** i.e., **by order of** the marshal of the lists

83. **conditions:** i.e., whatever is agreed upon

84. **like Hector:** i.e., with Hector's usual graciousness

85. **securely:** carelessly, overconfidently

86. **misprizing:** scorning, despising

92. **extremity:** extremes

95. **Weigh:** assess, evaluate

97. **Ajax . . . blood:** an acknowledgment that **Ajax** and **Hector** are first cousins (See line 136 and note.)

101. **maiden battle:** i.e., a **battle** without bloodshed; **perceive:** see through; understand

102. **gentle:** noble, courteous (The phrase **gentle knight** occurs frequently in literature of the fourteenth through the sixteenth centuries.)

104. **order:** ordering, regulation, control

105. **to the uttermost:** i.e., to the death (French: *à l'outrance*)

106. **a breath:** i.e., (the fight is simply for their) exercise

107. **stints:** checks, stops ("Stint the **strife**" was a familiar phrase.)

Pursue each other, or shall they be divided
By any voice or order of the field?
Hector bade ask.

AGAMEMNON Which way would Hector have it?

AENEAS
He cares not; he'll obey conditions.

AGAMEMNON
'Tis done like Hector.

⌜ACHILLES⌝ But securely done,
A little proudly, and great deal misprizing
The knight opposed.

AENEAS If not Achilles, sir,
What is your name?

ACHILLES If not Achilles, nothing.

AENEAS
Therefore Achilles. But whate'er, know this:
In the extremity of great and little,
Valor and pride excel themselves in Hector,
The one almost as infinite as all,
The other blank as nothing. Weigh him well,
And that which looks like pride is courtesy.
This Ajax is half made of Hector's blood,
In love whereof half Hector stays at home;
Half heart, half hand, half Hector comes to seek
This blended knight, half Trojan and half Greek.

ACHILLES
A maiden battle, then? O, I perceive you.

⌜Enter Diomedes.⌝

AGAMEMNON
Here is Sir Diomed.—Go, gentle knight;
Stand by our Ajax. As you and Lord Aeneas
Consent upon the order of their fight,
So be it, either to the uttermost
Or else a breath. The combatants being kin
Half stints their strife before their strokes begin.

107 SD. **lists:** arena set up for trials by combat (See picture below.)

108. **opposed:** standing face to face (in **the lists**)

109. **heavy:** sad

111. **matchless firm of word:** i.e., without equal in keeping his **word**

112. **deedless . . . tongue:** i.e., not bragging of or promising actions

117. **impair:** perhaps, unfit, unsuitable

119–20. **subscribes . . . objects:** i.e., negotiates with the defenseless or defeated **subscribes:** gives in, submits

120. **he:** i.e., **Troilus** (line 122)

121. **vindicative:** vindictive, vengeance-seeking

123. **as . . . Hector:** i.e., **as** fair **as** the **hope built** on **Hector**

125. **Even . . . inches:** i.e., in great detail; **private soul:** i.e., privately and personally

126. **translate:** interpret, explain

130. **disposed:** placed

Lists. (4.5.107 SD)
From [Sir William Segar,]
The booke of honor and armes . . . (1590).

⌜*Hector and Ajax enter the lists.*⌝

⟨ULYSSES They are opposed already.⟩

AGAMEMNON

What Trojan is that same that looks so heavy?

ULYSSES

The youngest son of Priam, a true knight,
Not yet mature, yet matchless firm of word,
Speaking ⟨in⟩ deeds, and deedless in his tongue,
Not soon provoked, nor being provoked soon calmed,
His heart and hand both open and both free.
For what he has, he gives; what thinks, he shows;
Yet gives he not till judgment guide his bounty,
Nor dignifies an impair thought with breath;
Manly as Hector, but more dangerous,
For Hector in his blaze of wrath subscribes
To tender objects, but he in heat of action
Is more vindicative than jealous love.
They call him Troilus, and on him erect
A second hope, as fairly built as Hector.
Thus says Aeneas, one that knows the youth
Even to his inches, and with private soul
Did in great Ilium thus translate him to me.

Alarum. ⌜*The fight begins.*⌝

AGAMEMNON They are in action.

NESTOR Now, Ajax, hold thine own!

TROILUS Hector, thou sleep'st. Awake thee!

AGAMEMNON

His blows are well disposed.—There, Ajax!

Trumpets cease.

DIOMEDES

You must no more.

AENEAS Princes, enough, so please you.

AJAX

I am not warm yet. Let us fight again.

DIOMEDES

As Hector pleases.

136. **my . . . son:** i.e., Priam's sister Hesione's **son** (See note to 2.2.82.)

137. **cousin-german . . . seed:** i.e., my first **cousin** **seed:** offspring

138. **blood:** i.e., blood relationship, kinship

139. **gory emulation:** bloody rivalry or contention

140. **commixtion . . . so:** i.e., mixture of **Greek and Trojan** such

144. **dexter:** right; **this sinister:** i.e., **this** left (**cheek**) Both **dexter** and **sinister** are drawn from the language of heraldry.

145. **multipotent:** most powerful

146. **member:** part of the body

147. **impressure:** impression

148. **rank feud:** violent hostility

152. **him that thunders:** i.e., Jove (See lines 2.3.10–11, note to 2.3.10, and picture, page 26.) **lusty:** strong, healthy

156. **gentle:** noble; **free:** generous

158. **addition:** title

159. **Not . . . mirable:** i.e., **not** even the marvelous **Neoptolemus** (Most editors agree that Shakespeare here refers to Achilles himself. See longer note, page 278.)

160. **Oyez:** i.e., "hear ye"

163. **There . . . sides:** i.e., **both** Greeks and Trojans are waiting to know

166. **issue:** outcome, conclusion; **embracement:** i.e., the act of embracing

HECTOR Why, then, will I no more.—
Thou art, great lord, my father's sister's son,
A cousin-german to great Priam's seed.
The obligation of our blood forbids
A gory emulation 'twixt us twain.
Were thy commixtion Greek and Trojan so
That thou couldst say "This hand is Grecian all,
And this is Trojan; the sinews of this leg
All Greek, and this all Troy; my mother's blood
Runs on the dexter cheek, and this sinister
Bounds in my father's," by Jove multipotent,
Thou shouldst not bear from me a Greekish member
Wherein my sword had not impressure made
⟨Of our rank feud.⟩ But the just gods gainsay
That any ⟨drop⟩ thou borrowd'st from thy mother,
My sacred aunt, should by my mortal sword
Be drained. Let me embrace thee, Ajax.
By him that thunders, thou hast lusty arms!
Hector would have them fall upon him thus.
Cousin, all honor to thee! ⌜*They embrace.*⌝

AJAX I thank thee, Hector.
Thou art too gentle and too free a man.
I came to kill thee, cousin, and bear hence
A great addition earnèd in thy death.

HECTOR
Not Neoptolemus so mirable—
On whose bright crest Fame with her loud'st "Oyez"
Cries "This is he"—could promise to himself
A thought of added honor torn from Hector.

AENEAS
There is expectance here from both the sides
What further you will do.

HECTOR We'll answer it;
The issue is embracement.—Ajax, farewell.
⌜*They embrace again.*⌝

168. **seld:** seldom; **chance:** i.e., opportunity (of entreating you); **desire:** invite

173. **signify:** announce; **interview:** meeting (specifically, a ceremonial meeting of princes or great persons)

174. **expecters . . . part:** i.e., those Trojans awaiting news

175. **Desire them home:** i.e., request that they return **home**

181. **portly:** majestic, imposing

182. **all arms:** i.e., complete warrior, at **all** points

184. **that's no welcome:** i.e., that doesn't sound welcoming

187. **extant:** present

187–90. **faith . . . welcome:** i.e., **faith and troth** (trustworthiness and honesty) . . . bid **thee . . . welcome** **Strained purely:** i.e., purified **hollow:** insincere or false **bias-drawing:** turning awry or away from the truth **integrity:** honesty, sincerity; completeness; perfection

191. **imperious:** majestic, imperial

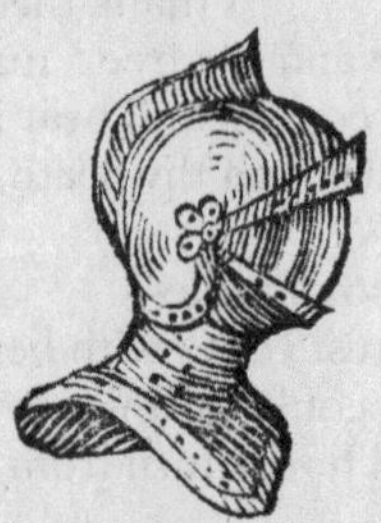

A casque. (5.2.200)
From Louis de Gaya,
Traité des armes, des machines de guerre . . . (1678).

AJAX
If I might in entreaties find success,
As seld I have the chance, I would desire
My famous cousin to our Grecian tents.

DIOMEDES
'Tis Agamemnon's wish; and great Achilles
Doth long to see unarmed the valiant Hector.

HECTOR
Aeneas, call my brother Troilus to me,
And signify this loving interview
To the expecters of our Trojan part;
Desire them home.
⌜*Aeneas speaks to Trojans, who exit; he then returns with Troilus.*⌝
⌜*To Ajax.*⌝ Give me thy hand, my cousin.
I will go eat with thee and see your knights.
⟨*Agamemnon and the rest* ⌜*come forward.*⌝⟩

AJAX
Great Agamemnon comes to meet us here.

HECTOR, ⌜*to Aeneas*⌝
The worthiest of them tell me name by name;
But for Achilles, my own searching eyes
Shall find him by his large and portly size.

AGAMEMNON
Worthy all arms! As welcome as to one
That would be rid of such an enemy—
⟨But that's no welcome. Understand more clear:
What's past and what's to come is strewed with husks
And formless ruin of oblivion;
But in this extant moment, faith and troth,
Strained purely from all hollow bias-drawing,
Bids thee, with most divine integrity,⟩
From heart of very heart, great Hector, welcome.

HECTOR
I thank thee, most imperious Agamemnon.

195. **Who . . . answer:** i.e., what is this person's name

197. **By Mars his gauntlet:** an oath, "by Mars's glove" (See longer note, page 279.)

198. **affect:** use ostentatiously; **untraded:** unfamiliar, unusual

199. **quondam:** former

204. **Laboring for destiny:** i.e., doing the work of **destiny** (one task of which is to end lives)

207. **hot:** ardent, fervent; **Perseus:** See longer note to 1.3.42, page 270. **Phrygian:** Trojan

208. **forfeits and subduments:** i.e., easy conquests (soldiers subdued and forfeit to death)

209. **hung . . . air:** i.e., allowed your raised **sword** to hang in the **air**

210. **the declined:** i.e., those already brought low or debased

212. **dealing life:** i.e., delivering **life** (instead of the customary "**dealing** or delivering blows")

215. **Olympian:** perhaps, god from Mount Olympus; or, perhaps, competitor at the **Olympian** games

216. **still . . . steel:** i.e., always enclosed in a **steel** helmet

217. **thy grandsire:** your grandfather (Laomedon)

219. **Mars, the captain:** i.e., **Mars,** who is **the captain** (See picture, page 158.)

AGAMEMNON, ⌜*to Troilus*⌝
My well-famed lord of Troy, no less to you.

MENELAUS
Let me confirm my princely brother's greeting:
You brace of warlike brothers, welcome hither.

HECTOR, ⌜*to Aeneas*⌝
Who must we answer?

AENEAS The noble Menelaus.

HECTOR
O, you, my lord? By Mars his gauntlet, thanks!
Mock not ⟨that I⟩ affect th' untraded ⟨oath;⟩
Your quondam wife swears still by Venus' glove.
She's well, but bade me not commend her to you.

MENELAUS
Name her not now, sir; she's a deadly theme.

HECTOR O, pardon! I offend.

NESTOR
I have, thou gallant Trojan, seen thee oft,
Laboring for destiny, make cruel way
Through ranks of Greekish youth; and I have seen thee,
As hot as Perseus, spur thy Phrygian steed,
Despising many forfeits and subduments,
When thou hast hung ⟨thy⟩ advanced sword i' th' air,
Not letting it decline on the declined,
That I have said to some my standers-by
"Lo, Jupiter is yonder, dealing life!"
And I have seen thee pause and take thy breath
When that a ring of Greeks have ⟨hemmed⟩ thee in,
Like an Olympian wrestling. This have I seen.
But this thy countenance, still locked in steel,
I never saw till now. I knew thy grandsire
And once fought with him; he was a soldier good,
But, by great Mars, the captain of us all,
Never like thee! O, let an old man embrace thee;
And, worthy warrior, welcome to our tents.

223. **chronicle:** i.e., (living) historical record

226. **would:** wish

230. **I . . . time:** i.e., I remember **the time** when I could **match thee in contention** (line 226) Proverbial: "**I have seen the** day."

232. **her base and pillar:** i.e., its foundation and support

233. **favor:** face

236. **embassy:** i.e., **embassy** of peace that, in many accounts, took place early in the Trojan War

238–41. **My prophecy . . . feet:** Ulysses **foretold** (line 237) that if the Trojans did not give up Helen, the **walls** and **towers** of Troy would be toppled to the ground. (See picture below.) **but half his journey:** i.e., only halfway fulfilled **pertly front:** boldly stand in front of **wanton:** amorous **Must . . . feet:** i.e., **must** (according to the **prophecy**) fall to the ground

242. **I must not:** i.e., I cannot

243. **modestly:** without exaggeration

245. **crowns all:** confirms everything previous

248. **to him we leave it:** i.e., let's **leave it to Time** (line 246) See picture, page 204.

The ruins of Troy.
From Pierre Belon, *Les observations* . . . (1555).

AENEAS, ⌜*to Hector*⌝ 'Tis the old Nestor.

HECTOR

Let me embrace thee, good old chronicle
That hast so long walked hand in hand with time.
Most reverend Nestor, I am glad to clasp thee.

⌜*They embrace.*⌝

NESTOR

I would my arms could match thee in contention
⟨As they contend with thee in courtesy.⟩

HECTOR I would they could.

NESTOR

Ha! By this white beard, I'd fight with thee tomorrow.
Well, welcome, welcome. I have seen the time!

ULYSSES

I wonder now how yonder city stands
When we have here her base and pillar by us.

HECTOR

I know your favor, Lord Ulysses, well.
Ah, sir, there's many a Greek and Trojan dead
Since first I saw yourself and Diomed
In Ilium, on your Greekish embassy.

ULYSSES

Sir, I foretold you then what would ensue.
My prophecy is but half his journey yet,
For yonder walls, that pertly front your town,
Yon towers, whose wanton tops do buss the clouds,
Must kiss their own feet.

HECTOR I must not believe you.
There they stand yet, and modestly I think
The fall of every Phrygian stone will cost
A drop of Grecian blood. The end crowns all,
And that old common arbitrator, Time,
Will one day end it.

ULYSSES So to him we leave it.
Most gentle and most valiant Hector, welcome.
After the General, I beseech you next
To feast with me and see me at my tent.

*Ulysses' prophesy of Troy's destruction see: 4.3,106

252. **thee, thou:** Achilles erupts into the dialogue, flaunting the familiar **thee** and **thou** in speaking to Ulysses, who is his elder, and then to Hector, who is a comparative stranger.

255. **quoted joint by joint:** observed you limb by limb (though **joint** carries also its meaning of a piece of meat for roasting, echoing the word **fed** in line 253)

258. **fair:** i.e., where I can see you

261. **brief:** hasty

262. **As I:** i.e., **as** if **I**

263. **book of sport:** i.e., handbook for hunters

265. **oppress me with thine eye:** i.e., stare at me

273. **Stand again:** Achilles perhaps knelt for his "prayer" in lines 266–71; or Hector may be repeating his request (line 258) that Achilles **stand fair.**

274. **catch:** i.e., take; **pleasantly:** playfully, jocosely

275. **prenominate:** name in advance; **nice:** precise, exact

279. **guard thee:** i.e., protect yourself

A screech-owl. (5.11.17)
From Konrad Gesner,
Icones animalium quadrupedum . . . (1560).

ACHILLES
I shall forestall thee, Lord Ulysses, thou!—
Now, Hector, I have fed mine eyes on thee;
I have with exact view perused thee, Hector,
And quoted joint by joint.

HECTOR
Is this Achilles?

ACHILLES I am Achilles.

HECTOR
Stand fair, I pray thee. Let me look on thee.

ACHILLES
Behold thy fill.

HECTOR Nay, I have done already.

ACHILLES
Thou art too brief. I will the second time,
As I would buy thee, view thee limb by limb.

HECTOR
O, like a book of sport thou'lt read me o'er;
But there's more in me than thou understand'st.
Why dost thou so oppress me with thine eye?

ACHILLES
Tell me, you heavens, in which part of his body
Shall I destroy him—whether there, or there, or
there—
That I may give the local wound a name
And make distinct the very breach whereout
Hector's great spirit flew. Answer me, heavens!

HECTOR
It would discredit the blest gods, proud man,
To answer such a question. Stand again.
Think'st thou to catch my life so pleasantly
As to prenominate in nice conjecture
Where thou wilt hit me dead?

ACHILLES I tell thee, yea.

HECTOR
Wert thou an oracle to tell me so,
I'd not believe thee. Henceforth guard thee well,

281. **that stithied Mars his helm:** i.e., **that** forged Mars's helmet (See picture, page 158.)

285. **endeavor:** attempt

287. **chafe thee:** i.e., get angry

291. **stomach:** inclination; courage; **general state:** i.e., Greek council

292. **odd:** i.e., at odds, in conflict

294. **pelting:** paltry, petty

297. **fell:** cruel, dreadful

299. **match:** agreement, compact

300. **peers:** nobles

301. **in the full convive we:** i.e., we will feast together fully

303. **severally entreat:** individually invite

304. **taborins:** drums

307. **keep:** reside, stay

"That old common arbitrator, Time." (4.5.246)
From Jean de Serres,
A generall historie of France . . . (1611).

For I'll not kill thee there, nor there, nor there,
But, by the forge that stithied Mars his helm,
I'll kill thee everywhere, yea, o'er and o'er.—
You wisest Grecians, pardon me this brag;
His insolence draws folly from my lips.
But I'll endeavor deeds to match these words,
Or may I never—

AJAX Do not chafe thee, cousin.—
And you, Achilles, let these threats alone
Till accident or purpose bring you to 't.
You may have every day enough of Hector
If you have stomach. The general state, I fear,
Can scarce entreat you to be odd with him.

HECTOR, ⌜*to Achilles*⌝
I pray you, let us see you in the field.
We have had pelting wars since you refused
The Grecians' cause.

ACHILLES Dost thou entreat me, Hector?
Tomorrow do I meet thee, fell as death;
Tonight all friends.

HECTOR Thy hand upon that match.

AGAMEMNON
First, all you peers of Greece, go to my tent;
There in the full convive we. Afterwards,
As Hector's leisure and your bounties shall
Concur together, severally entreat him.
⟨Beat loud the taborins;⟩ let the trumpets blow,
That this great soldier may his welcome know.

⌜*Flourish.*⌝

⌜*All but Troilus and Ulysses*⌝ *exit.*

TROILUS
My Lord Ulysses, tell me, I beseech you,
In what place of the field doth Calchas keep?

ULYSSES
At Menelaus' tent, most princely Troilus.
There Diomed doth feast with him tonight,

310. **neither looks upon:** i.e., **looks upon neither**

311. **bent:** inclination, bending

313. **be bound . . . much:** i.e., dare to ask you (and thus put myself under obligation to you)

317. **As gentle:** i.e., **as** courteously; **honor:** reputation

322. **she is, and doth:** i.e., she **is** loved **and she doth** love

323. **sweet . . . tooth:** a combining of the proverbial "to have a **sweet tooth**" with the commonplace that **love** is subject to Fortune

Winged Cupid. (3.1.110; 3.2.13)
From Philippe Galle, *De deis gentium imagines* . . . (1581).

Who neither looks upon the heaven nor earth,
But gives all gaze and bent of amorous view
On the fair Cressid.

TROILUS

Shall I, sweet lord, be bound to you so much,
After we part from Agamemnon's tent,
To bring me thither?

ULYSSES You shall command me, sir.
⟨As⟩ gentle tell me, of what honor was
This Cressida in Troy? Had she no lover there
That wails her absence?

TROILUS

O sir, to such as boasting show their scars
A mock is due. Will you walk on, my lord?
She was beloved, ⟨she loved;⟩ she is, and doth;
But still sweet love is food for Fortune's tooth.

They exit.

TROILUS AND CRESSIDA

ACT 5

5.1 Achilles receives a letter from Queen Hecuba of Troy requiring him to keep an oath he has sworn to seek peace with the Trojans. He decides to keep the oath, in spite of his challenge to Hector. As Hector and some of the Greeks gather at Achilles' tent, Diomedes leaves to join Cressida. Ulysses and Troilus follow him, followed in turn by Thersites.

---

2. **scimitar:** See picture, page 254.

3. **height:** utmost

5. **core:** heart, with wordplay on "mass of dead tissue at the center of a boil" (The image continues in line 6 with **crusty botch,** or "scabby boil.")

7. **picture:** image, statue

9. **fragment:** a term of contempt

10. **full dish:** playing on **fragment** (line 9) as leftover bit of food; **fool:** wordplay on (1) foolishness; (2) a dessert of clotted cream or custard, also called trifle

11. **Who . . . tent:** probably alluding to Thersites' duties (See line 46.) **keeps:** is taking care of

12. **surgeon's . . . wound:** wordplay on **tent** as a medical probe and on **keeps** (line 11) as "possesses, holds onto"

13. **adversity:** i.e., perverse one, quibbler

14. **tricks:** perhaps, quibbles

16. **varlet:** attendant; rogue; valet

19. **guts-griping:** abdominal spasm; **ruptures:** hernias

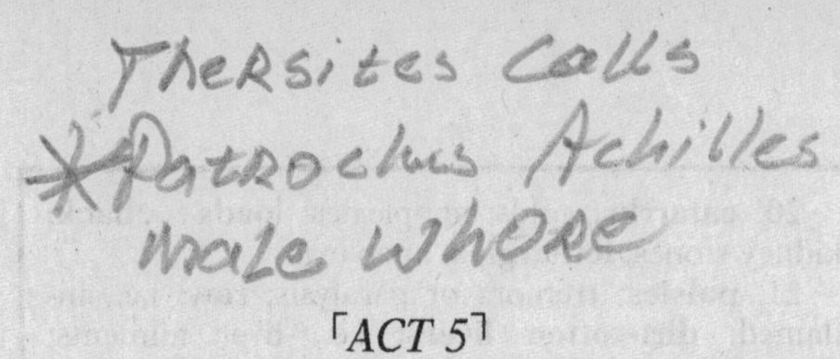

⌜ACT 5⌝

⌜Scene 1⌝

Enter Achilles and Patroclus.

ACHILLES
I'll heat his blood with Greekish wine tonight,
Which with my scimitar I'll cool tomorrow.
Patroclus, let us feast him to the height.

PATROCLUS
Here comes Thersites.

Enter Thersites.

ACHILLES How now, thou ⟨core⟩ of envy?
Thou crusty ⌜botch⌝ of nature, what's the news?

THERSITES Why, thou picture of what thou seemest and idol of idiot-worshippers, here's a letter for thee.

ACHILLES From whence, fragment?

THERSITES Why, thou full dish of fool, from Troy.

⌜*Achilles takes the letter and moves aside to read it.*⌝

PATROCLUS Who keeps the tent now?

THERSITES The surgeon's box or the patient's wound.

PATROCLUS Well said, adversity. And what ⟨need these⟩ tricks?

THERSITES Prithee, be silent, ⟨boy.⟩ I profit not by thy talk. Thou art said to be Achilles' male varlet.

PATROCLUS "Male varlet," you rogue! What's that?

THERSITES Why, his masculine whore. Now the rotten diseases of the south, the guts-griping, ruptures,

20. **catarrhs:** colds; apoplexies; **loads . . . back:** kidney stones; **lethargies:** apoplexies

21. **palsies:** tremors or paralysis; **raw:** i.e., inflamed; **dirt-rotten livers:** i.e., liver ailments; **whissing:** wheezing

22. **impostume:** abscesses

23. **limekilns . . . palm:** skin disease (perhaps psoriasis)

24. **rivelled . . . tetter:** i.e., permanent wrinkles caused by skin eruptions **fee-simple:** literally, an estate belonging to the owner forever

24–25. **take . . . again:** i.e., attack repeatedly

25. **preposterous discoveries:** i.e., perverse or unnatural revelations

26. **box of envy:** container of malice

27. **to curse:** i.e., by cursing

29. **ruinous butt:** dilapidated cask (with wordplay on **ruinous** as "destructive" and on **butt** as "broad end of a tool or instrument," "mound on which a target is set up," and "buttock")

30. **indistinguishable:** i.e., deformed

31. **exasperate:** i.e., exasperated

32. **immaterial:** flimsy; **sleave-silk:** i.e., silk thread

33. **flap:** i.e., patch

35. **waterflies:** small iridescent insects

36. **gall:** bile, bitterness, rancor

37. **Finch egg:** a contemptuous epithet that, like **diminutives** (line 35), refers to Patroclus's small size

42. **taxing:** ordering (or, perhaps, reproving); **gaging:** binding

44. **or go:** i.e., either **go**

(continued)

⟨catarrhs,⟩ loads o' gravel in the back, lethargies, cold palsies, [raw eyes, dirt-rotten livers, whissing lungs, bladders full of impostume, sciaticas, limekilns i' th' palm, incurable bone-ache, and the rivelled fee-simple of the tetter,] take and take again such preposterous discoveries.

PATROCLUS Why, thou damnable box of envy, thou, what means thou to curse thus?

THERSITES Do I curse thee?

PATROCLUS Why, no, you ruinous butt, you whoreson indistinguishable cur, no.

THERSITES No? Why art thou then exasperate, thou idle immaterial skein of sleave-silk, thou green sarsenet flap for a sore eye, thou tassel of a prodigal's purse, thou? Ah, how the poor world is pestered with such waterflies, diminutives of nature!

PATROCLUS Out, gall!

THERSITES Finch egg!

ACHILLES, ⌜*coming forward*⌝

My sweet Patroclus, I am thwarted quite
From my great purpose in tomorrow's battle.
Here is a letter from Queen Hecuba,
A token from her daughter, my fair love,
Both taxing me and gaging me to keep
An oath that I have sworn. I will not break it.
Fall, Greeks; fail, fame; honor, or go or stay;
My major vow lies here; this I'll obey.
Come, come, Thersites, help to trim my tent.
This night in banqueting must all be spent.
Away, Patroclus. ⟨*He exits* ⌜*with Patroclus.*⌝⟩

THERSITES With too much blood and too little brain, these two may run mad; but if with too much brain and too little blood they do, I'll be a curer of madmen. Here's Agamemnon, an honest fellow enough and one that loves quails, but he has not so much brain as earwax. And the goodly transformation

45. **here:** i.e., in the **letter** (line 40)

46. **trim:** prepare

49. **blood:** passion

53. **quails:** i.e., prostitutes

54. **as earwax:** i.e., **as** he has **earwax**

54–55. **goodly . . . bull:** i.e., Menelaus, who, as a **bull** (i.e., a horned creature or cuckold) is a **goodly** (splendid) image of **Jupiter** when he transformed himself into a **bull** to carry off Europa (See picture, page 228.)

55–58. **the primitive . . . leg:** a parenthetical description of Menelaus's status as a cuckold (See longer note, page 279.)

58. **form but that he is:** i.e., shape other than what **he** already **is**

59. **larded:** i.e., intermingled; **forced:** i.e., farced, stuffed

60. **turn him to:** i.e., transform him into; **were nothing:** would be trivial; would accomplish **nothing**

61. **ass and ox:** An **ass** typifies ignorance and stupidity; an **ox** typifies a fool, and its horns also associate it with a cuckold.

62. **fitchew:** polecat (See picture, page 218.)

63. **puttock:** hawk or kite (See picture, page 222.)

63–64. **herring . . . roe:** i.e., thin and weakened **herring** (having already spawned)

66. **care not to be:** i.e., I don't **care** if I am

67. **lazar:** leper (See picture, page 164.)

68. **Sprites and fires:** alluding to the **lights** (line 67 SD) **Sprites:** spirits

76. **to tend on:** i.e., who will attend

79. **sweet:** a complimentary form of address

of Jupiter there, his ⟨brother,⟩ the bull—the primitive statue and oblique memorial of cuckolds, a thrifty shoeing-horn in a chain, ⟨hanging⟩ at his ⟨brother's⟩ leg—to what form but that he is should wit larded with malice and malice ⟨forced⟩ with wit turn him to? To an ass were nothing; he is both ass and ox. To an ox were nothing; ⟨he is⟩ both ox and ass. To be a ⟨dog,⟩ a ⟨mule,⟩ a cat, a fitchew, a toad, a lizard, an owl, a puttock, or a herring without a roe, I would not care; but to be Menelaus! I would conspire against destiny. Ask me ⟨not⟩ what I would be, if I were not Thersites, for I care not to be the louse of a lazar so I were not Menelaus.

Enter ⟨Hector,⟩ ⌜Troilus,⌝ ⟨Ajax,⟩ Agamemnon, Ulysses, Nestor, ⌜Menelaus,⌝ and Diomedes, with lights.

Heyday! Sprites and fires!

AGAMEMNON We go wrong, we go wrong.

AJAX
No, yonder—'tis there, where we see the lights.

HECTOR I trouble you.

AJAX No, not a whit.

⟨Enter Achilles.⟩

ULYSSES, ⌜*to Hector*⌝ Here comes himself to guide you.

ACHILLES
Welcome, brave Hector. Welcome, princes all.

AGAMEMNON, ⌜*to Hector*⌝
So now, fair prince of Troy, I bid good night.
Ajax commands the guard to tend on you.

HECTOR
Thanks, and good night to the Greeks' general.

MENELAUS
Good night, my lord.

HECTOR Good night, sweet lord
Menelaus.

81. **Sweet:** flavorful, fragrant, wholesome

81–82. **draught, sink, sewer:** i.e., cesspool

89. **tide:** opportune time

91. **his torch:** i.e., Diomedes' **torch**

98. **leers:** casts glances aside; **he hisses:** i.e., it **hisses**

99. **spend his mouth:** i.e., bark, bray

102. **borrows of:** i.e., **borrows** light from

103. **leave to see:** i.e., forgo seeing

105. **Calchas his:** i.e., Calchas's

106. **incontinent varlets:** i.e., lecherous rogues

The Greeks' "brave pavilions" and Troy's walls. (Prologue, 15)
From [John Lydgate,]
The hystorye sege and dystruccyon of Troye [1513].

THERSITES, ⌜*aside*⌝ Sweet draught. "Sweet," quoth he?
Sweet sink, sweet sewer.

ACHILLES
Good night and welcome, both ⟨at once⟩, to those
That go or tarry.

AGAMEMNON Good night.

Agamemnon ⌜and⌝ Menelaus exit.

ACHILLES
Old Nestor tarries, and you too, Diomed.
Keep Hector company an hour or two.

DIOMEDES
I cannot, lord. I have important business,
The tide whereof is now.—Good night, great Hector.

HECTOR
Give me your hand.

ULYSSES, ⌜*aside to Troilus*⌝
Follow his torch; he goes to Calchas' tent.
I'll keep you company.

TROILUS Sweet sir, you honor me.

HECTOR And so, good night.

⌜*Diomedes exits, followed by Troilus and Ulysses.*⌝

ACHILLES Come, come, enter my tent.

⌜*Achilles, Ajax, Nestor, and Hector*⌝ *exit.*

THERSITES That same Diomed's a false-hearted rogue, a most unjust knave. I will no more trust him when he leers than I will a serpent when he hisses. He will spend his mouth and promise like Brabbler the hound, but when he performs, astronomers foretell it; it is prodigious, there will come some change. The sun borrows of the moon when Diomed keeps his word. I will rather leave to see Hector than not to dog him. They say he keeps a Trojan drab and uses the traitor Calchas ⟨his⟩ tent. I'll after. Nothing but lechery! All incontinent varlets!

⌜*He exits.*⌝

5.2 Diomedes pressures Cressida to keep her promise to have sex with him; they are overheard by an enraged Troilus, an anxious Ulysses, and a bitterly satirical Thersites. When Cressida gives Diomedes the love token that Troilus gave her, Troilus cannot reconcile her betrayal with his earlier experience of her. He vows to avenge himself on Diomedes.

---

6. **discover:** reveal
8. **my charge:** i.e., person entrusted to my care
10. **familiar:** intimate
14. **clef:** musical notation indicating the pitch of the notes (with possible wordplay on "cleft," a word for the external female genitalia); **noted:** wordplay on (1) observed, infamous; (2) full of musical notes
17–18. **let . . . words:** i.e., don't lie
20. **List:** listen
21. **folly:** unwise behavior; lewdness, wantonness

A fitchew, or polecat. (5.1.62)
From Edward Topsell,
The historie of foure-footed beastes . . . (1607).

⌜Scene 2⌝

Enter Diomedes.

DIOMEDES What, are you up here, ho? Speak.

CALCHAS, ⌜*within*⌝ Who calls?

DIOMEDES Diomed. Calchas, I think? Where's your daughter?

CALCHAS, ⌜*within*⌝ She comes to you.

⟨*Enter Troilus and Ulysses,*⟩ ⌜*at a distance, and then, apart from them, Thersites.*⌝

ULYSSES, ⌜*aside to Troilus*⌝
Stand where the torch may not discover us.

Enter Cressida.

TROILUS, ⌜*aside to Ulysses*⌝
Cressid comes forth to him.

DIOMEDES How now, my charge?

CRESSIDA
Now, my sweet guardian. Hark, a word with you.

⌜*She whispers to him.*⌝

TROILUS, ⌜*aside*⌝ Yea, so familiar?

ULYSSES, ⌜*aside to Troilus*⌝ She will sing any man at first sight. *

THERSITES, ⌜*aside*⌝ And any man may sing her, if he can take her clef. She's noted.

DIOMEDES Will you remember?

⌜CRESSIDA⌝ Remember? Yes.

DIOMEDES Nay, but do, then, and let your mind be coupled with your words.

TROILUS, ⌜*aside*⌝ What ⟨should⟩ she remember?

ULYSSES, ⌜*aside to Troilus*⌝ List!

CRESSIDA
Sweet honey Greek, tempt me no more to folly.

THERSITES, ⌜*aside*⌝ Roguery!

DIOMEDES Nay, then—

* See 4.1. 71-72
4.5. 71-72

25. **a pin:** i.e., something worthless; **are forsworn:** have sworn falsely

27. **juggling trick:** magician's sleight of hand or deceptive illusion; **secretly open:** perhaps, modestly wanton (See longer note, page 279.)

35. **fool:** dupe

39. **moved:** angry, agitated, disturbed

41. **wrathful terms:** i.e., enraged language

45. **flow:** i.e., overflow; **distraction:** violent mental perturbation

Pluto, god of the underworld. (3.3.206; 4.4.136)
From Philippe Galle, *De deis gentium imagines* . . . (1581).

CRESSIDA I'll tell you what—
DIOMEDES
Foh, foh, come, tell a pin! You are forsworn.
CRESSIDA
In faith, I cannot. What would you have me do?
THERSITES, ⌜*aside*⌝ A juggling trick: to be secretly open!
DIOMEDES
What did you swear you would bestow on me?
CRESSIDA
I prithee, do not hold me to mine oath.
Bid me do anything but that, sweet Greek.
DIOMEDES Good night.
TROILUS, ⌜*aside*⌝ Hold, patience!
ULYSSES, ⌜*aside to Troilus*⌝ How now, Trojan?
CRESSIDA Diomed—
DIOMEDES
No, no, good night. I'll be your fool no more.
TROILUS, ⌜*aside*⌝ Thy better must.
CRESSIDA Hark, a word in your ear.
⌜*She whispers to him.*⌝
TROILUS, ⌜*aside*⌝ O plague and madness!
ULYSSES, ⌜*aside to Troilus*⌝
You are moved, prince. Let us depart, I pray ⟨you,⟩
Lest your displeasure should enlarge itself
To wrathful terms. This place is dangerous;
The time right deadly. I beseech you, go.
TROILUS, ⌜*aside to Ulysses*⌝
Behold, I pray you.
ULYSSES, ⌜*aside to Troilus*⌝ ⟨Nay,⟩ good my lord, go off.
You flow to great ⟨distraction.⟩ Come, my lord.
TROILUS, ⌜*aside to Ulysses*⌝
I prithee, stay.
ULYSSES, ⌜*aside to Troilus*⌝ You have not patience. Come.
TROILUS, ⌜*aside to Ulysses*⌝
I pray you, stay. By hell and all hell's torments,
I will not speak a word.

51. **part:** depart, leave; or, **part** from me

53. **truth:** fidelity

57. **palter:** waver, shift position

60. **break out:** perhaps, **break** your silence

64. **will:** i.e., that which pushes me to act; inclination, desire; **offenses:** perhaps, offensive words or actions on my part; or, perhaps, insults or damages done to me

65. **guard:** protection, defense

66. **Luxury:** lecherousness

67. **potato finger:** an allusion to the alleged aphrodisiac quality of the sweet **potato; tickles:** arouses

68. **Fry:** i.e., burn (with passion, or in hell)

71. **for the surety:** perhaps, **for the** certainty; or, perhaps, as a bond or guarantee

A "puttock," or kite. (5.1.63)
From Konrad Gesner,
Historiae animalium . . . (1585-1604).

DIOMEDES
And so good night. ⌜*He starts to leave.*⌝

CRESSIDA Nay, but you part in anger.

TROILUS, ⌜*aside*⌝ Doth that grieve thee? O withered truth!

ULYSSES, ⌜*aside to Troilus*⌝
How now, my lord?

TROILUS, ⌜*aside to Ulysses*⌝ By Jove, I will be patient.

CRESSIDA
Guardian! Why, Greek!

DIOMEDES Foh foh! ⟨Adieu.⟩ You palter.

CRESSIDA
In faith, I do not. Come hither once again.

ULYSSES, ⌜*aside to Troilus*⌝
You shake, my lord, at something. Will you go?
You will break out.

TROILUS, ⌜*aside*⌝ She strokes his cheek!

ULYSSES, ⌜*aside to Troilus*⌝ Come, come.

TROILUS, ⌜*aside to Ulysses*⌝
Nay, stay. By Jove, I will not speak a word.
There is between my will and all offenses
A guard of patience. Stay a little while.

THERSITES, ⌜*aside*⌝ How the devil Luxury, with his fat rump and potato finger, tickles ⟨these⟩ together. Fry, lechery, fry!

DIOMEDES ⟨But⟩ will you, then?

CRESSIDA
In faith, I will, ⌜la.⌝ Never trust me else.

DIOMEDES
Give me some token for the surety of it.

CRESSIDA I'll fetch you one. *She exits.*

ULYSSES, ⌜*aside to Troilus*⌝
You have sworn patience.

TROILUS, ⌜*aside to Ulysses*⌝ Fear me not, my lord.
I will not be myself nor have cognition
Of what I feel. I am all patience.

77. **pledge:** i.e., the **token** (line 71) being fetched by Cressida

80. **faith:** constancy, loyalty

84. **false:** unfaithful; **wench:** perhaps, girl or woman; or, perhaps, unchaste or lascivious woman

86. **ha 't:** i.e., have it

89. **sharpens:** i.e., acts as a **whetstone** (lines 89–90) for honing Diomedes' desire

94. **pledge:** i.e., **token** (line 71) given as a guarantee of good faith

97. **memorial:** commemorative

100. **withal:** with it

Pressing to death. (3.2.211)
From *The life and death of Griffin Flood informer . . .* (1623).

Enter Cressida ⌜with Troilus's sleeve.⌝

THERSITES, ⌜*aside*⌝ Now the pledge, now, now, now!

CRESSIDA, ⌜*giving the sleeve*⌝ Here, Diomed. Keep this sleeve.

TROILUS, ⌜*aside*⌝ O beauty, where is thy faith?

ULYSSES, ⌜*aside to Troilus*⌝ My lord—

TROILUS, ⌜*aside to Ulysses*⌝
⟨I will be patient; outwardly I will.

CRESSIDA⟩
You look upon that sleeve? Behold it well.
He loved me—O false wench!—Give 't me again.

⌜She snatches the sleeve from Diomedes.⌝

DIOMEDES Whose was 't?

CRESSIDA
It is no matter, now I ha 't again.
I will not meet with you tomorrow night.
I prithee, Diomed, visit me no more.

THERSITES, ⌜*aside*⌝ Now she sharpens. Well said, whetstone.

DIOMEDES I shall have it.

CRESSIDA What, this?

DIOMEDES Ay, that.

CRESSIDA
O all you gods!—O pretty, pretty pledge!
Thy master now lies thinking on his bed
Of thee and me, and sighs, and takes my glove,
And gives memorial dainty kisses to it
As I kiss thee.

⌜He grabs the sleeve, and she tries to retrieve it.⌝

DIOMEDES Nay, do not snatch it from me.

CRESSIDA
He that takes that doth take my heart withal.

DIOMEDES
I had your heart before. This follows it.

TROILUS, ⌜*aside*⌝ I did swear patience.

103. **faith:** i.e., in **faith** (a mild oath)

111–12. **By . . . herself:** i.e., by the stars and the moon (Diana, goddess of chastity, is also goddess of the moon. Here, the stars are imagined as her **waiting-women.**) See picture below. **yond:** yonder

113. **helm:** helmet

114. **his spirit:** i.e., the **spirit** of the owner of the **pledge** (line 94)

115. **wor'st:** worest (i.e., wore)

122. **straight starts:** i.e., immediately startles

123. **fooling:** trifling, idling

124. **that likes not you:** i.e., which you dislike

127. **plagued:** afflicted, tormented

Diana. (5.2.111)
From Robert Whitcombe, *Janua divorum* . . . (1678).

⟨CRESSIDA⟩
You shall not have it, Diomed, faith, you shall not.
I'll give you something else.

DIOMEDES I will have this. Whose was it?

CRESSIDA It is no matter.

DIOMEDES Come, tell me whose it was.

CRESSIDA
'Twas one's that loved me better than you will.
But now you have it, take it.

DIOMEDES Whose was it?

CRESSIDA
By all Diana's waiting-women yond,
And by herself, I will not tell you whose.

DIOMEDES
Tomorrow will I wear it on my helm
And grieve his spirit that dares not challenge it.

TROILUS, ⌜*aside*⌝
Wert thou the devil and wor'st it on thy horn,
It should be challenged.

CRESSIDA
Well, well, 'tis done, 'tis past. And yet it is not.
I will not keep my word.

DIOMEDES Why, then, farewell.
Thou never shalt mock Diomed again.
⌜*He starts to leave.*⌝

CRESSIDA
You shall not go. One cannot speak a word
But it straight starts you.

DIOMEDES I do not like this fooling.

⌜TROILUS, *aside*⌝
Nor I, by Pluto! But that that likes not you
Pleases me best.

DIOMEDES What, shall I come? The hour?

CRESSIDA
Ay, come.—O Jove!—Do, come.—I shall be plagued.

132. **poor our:** i.e., our inferior (or, our unfortunate or pitiable)

136. **proof of strength:** i.e., strong evidence in this case; **publish:** announce, make generally known

141. **recordation:** commemorative account

143. **co-act:** act together

145. **Sith:** since; **credence:** belief

146. **esperance:** expectation, hope

147. **th' attest:** the evidence or testimony

148. **deceptious:** deceiving, misleading

149. **calumniate:** utter maliciously false statements, slander

151. **conjure:** call up a spirit (that looks like Cressida)

152. **sure:** i.e., surely, certainly

154. **negation:** statement that **she was not** here (line 152)

155. **but now:** only this moment, just **now**

Jupiter, as a bull, with Europa. (5.1.54–55)
From Gabriele Simeoni, *La vita* . . . (1559).

DIOMEDES
Farewell, till then.
CRESSIDA Good night. I prithee, come.—
⟨*He exits.*⟩
Troilus, farewell. One eye yet looks on thee,
But with my heart the other eye doth see.
Ah, poor our sex! This fault in us I find:
The error of our eye directs our mind.
What error leads must err. O, then conclude:
Minds swayed by eyes are full of turpitude. *She exits.*
THERSITES, ⌜*aside*⌝
A proof of strength she could not publish more,
Unless she said "My mind is now turned whore."
ULYSSES
All's done, my lord.
TROILUS It is.
ULYSSES Why stay we then?
TROILUS
To make a recordation to my soul
Of every syllable that here was spoke.
But if I tell how these two did ⟨co-act,⟩
Shall I not lie in publishing a truth?
Sith yet there is a credence in my heart,
An esperance so obstinately strong,
That doth invert th' attest of eyes and ears,
As if those organs ⟨had deceptious⟩ functions,
Created only to calumniate.
Was Cressid here?
ULYSSES I cannot conjure, Trojan.
TROILUS She was not, sure.
ULYSSES Most sure she was.
TROILUS
Why, my negation hath no taste of madness.
ULYSSES
Nor mine, my lord. Cressid was here but now.

156. **for womanhood:** i.e., for the sake of women (and their reputation)

158. **stubborn:** fierce or obstinate

158–59. **theme . . . depravation:** i.e., grounds for vilification or detraction

159–60. **square . . . rule:** i.e., frame the idea of woman in accord with Cressida's behavior (with wordplay on **square** and **rule** as "measure with a carpenter's square" and **rule** as "a measuring stick")

161. **soil:** sully, discredit

164. **swagger:** bluster

164–65. **out . . . eyes:** i.e., **out** of (believing what he has seen with) his **own eyes** **on 's:** i.e., of his

168. **sanctimonies:** i.e., sacred things

169. **sanctimony:** holiness of life and character

170. **rule in unity:** a principle governing oneness (i.e., that **unity** means indivisibility) See longer note, page 279.

171. **discourse:** i.e., (such) reasoning

172. **cause . . . itself:** i.e., advocates both sides of the case

173. **Bifold authority:** perhaps, the power of doubleness, of divisibility (See line 170 and note.) **reason:** reasoning; **revolt:** i.e., contradict itself

174. **perdition, loss:** being totally destroyed; **assume:** i.e., **can** put on the garb of

175. **revolt:** i.e., apparent contradiction

176. **conduce:** perhaps, conduct itself

177. **inseparate:** incapable of being separated

178. **Divides more wider:** i.e., is **more** widely separated

180. **Admits no orifex:** i.e., allows **no** orifice or opening; **subtle:** thin, fine

(continued)

TROILUS
Let it not be believed for womanhood!
Think, we had mothers. Do not give advantage
To stubborn critics, apt, without a theme
For depravation, to square the general sex
By Cressid's rule. Rather, think this not Cressid.

ULYSSES
What hath she done, prince, that can ⟨soil⟩ our
mothers?

TROILUS
Nothing at all, unless that this were she.

THERSITES, ⌜*aside*⌝ Will he swagger himself out on 's
own eyes?

TROILUS
This she? No, this is Diomed's Cressida.
If beauty have a soul, this is not she;
If souls guide vows, if vows be sanctimonies,
If sanctimony be the gods' delight,
If there be rule in unity itself,
This ⟨is⟩ not she. O madness of discourse,
That cause sets up with and against itself!
Bifold authority, where reason can revolt
Without perdition, and loss assume all reason
Without revolt. This is and is not Cressid.
Within my soul there doth conduce a fight
Of this strange nature, that a thing inseparate
Divides more wider than the sky and earth,
And yet the spacious breadth of this division
Admits no orifex for a point as subtle
As Ariachne's broken woof to enter.
Instance, O instance, strong as Pluto's gates,
Cressid is mine, tied with the bonds of heaven;
Instance, O instance, strong as heaven itself,
The bonds of heaven are slipped, dissolved, and
loosed,
And with another knot, ⟨five-finger-tied,⟩

181. **Ariachne's broken woof:** i.e., the thinnest of threads (See longer note, page 280.)

182. **Instance:** evidence, proof; **Pluto's gates:** i.e., the **gates** to the underworld

185. **are slipped:** i.e., have lost their hold

187. **five-finger-tied:** i.e., firmly **tied, tied** with all the fingers of the hand; or, perhaps, **tied** with the hand given to Diomedes

188–90. **fractions . . . her o'er-eaten faith:** i.e., what's left **of her** fidelity and **love** **fractions, orts, relics:** fragments, leavings, remains **o'er-eaten:** i.e., nibbled all over or on all sides

191–92. **attached / With:** seized by

193–95. **divulgèd . . . Venus:** i.e., revealed in symbols (**characters**) written in **red** blood **Mars his:** Mars's **Inflamed with:** i.e., when it was on fire with love for

195. **fancy:** love

196. **fixed:** steadfast, constant

198. **So much by weight:** i.e., in equal measure

199–200. **helm, casque:** helmet (See picture, page 196.)

200. **composed:** formed, constructed; **Vulcan's skill:** i.e., the metalwork of the god Vulcan (See picture, page 88.)

201. **spout:** waterspout (a violent storm or tornado over water)

202. **hurricano:** i.e., hurricane

203. **Constringed:** compressed; **almighty:** all-powerful

204. **Neptune's:** i.e., the god of the sea's

205. **his descent:** i.e., its (the waterspout's) **descent**

(continued)

The fractions of her faith, orts of her love,
The fragments, scraps, the bits and greasy relics
Of her o'er-eaten faith are given to Diomed.

ULYSSES
May worthy Troilus be half attached
With that which here his passion doth express?

TROILUS
Ay, Greek, and that shall be divulgèd well
In characters as red as Mars his heart
Inflamed with Venus. Never did young man fancy
With so eternal and so fixed a soul.
Hark, Greek: as much ⌜as⌝ I do Cressid love,
So much by weight hate I her Diomed.
That sleeve is mine that he'll bear on his helm.
Were it a casque composed by Vulcan's skill,
My sword should bite it. Not the dreadful spout
Which shipmen do the hurricano call,
Constringed in mass by the almighty sun,
Shall dizzy with more clamor Neptune's ear
In his descent than shall my prompted sword
Falling on Diomed.

THERSITES, ⌜*aside*⌝ He'll tickle it for his concupy.

TROILUS
O Cressid! O false Cressid! False, false, false!
Let all untruths stand by thy stainèd name,
And they'll seem glorious.

ULYSSES O, contain yourself.
Your passion draws ears hither.

Enter Aeneas.

AENEAS, ⌜*to Troilus*⌝
I have been seeking you this hour, my lord.
Hector, by this, is arming him in Troy.
Ajax, your guard, stays to conduct you home.

TROILUS
Have with you, prince.—My courteous lord, adieu.—

207. **tickle it:** beat or chastise Diomedes (with wordplay on **tickle** as "tease, annoy"); **concupy:** perhaps, concubine; or, perhaps, concupiscence

209. **stand by:** i.e., place themselves beside

212. **passion:** outburst of anger

213. **this hour:** i.e., for an **hour**

214. **by this:** i.e., **by this** time; **him:** himself

215. **guard:** i.e., escort and safe-conduct; **stays:** waits

216. **Have with you:** i.e., I'm coming

217. **revolted fair:** i.e., disloyal beauty (To *revolt* is to cast off allegiance.)

220. **distracted thanks:** i.e., **thanks** from a perplexed (or deranged) mind

222. **bode:** foretell, predict

223–24. **the intelligence of:** i.e., information about, news of

225. **than he:** i.e., **than Patroclus** (line 223); **commodious:** accommodating, serviceable, handy

226. **still:** always, invariably

5.3 Andromache and Cassandra enlist Priam in their efforts to persuade Hector to refrain from battle. He, in turn, futilely attempts to keep Troilus from the fight. With Priam's reluctant blessing on Hector, both young men leave to fight, with Troilus delayed a moment by Pandarus, who gives him a letter from Cressida that Troilus reads and then tears up.

---

1. **so much ungently tempered:** i.e., in such a discourteous mood

(continued)

Farewell, revolted fair!—And, Diomed,
Stand fast, and wear a castle on thy head!

ULYSSES I'll bring you to the gates.

TROILUS Accept distracted thanks.

Troilus, Aeneas, and Ulysses exit.

THERSITES Would I could meet that rogue Diomed! I would croak like a raven; I would bode, I would bode. Patroclus will give me anything for the intelligence of this whore. The parrot will not do more for an almond than he for a commodious drab. Lechery, lechery, still wars and lechery! Nothing else holds fashion. A burning devil take them!

He exits.

⌜Scene 3⌝

Enter Hector, ⌜armed,⌝ and Andromache.

ANDROMACHE
When was my lord so much ungently tempered
To stop his ears against admonishment?
Unarm, unarm, and do not fight today.

HECTOR
You train me to offend you. Get you in.
By all the everlasting gods, I'll go!

ANDROMACHE
My dreams will sure prove ominous to the day.

HECTOR
No more, I say.

Enter Cassandra.

CASSANDRA Where is my brother Hector?

ANDROMACHE
Here, sister, armed and bloody in intent.
Consort with me in loud and dear petition;
Pursue we him on knees. For I have dreamt

2. **stop . . . admonishment:** i.e., refuse to listen to advice or warning

4. **train:** persuade, induce

6. **sure:** surely; **ominous to:** prophetic about

9. **bloody:** bloodthirsty

10. **Consort:** join; **dear:** heartfelt, earnest

16. **sally:** sortie, attack

18. **peevish:** obstinate, foolish

20. **spotted:** blemished

22. **just:** righteous

23. **For . . . much:** i.e., on the grounds that we wish to be generous; **use:** practice

26. **to every purpose:** i.e., **to** each and **every purpose; hold:** i.e., be held inviolate

29. **keeps the weather of:** i.e., lies to the windward of, has the advantage over

30. **dear man:** honorable, worthy **man**

33. **father:** i.e., **father**-in-law, Priam

34. **harness:** armor

35. **i' th' vein of chivalry:** i.e., in the mood for gallant deeds

36. **sinews:** muscles; **till . . . strong:** perhaps, until they have become knotted and protuberant

Of bloody turbulence, and this whole night
Hath nothing been but shapes and forms of slaughter.

CASSANDRA

O, 'tis true!

HECTOR, ⌜*calling out*⌝ Ho! Bid my trumpet sound!

⟨CASSANDRA⟩

No notes of sally, for the heavens, sweet brother!

HECTOR

Begone, I say. The gods have heard me swear.

CASSANDRA

The gods are deaf to hot and peevish vows.
They are polluted off'rings more abhorred
Than spotted livers in the sacrifice.

ANDROMACHE, ⌜*to Hector*⌝

O, be persuaded! Do not count it holy
⟨To hurt by being just. It is as lawful,
For we would give much, to ⌜use⌝ violent thefts
And rob in the behalf of charity.

CASSANDRA⟩

It is the purpose that makes strong the vow,
But vows to every purpose must not hold.
Unarm, sweet Hector.

HECTOR Hold you still, I say.

Mine honor keeps the weather of my fate.
Life every man holds dear, but the dear man
Holds honor far more precious-dear than life.

Enter Troilus, ⌜*armed.*⌝

How now, young man? Meanest thou to fight today?

ANDROMACHE

Cassandra, call my father to persuade.

Cassandra exits.

HECTOR

No, faith, young Troilus, doff thy harness, youth.
I am today i' th' vein of chivalry.
Let grow thy sinews till their knots be strong,

37. **brushes:** hostile encounters

38. **doubt:** fear

41. **better . . . lion:** Proverbial: "The **lion** spares the suppliant."

44. **Even . . . sword:** i.e., knocked down just by the rush of air from **your sword**

50. **hermit Pity:** The virtue **pity** is here imaged as a monastic who lives apart from the world, praying for others.

52. **venomed:** noxious, malevolent

53. **ruthful:** lamentable, piteous; **ruth:** compassion

59. **Beck'ning . . . retire:** i.e., signaling me to withdraw **truncheon:** warder or staff used by an official to signal the beginning or end of hostilities **retire:** act of withdrawing or retreating

61. **o'er-gallèd:** i.e., red and raw (literally, over-irritated); **recourse:** flow

64. **ruin:** destruction

Fame. (3.3.219)
From August Casimir Redel,
Apophtegmata symbolica . . . [n.d.].

And tempt not yet the brushes of the war.
Unarm thee, go, and doubt thou not, brave boy,
I'll stand today for thee and me and Troy.

TROILUS
Brother, you have a vice of mercy in you
Which better fits a lion than a man.

HECTOR
What vice is that? Good Troilus, chide me for it.

TROILUS
When many times the captive Grecian falls,
Even in the fan and wind of your fair sword,
You bid them rise and live.

HECTOR
O, 'tis fair play.

TROILUS Fool's play, by heaven, Hector.

HECTOR
How now? How now?

TROILUS For th' love of all the gods,
Let's leave the hermit Pity with our mother,
And when we have our armors buckled on,
The venomed Vengeance ride upon our swords,
Spur them to ruthful work, rein them from ruth.

HECTOR
Fie, savage, fie!

TROILUS Hector, then 'tis wars.

HECTOR
Troilus, I would not have you fight today.

TROILUS Who should withhold me?
Not fate, obedience, nor the hand of Mars,
Beck'ning with fiery truncheon my retire;
Not Priamus and Hecuba on knees,
Their eyes o'er-gallèd with recourse of tears;
Nor you, my brother, with your true sword drawn
Opposed to hinder me, should stop my way,
⟨But by my ruin.⟩

66. **loose thy stay:** i.e., let go your support

72. **enrapt:** i.e., carried away in prophetic inspiration

76. **do stand engaged to:** i.e., have promised

77, 80. **faith:** pledge, promise

81. **dutiful:** i.e., filled with the regard due (to you as my father)

82. **respect:** deferential esteem (shown toward, e.g., a parent); **leave:** permission

83. **voice:** support, approval

88. **Upon . . . me:** i.e., in accordance with your proper wifely **love**

89. **This . . . girl:** i.e., Cassandra

90. **bodements:** omens

The Greeks attack Troy.
From [John Lydgate,]
The hystorye sege and dystruccyon of Troye [1513].

Enter Priam and Cassandra.

CASSANDRA, ⌜*indicating Hector*⌝
Lay hold upon him, Priam; hold him fast.
He is thy crutch. Now if thou loose thy stay,
Thou on him leaning, and all Troy on thee,
Fall all together.

PRIAM Come, Hector, come. Go back.
Thy wife hath dreamt, thy mother hath had visions,
Cassandra doth foresee, and I myself
Am like a prophet suddenly enrapt
To tell thee that this day is ominous.
Therefore, come back.

HECTOR Aeneas is afield,
And I do stand engaged to many Greeks,
Even in the faith of valor, to appear
This morning to them.

PRIAM Ay, but thou shalt not go.

HECTOR I must not break my faith.
You know me dutiful; therefore, dear sir,
Let me not shame respect, but give me leave
To take that course by your consent and voice
Which you do here forbid me, royal Priam.

CASSANDRA.
O Priam, yield not to him!

ANDROMACHE Do not, dear father.

HECTOR
Andromache, I am offended with you.
Upon the love you bear me, get you in.
Andromache exits.

TROILUS
This foolish, dreaming, superstitious girl
Makes all these bodements.

CASSANDRA O farewell, dear Hector.
Look how thou diest! Look how thy eye turns pale!
Look how thy wounds do bleed at many vents!

96. **distraction:** madness; **amazement:** mental stupefaction

97. **antics:** performers who play grotesque parts (The word **witless** [i.e., lunatic, deranged] refers to the roles the **antics** play.)

100. **soft:** i.e., wait a minute; **take my leave:** i.e., bid farewell, say good-bye

101. **deceive:** betray

102. **amazed:** stunned; **liege:** i.e., liege lord, the superior to whom one owes obedience; **exclaim:** outcry

112. **whoreson phthisic:** vile cough

116. **rheum in:** flow or discharge from

116–17. **ache . . . bones:** associated with syphilis (See note to 2.3.19–20.)

118. **on 't:** i.e., of it

119. **no matter:** i.e., nothing substantive

120. **Th' effect:** i.e., the reality (as opposed to what she says)

A sweating tub for treating venereal disease. (5.11.58)
From Thomas Randolph, *Cornelianum dolium* . . . (1638).

Hark, how Troy roars, how Hecuba cries out,
How poor Andromache shrills her ⟨dolor⟩ forth!
Behold, ⟨distraction,⟩ frenzy, and amazement,
Like witless antics, one another meet,
And all cry "Hector! Hector's dead! O, Hector!"

TROILUS Away, away!

CASSANDRA
Farewell.—Yet soft! Hector, I take my leave.
Thou dost thyself and all our Troy deceive. ⟨*She exits.*⟩

HECTOR
You are amazed, my liege, at her exclaim.
Go in and cheer the town. We'll forth and fight,
Do deeds worth praise, and tell you them at night.

PRIAM
Farewell. The gods with safety stand about thee!
⌜*Hector and Priam exit at separate doors.*⌝
Alarum.

TROILUS
They are at it, hark! Proud Diomed, believe,
I come to lose my arm or win my sleeve.

Enter Pandarus, ⌜with a paper.⌝

PANDARUS Do you hear, my lord? Do you hear?
TROILUS What now?
PANDARUS Here's a letter come from yond poor girl.
TROILUS Let me read. ⌜*He reads.*⌝
PANDARUS A whoreson phthisic, a whoreson rascally phthisic so troubles me, and the foolish fortune of this girl, and what one thing, what another, that I shall leave you one o' ⌜these⌝ days. And I have a rheum in mine eyes too, and such an ache in my bones that, unless a man were cursed, I cannot tell what to think on 't.—What says she there?

TROILUS
Words, words, mere words, no matter from the heart.
Th' effect doth operate another way.

121. **Go, wind, to wind:** i.e., **go** words into the **wind** (Proverbial: "Words are but **wind.**") **turn and change:** Both words have several meanings that may be pertinent. See longer note, page 280.

122. **errors:** perhaps, illusions; or, perhaps, things that mislead or delude (An error is, at root, a devious or winding course or a mistaken belief.)

123. **edifies:** i.e., establishes, strengthens (and, ironically, improves in a moral sense)

5.4 A railing Thersites watches Troilus and Diomedes go off fighting and, surprised by Hector, escapes death only through the Trojan's contemptuous mercy.

---

0 SD. **Excursions:** skirmishes

1. **clapper-clawing:** thrashing, drubbing

3. **that same:** a phrase that connotes contempt (as also at lines 5 and 11); **doting:** foolishly in love

5. **fain:** happily

7. **whoremasterly:** lecherous

8. **luxurious:** lecherous

8–9. **of . . . errand:** i.e., on an empty or pointless **errand** (with obvious wordplay on **sleeveless**)

9. **policy:** cunning

11. **dog-fox:** i.e., male **fox** (known for its cunning)

12. **blackberry:** a wild fruit so plentiful at the time as to be of little value

13. **set me up:** i.e., **set up; in policy:** i.e., in a trick or stratagem

(continued)

Go, wind, to wind! There turn and change together.
⌜*He tears up the paper and throws the pieces in the air.*⌝
My love with words and errors still she feeds,
But edifies another with her deeds.
They exit.

⌜Scene 4⌝

⟨*Alarum.*⟩ *Excursions. Enter Thersites.*

THERSITES Now they are clapper-clawing one another. I'll go look on. That dissembling abominable varlet, Diomed, has got that same scurvy doting foolish ⟨young⟩ knave's sleeve of Troy there in his helm. I would fain see them meet, that that same young Trojan ass that loves the whore there might send that Greekish whoremasterly villain with the sleeve back to the dissembling luxurious drab, of a sleeveless errand. O' th' t'other side, the policy of those crafty swearing rascals—that stale old mouse-eaten dry cheese, Nestor, and that same dog-fox, Ulysses—is ⌜proved not⌝ worth a blackberry. They set me up, in policy, that mongrel cur, Ajax, against that dog of as bad a kind, Achilles. And now is the cur Ajax prouder than the cur Achilles, and will not arm today, whereupon the Grecians ⌜begin⌝ to proclaim barbarism, and policy grows into an ill opinion.

⟨*Enter Diomedes, and Troilus* ⌜*pursuing him.*⌝⟩

Soft! Here comes sleeve and t' other.
⌜*Thersites moves aside.*⌝

TROILUS, ⌜*to Diomedes*⌝
Fly not, for shouldst thou take the river Styx
I would swim after.

DIOMEDES Thou dost miscall retire.

15. **prouder:** more arrogant, more contemptuous

16–17. **Grecians . . . barbarism:** i.e., Greeks announce (the superiority of) uncivilized ignorance

17–18. **policy . . . opinion:** i.e., political cunning achieves a bad reputation **grows:** becomes fixed

20. **Fly not:** i.e., do **not** run away; **take:** i.e., escape into; **the river Styx:** See notes to 3.2.8–9.

22. **miscall:** misname; **retire:** withdrawal

23. **fly:** flee; **advantageous care:** i.e., regard or concern for (my own) advantage

24. **multitude:** great numbers (against me)

25. **Have at thee:** i.e., I am ready to fight

26. **Hold:** i.e., defend your possession of

28–29. **Art . . . honor:** See longer note, page 280. **blood:** i.e., noble birth

33. **God-a-mercy:** i.e., thank you

34. **a plague:** i.e., a calamity, divine punishment

37. **lechery eats itself:** i.e., lust is no sooner "enjoyed . . . but despisèd straight" (Sonnet 129)

5.5 Diomedes sends the horse he has won from Troilus to Cressida. Agamemnon and Nestor recount the slaughter of Greeks by the Trojans, but Ulysses announces that Achilles and Ajax are arming to join the fight.

---

5. **proof:** i.e., proved or tested power

I do not fly, but advantageous care
Withdrew me from the odds of multitude.
Have at thee! ⌜*They fight.*⌝

THERSITES Hold thy whore, Grecian! Now for thy whore, Trojan! Now the sleeve, now the sleeve!

⌜*Diomedes and Troilus exit fighting.*⌝

Enter Hector.

HECTOR
What art ⟨thou,⟩ Greek? Art thou for Hector's match?
Art thou of blood and honor?

THERSITES No, no, I am a rascal, a scurvy railing knave, a very filthy rogue.

HECTOR I do believe thee. Live. ⌜*He exits.*⌝

THERSITES God-a-mercy, that thou wilt believe me! But a plague break thy neck for frighting me! What's become of the wenching rogues? I think they have swallowed one another. I would laugh at that miracle—yet, in a sort, lechery eats itself. I'll seek them.

He exits.

⌜Scene 5⌝

Enter Diomedes and ⌜*Servingman.*⌝

DIOMEDES
Go, go, my servant, take thou Troilus' horse;
Present the fair steed to my Lady Cressid.
Fellow, commend my service to her beauty.
Tell her I have chastised the amorous Trojan
And am her knight by proof.

MAN I go, my lord. ⌜*He exits.*⌝

Enter Agamemnon.

7. **Renew:** i.e., **renew** the fight; **Polydamas:** a bastard son of Priam (The remaining names in lines 8–14 [except for **Margareton,** a Trojan] are from the Greek army. Only **Patroclus,** line 14, appears as a character in the play.)

9. **Hath Doreus:** i.e., has taken **Doreus**

10. **colossus-wise:** i.e., like the **Colossus** of Rhodes, a huge statue of Helios at the harbor entrance to Rhodes (See picture, page 252.) **beam:** i.e., sword (literally, a large piece of timber, here serving as the shaft of the colossus's sword)

11. **pashèd corses:** i.e., battered corpses

15. **Sore:** seriously; **Sagittary:** the name of the centaur (half-horse, half-human) who fought on the Trojan side against the Greeks (See picture, page 258.)

16. **Appals our numbers:** i.e., terrifies or dismays our company

17. **To reinforcement:** i.e., to reinforce our troops

19. **for shame:** i.e., from a sense of **shame**

21. **Galathe:** pronounced as three syllables

23. **fly:** flee; **scalèd schools:** i.e., **schools** of fish

24. **belching:** spouting

25. **strawy:** i.e., strawlike; or, worthless as straw; **ripe . . . edge:** i.e., ready to be reaped with his scythe-like sword

28. **appetite:** desire, inclination

30. **proof:** i.e., evidence (of what he has done)

34. **Myrmidons:** See note to 1.3.386.

AGAMEMNON

Renew, renew! The fierce Polydamas
Hath beat down Menon; bastard Margareton
Hath Doreus prisoner,
And stands colossus-wise, waving his beam
Upon the pashèd corses of the kings
Epistrophus and Cedius. Polyxenes is slain,
Amphimachus and Thoas deadly hurt,
Patroclus ta'en or slain, and Palamedes
Sore hurt and bruised. The dreadful Sagittary
Appals our numbers. Haste we, Diomed,
To reinforcement, or we perish all.

Enter Nestor, ⌜with Soldiers bearing the body of Patroclus.⌝

NESTOR

Go, bear Patroclus' body to Achilles,
And bid the snail-paced Ajax arm for shame.
⌜Soldiers exit with Patroclus's body.⌝
There is a thousand Hectors in the field.
Now here he fights on Galathe his horse,
And ⌜here⌝ lacks work; anon he's there afoot
And there they fly or die, like ⟨scalèd⟩ schools
Before the belching whale; then is he yonder,
And there the strawy Greeks, ripe for his edge,
Fall down before him like a mower's swath.
Here, there, and everywhere he leaves and takes,
Dexterity so obeying appetite
That what he will he does, and does so much
That proof is called impossibility.

Enter Ulysses.

ULYSSES

O, courage, courage, princes! Great Achilles
Is arming, weeping, cursing, vowing vengeance.
Patroclus' wounds have roused his drowsy blood,
Together with his mangled Myrmidons,

37. **Crying on:** exclaiming against

40. **execution:** wordplay on (1) performance; (2) damage or slaughter

41. **Engaging and redeeming of himself:** possible wordplay on (1) attacking and rescuing **himself;** (2) offering his life as a guarantee and saving **himself**

42. **careless:** i.e., effortless; reckless; **forceless:** i.e., unstrained or easy (literally, without exertion or intensity)

43. **As . . . luck:** i.e., **as if** Fortune; **in . . . cunning:** i.e., **in** the **very** face **of** (his enemies') craftiness

47. **we draw together:** i.e., **we** (the Greeks) pull **together** (perhaps a response to Achilles' entry [line 47])

49. **boy-queller:** i.e., **boy** killer (killer of Patroclus)

5.6 Troilus fights both Diomedes and Ajax. Hector bests Achilles but allows him to live, and pursues another Greek in order to take his splendid armor.

---

4. **correct:** punish; tame

That noseless, handless, hacked and chipped, come to him,
Crying on Hector. Ajax hath lost a friend
And foams at mouth, and he is armed and at it,
Roaring for Troilus, who hath done today
Mad and fantastic execution,
Engaging and redeeming of himself
With such a careless force and forceless care
As if that ⟨luck,⟩ in very spite of cunning,
Bade him win all.

Enter Ajax.

⟨AJAX⟩ Troilus, thou coward Troilus! *He exits.*
DIOMEDES Ay, there, there! *He exits.*
NESTOR So, so, we draw together.

Enter Achilles.

ACHILLES Where is this Hector?—
Come, come, thou boy-queller, show thy face!
Know what it is to meet Achilles angry.
Hector! Where's Hector? I will none but Hector.
He exits, ⌜with the others.⌝

⌜Scene 6⌝

Enter Ajax.

⟨AJAX⟩
Troilus, thou coward Troilus, show thy head!

Enter Diomedes.

⟨DIOMEDES⟩ Troilus, I say! Where's Troilus?
AJAX What wouldst thou?
DIOMEDES I would correct him.
AJAX
Were I the General, thou shouldst have my office
Ere that correction.—Troilus, I say! What, Troilus!

7. **false:** deceitful, faithless

10. **Stand:** a command to halt

11. **prize:** reward, trophy; **look upon:** i.e., be a mere spectator

12. **cogging:** cunning, cheating; **Have at you:** See note to line 5.4.25.

17. **out of use:** i.e., **out of** practice

The Colossus of Rhodes. (5.5.10)
From Henry Peacham, *Minerua Britanna* . . . (1612).

Enter Troilus.

TROILUS
O traitor Diomed! Turn thy false face, thou traitor,
And pay ⌜the⌝ life thou owest me for my horse!

DIOMEDES Ha! Art thou there?

AJAX
I'll fight with him alone. Stand, Diomed.

DIOMEDES
He is my prize. I will not look upon.

TROILUS
Come, both you cogging Greeks. Have at you both!

⟨*Enter Hector.*⟩

⟨*Troilus exits,* ⌜*fighting Diomedes and Ajax.*⌝⟩

HECTOR
Yea, Troilus? O, well fought, my youngest brother!

Enter Achilles.

⟨ACHILLES⟩
Now do I see thee. Ha! Have at thee, Hector!
⌜*They fight.*⌝

HECTOR Pause if thou wilt.

ACHILLES
I do disdain thy courtesy, proud Trojan.
Be happy that my arms are out of use.
My rest and negligence befriends thee now,
But thou anon shalt hear of me again;
Till when, go seek thy fortune. *He exits.*

HECTOR Fare thee well.
I would have been much more a fresher man
Had I expected thee.

Enter Troilus.

How now, my brother?

27. **carry:** i.e., capture

28. **bring him off:** i.e., rescue him

29. **reck:** care

30. **goodly mark:** i.e., splendid (or, convenient) target or quarry

32–33. **frush . . . of it:** i.e., crush it and knock out its **rivets** (if I have to) in order to own it

34. **abide:** stop

35. **fly on:** i.e., run away

5.7 Achilles, now accompanied by Myrmidons, searches for Hector.

---

2. **Mark:** listen to; **Attend:** follow; **wheel:** i.e., search (literally, walk in an arc)

4. **bloody:** bloodthirsty

5. **Empale him:** enclose or surround him (with wordplay on "make him pale")

6. **fellest:** cruelest, deadliest; **execute your arms:** use your weapons

7. **eye:** observe

A scimitar. (5.1.2)
From Louis de Gaya, *A treatise of the arms ....* (1678).

TROILUS

Ajax hath ta'en Aeneas. Shall it be?
No, by the flame of yonder glorious heaven,
He shall not carry him. I'll be ta'en too
Or bring him off. Fate, hear me what I say!
I reck not though I end my life today.

He exits.

Enter one in ⌜Greek⌝ armor.

HECTOR

Stand, stand, thou Greek! Thou art a goodly mark.
No? Wilt thou not? I like thy armor well.
I'll frush it and unlock the rivets all,
But I'll be master of it. ⌜*The Greek exits.*⌝
Wilt thou not, beast, abide?
Why then, fly on. I'll hunt thee for thy hide.

He exits.

⌜Scene 7⌝

Enter Achilles, with Myrmidons.

⟨ACHILLES⟩

Come here about me, you my Myrmidons.
Mark what I say. Attend me where I wheel.
Strike not a stroke, but keep yourselves in breath,
And, when I have the bloody Hector found,
Empale him with your weapons round about.
In fellest manner execute your arms.
Follow me, sirs, and my proceedings eye.
It is decreed Hector the great must die.

⌜*They*⌝ *exit.*

5.8 Thersites comments on the combat between Menelaus and Paris. Then, surprised by Priam's bastard son, Thersites escapes by refusing to fight.

1–4. **The cuckold . . . horns, ho:** In this metaphoric bullbaiting, the **cuckold** Menelaus, the **bull,** is baited by the **dog** Paris. **Loo:** a cry encouraging the bulldogs **Spartan:** Menelaus is king of Sparta. **Ware:** i.e., beware of (the cuckold's) **horns** (See longer note to 1.1.115, page 269, and note to 5.1.54–55.)

5. **slave:** a term of contempt

10–11. **One . . . another:** proverbial

11. **wherefore:** why

14. **tempts judgment:** i.e., invites punishment as a token of divine displeasure

5.9 Hector, having killed the Greek in the splendid armor, unarms himself and is surprised by Achilles, who orders his Myrmidons to slaughter the Trojan.

---

1. **putrefied . . . without:** See Matthew 23.27: "ye are like unto whited [i.e., whitewashed] tombs, which appear beautiful outward [i.e., **fair without**], but are within full of dead men's bones, and all filthiness." **core:** possible wordplay on "corse, corpse"

2. **goodly:** splendid

⌜Scene 8⌝

Enter Thersites; ⌜then⌝ Menelaus ⌜fighting⌝ Paris.

THERSITES The cuckold and the cuckold-maker are at it. Now, bull! Now, dog! Loo, Paris, loo! Now, my ⌜double-horned⌝ Spartan! Loo, Paris, loo! The bull has the game. Ware horns, ho!

Paris and Menelaus exit, ⌜fighting.⌝

Enter Bastard.

BASTARD Turn, slave, and fight.

THERSITES What art thou?

BASTARD A bastard son of Priam's.

THERSITES I am a bastard too. I love bastards. I am bastard begot, bastard instructed, bastard in mind, bastard in valor, in everything illegitimate. One bear will not bite another, and wherefore should one bastard? Take heed: the quarrel's most ominous to us. If the son of a whore fight for a whore, he tempts judgment. Farewell, bastard. ⌜*He exits.*⌝

BASTARD The devil take thee, coward!

He exits.

⌜Scene 9⌝

Enter Hector, ⌜with the body of the Greek in armor.⌝

HECTOR

Most putrefied core, so fair without,
Thy goodly armor thus hath cost thy life.
Now is my day's work done. I'll take my breath.
Rest, sword; thou hast thy fill of blood and death.

⌜*He begins to disarm.*⌝

Enter Achilles and ⟨his⟩ Myrmidons.

6. **his:** its (the sun's)

7. **vail:** setting, going down

12. **sinews:** muscles, strength

13. **amain:** with all your strength

15. **retire:** (signal to) withdraw

16. **sound the like:** i.e., send the same signal

18. **And . . . separates:** i.e., **and,** like a referee or umpire, **night** (line 17) **separates the armies**

19. **frankly:** unrestrainedly

20. **dainty bait:** choice snack

5.10 The rest of the Greek forces hear the shouts of the Myrmidons announcing Hector's death.

"The dreadful Sagittary." (5.5.15)
From [Dirck Pietersz Pers,]
Bellerophon, of Lust tot wysheyt . . . [n.d.].

ACHILLES
Look, Hector, how the sun begins to set,
How ugly night comes breathing at his heels.
Even with the vail and dark'ning of the sun
To close the day up, Hector's life is done.

HECTOR
I am unarmed. Forgo this vantage, Greek.

ACHILLES
Strike, fellows, strike! This is the man I seek.
⌜*The Myrmidons kill Hector.*⌝
So, Ilium, fall thou next! Come, Troy, sink down!
Here lies thy heart, thy sinews, and thy bone.
On, Myrmidons, and cry you all amain
"Achilles hath the mighty Hector slain."
Retreat ⌜*sounded from both armies.*⌝
Hark! A retire upon our Grecian part.

⌜A MYRMIDON⌝
The ⟨Trojan trumpets⟩ sound the like, my lord.

ACHILLES
The dragon wing of night o'erspreads the earth
And, stickler-like, the armies separates.
My half-supped sword, that frankly would have fed,
Pleased with this dainty bait, thus goes to bed.
⌜*He sheathes his sword.*⌝
Come, tie his body to my horse's tail;
Along the field I will the Trojan trail.
They exit ⌜*with the bodies.*⌝

⌜Scene 10⌝

⟨*Sound retreat.*⟩ *Enter Agamemnon, Ajax, Menelaus, Nestor, Diomedes, and the rest, marching* ⌜*to the beat of drums.*⌝ ⟨*Shout* ⌜*within.*⌝⟩

AGAMEMNON Hark, hark, what ⟨shout⟩ is this?
NESTOR Peace, drums! ⌜*The drums cease.*⌝

4. **bruit:** news, rumor

7. **patiently:** calmly, quietly

8. **pray:** ask, invite; **us, our:** i.e., me, my (the royal plural)

9. **his death:** i.e., Hector's **death**

10. **sharp:** fierce

5.11 Troilus announces Hector's death to the Trojans. Marching back to Troy, Troilus meets Pandarus and reviles him.

---

2. **starve . . . night:** i.e., we will endure the cold of **the night;** or, perhaps, we will cause **the night** to wither

6. **In beastly sort:** i.e., in a brutal manner

7. **effect:** fulfill

9. **brief plagues:** i.e., afflictions, punishments, or blows which end quickly; **be mercy:** i.e., show your **mercy**

10. **linger . . . on:** i.e., do **not** protract (or, perhaps, delay, put off) **our** certain ruin

11. **discomfort:** discourage, dishearten; **host:** army, company

SOLDIERS, *within*
Achilles! Achilles! Hector's slain! Achilles!

DIOMEDES
The bruit is Hector's slain, and by Achilles.

AJAX
If it be so, yet bragless let it be.
Great Hector was as good a man as he.

AGAMEMNON
March patiently along. Let one be sent
To pray Achilles see us at our tent.
If in his death the gods have us befriended,
Great Troy is ours, and our sharp wars are ended.

They exit, ⌜*marching.*⌝

⌜Scene 11⌝

Enter Aeneas, Paris, Antenor, Deiphobus, ⌜*and Trojan soldiers.*⌝

AENEAS
Stand, ho! Yet are we masters of the field.
Never go home; here starve we out the night.

Enter Troilus.

TROILUS
Hector is slain.

ALL Hector! The gods forbid!

TROILUS
He's dead, and at the murderer's horse's tail,
In beastly sort, dragged through the shameful field.
Frown on, you heavens; effect your rage with speed.
Sit, gods, upon your thrones, and ⌜smite⌝ at Troy!
I say at once: let your brief plagues be mercy,
And linger not our sure destructions on!

AENEAS
My lord, you do discomfort all the host.

14. **imminence:** impending evil or peril

15. **Address:** (1) arrange, order; (2) apparel, clothe; (3) apply, direct; **dangers:** mischiefs, harms, perils

17. **aye:** forever

20. **wells and Niobes:** i.e., springs or streams of water (Niobe, in Greek mythology, was so grief-stricken at the loss of her children that she could not cease weeping and was turned into a stone from which water continually flows.)

26. **Titan:** a poetic name for the sun

27–28. **great-sized coward:** i.e., massive or brawny Achilles

30. **still:** always, continually

31. **moldeth goblins:** i.e., creates demons; **swift:** i.e., as quickly; **frenzy's:** i.e., delirium's, insanity's

32. **Strike a free march:** i.e., sound the drum for **a march** that will take us quickly

33. **hide:** shield or protect

35. **broker:** go-between, pimp; **lackey:** hanger-on, camp follower; **Ignomy:** i.e., ignominy, disgrace

38. **agent:** one who acts for another, emissary

40. **ill:** badly

41. **endeavor:** effort, exertion; **performance:** achievement, accomplishment

42. **verse:** poem; **instance:** illustrative example

TROILUS

You understand me not that tell me so.
I do not speak of flight, of fear, of death,
But dare all imminence that gods and men
Address their dangers in. Hector is gone.
Who shall tell Priam so, or Hecuba?
Let him that will a screech-owl aye be called
Go into Troy and say their Hector's dead.
There is a word will Priam turn to stone,
Make wells and Niobes of the maids and wives,
Cold statues of the youth and, in a word,
Scare Troy out of itself. ⟨But march away.
Hector is dead.⟩ There is no more to say.
Stay yet. You ⟨vile⟩ abominable tents,
Thus proudly pitched upon our Phrygian plains,
Let Titan rise as early as he dare,
I'll through and through you! And, thou great-sized
  coward,
No space of earth shall sunder our two hates.
I'll haunt thee like a wicked conscience still,
That moldeth goblins swift as frenzy's thoughts.
Strike a free march to Troy! With comfort go.
Hope of revenge shall hide our inward woe.

Enter Pandarus.

PANDARUS But hear you, hear you!

TROILUS

Hence, broker, lackey! ⟨Ignomy and⟩ shame
Pursue thy life, and live aye with thy name!

All but Pandarus exit.

PANDARUS A goodly medicine for my aching bones! O world, world, ⟨world⟩! Thus is the poor agent despised. O traitors and bawds, how earnestly are you set a-work, and how ill requited! Why should our endeavor be so loved and the performance so loathed? What verse for it? What instance for it?

44. **humble-bee:** i.e., bumblebee

46. **being . . . tail:** i.e., **once** its **sting** (line 45) or **armèd tail** has been lost

48. **traders in the flesh:** i.e., fleshmongers, panders (This and the following lines are addressed to the audience, as if they—or some of them—are pimps and bawds.)

48–49. **painted cloths:** wall hangings painted with pictures and brief moral sentences

50. **of panders' hall:** i.e., who are members of the guild of panders

51. **half out:** i.e., almost blind (with venereal disease)

53. **Though:** even if; **aching bones:** See note to 5.3.116–17.

54. **hold-door trade:** i.e., the **trade** of pimps and bawds (In *Pericles,* a pimp at a brothel is addressed as "damnèd doorkeeper" [4.6.125]. See also *Othello* 4.2.105–10.)

57. **gallèd goose of Winchester:** slang for (1) prostitute; (2) a pustule of syphilitic infection (See Jonathan Gil Harris, "Shakespeare's Hair: Staging the Object of Material Culture," *Shakespeare Quarterly* 52 [2001]: 488, n. 21.)

58. **sweat:** i.e., spend time in a sweating tub (the Elizabethan treatment for syphilis) See picture, page 242. **eases:** means of relieving my symptoms

Let me see:
  Full merrily the humble-bee doth sing,
  Till he hath lost his honey and his sting;
  And being once subdued in armèd tail,
  Sweet honey and sweet notes together fail.
Good traders in the flesh, set this in your painted cloths:
As many as be here of panders' hall,
Your eyes, half out, weep out at Pandar's fall;
Or if you cannot weep, yet give some groans,
Though not for me, yet for ⟨your⟩ aching bones.
Brethren and sisters of the hold-door trade,
Some two months hence my will shall here be made.
It should be now, but that my fear is this:
Some gallèd goose of Winchester would hiss.
Till then I'll sweat and seek about for eases,
And at that time bequeath you my diseases.

⌜*He exits.*⌝

Longer Notes

Pr. 15–19. **Priam's . . . Troy: Dardan, Timbria, Helias, Chetas, Troien,** and **Antenorides** are the names of the city's gates. **Staples** are U-shaped metal bars driven into posts to hold hooks or **bolts** that secure doors or gates. **Corresponsive** means "corresponding, answering," and **fulfilling** means "complementary" (with possible wordplay on the sense that the **bolts** fill the space within the **staples**). **Spar up** means "enclose (and thus protect)."

Pr. 23–24. **A prologue . . . voice:** The relevant lines of the Prologue of Jonson's *Poetaster* read as follows:

If any muse why I salute the Stage,
An armed Prologue; know, 'tis a dangerous Age:
Wherein, who writes, had need present his Scenes
Forty-fold proof against the conjuring means
Of base Detractors, and illiterate Apes,
That fill up Rooms in fair and formal shapes.
'Gainst these, have we put on this forc't defence:
Whereof the Allegory and hid sense
Is, that a well erected Confidence
Can fright their Pride, and laugh their Folly hence.
(*Poetaster,* Prologue, 5–14)

Pr. 28. **Beginning in the middle:** Epic poems conventionally begin in the middle of the story they narrate. Shakespeare's *Troilus and Cressida* here points out its use of this epic convention. It also points to the poem that provides much of its subject matter and its general structure, Homer's great epic the *Iliad.* This poem is the first to tell the story of the Trojan War, and Shakespeare's play (beyond the Troilus and Cressida plot) follows the *Iliad* in its structure, focusing on the stand-off between Achilles and Agamemnon and on that quarrel's ramifications. Like the *Iliad,* the play begins with Achilles' anger, many years after the beginning of the war, and ends with the death and degradation of Hector.

1.1.59. **spirit of sense:** Troilus here is reaching for an image of something even softer than "cygnet's down" with which to compare the touch of Cressida's hand. He chooses "**spirit of sense,**" an unusual phrase that brings together the "sensible soul" (i.e., the soul housed in the brain and responsible for all human and animal senses, inward and outward) and the **spirit** that carries out the work of the soul. In the humoral psychology of Shakespeare's time, spirit is "a most subtle vapour, which is expressed from the blood, and [is] the instrument of the soul, to perform all his [its] actions." The spirits that serve the sensible soul in the brain are especially rarefied, in that the spirits brought into the ventricles of the brain by the arteries "are there refined to a more heavenly nature, to perform the actions of the soul" (Robert Burton, *The Anatomy of Melancholy* [1621], pt. 1, sec. 1, mem. 2, subs. 6, 4). It seems likely that the **sense** to which Troilus most immediately points is that of touch (a sense that is "exquisite in men" [Burton, subs. 6]), since the context is that of Cressida's "hand," its "soft seizure," and the "hard . . . palm of plowman."

1.1.78. **o' Friday, on Sunday:** The distinction made in this line is anachronistic, since it is based in Christian doctrine and practice. Such anachronisms are found often in this play, which is set in ancient, pre-Christian times.

1.1.100. **Apollo . . . love:** It can be argued, as some editors have done, that Troilus is here equating his situation with Apollo's. He sees Cressida as "stubborn-chaste against all suit," as was Daphne, and his description (lines 102–6) of his pursuit of Cressida (as a merchant in a risky ship crossing the wild seas to obtain a pearl) presents an attempt as apparently hopeless as Apollo's pursuit of Daphne.

1.1.114. **to scorn:** Editors argue that the phrase "a scar to scorn" is ambiguous, and that it might just as well mean "a scar given in retaliation for Paris's scorn" of Menelaus. This reading, though, puts considerable pressure on the preposition *to.*

1.1.115. **gored . . . horn:** The association of the cuckold (a man whose wife is unfaithful to him) with horns growing from the man's forehead goes back to ancient times and may originate with the early and prevalent practice of "grafting the spurs of a castrated cock on the root of the excised comb, where they grew and became horns, sometimes of several inches long" (*OED, horn* 7a).

1.2.26. **humors:** According to the Greek medical writer Galen, the relative proportions of the four **humors** within a person determined his or her appearance and disposition. The word *humor* could refer to the bodily fluids themselves (blood, phlegm, yellow bile, and black bile) or to the dispositions, character traits, or moods thought to be caused by these fluids. In a weakened sense, the word could simply refer to whims or moods in general. In 1.2.26, since the **humors** are said to be "**crowded**" into the man being described, it seems likely that the reference is to the fluids themselves rather than to less tangible moods or character traits—though these too are inevitably alluded to.

1.2.77. **Condition:** Some editors have suggested that in this line, Pandarus means "even if I had been forced to go barefoot to India to prove that Troilus is not himself"; other editors read the line as Pandarus's lamentation that Troilus will recover his true self no more quickly than Pandarus would walk barefoot to India, or, conversely, his pledge that he would walk barefoot to India if it would help to restore Troilus to himself. These readings seem equally plausible (or implausible).

1.3.22. **fineness of which metal:** Testing of a man's strength and character (i.e., the man's "mettle") through prolonged suffering, as if it were **metal** being refined and purged, is found in such biblical passages as Job 23.10 ("when he hath tried me, I shall come forth as gold") and Zechariah 13.8–9 ("And it shall come to pass . . . saith the Lord, [that] I will bring the third part [of mankind] through the fire, and will refine them as silver is refined, and will try them as gold is tried, . . . and . . . I will say, 'It is my people' ").

1.3.42. **Perseus' horse:** Pegasus is the mythological winged horse that sprang from the neck of Medusa when Perseus cut off her head. Pegasus was later captured by Bellerophon and should more appropriately be called "Bellerophon's horse." Perseus himself used winged shoes to speed through the air.

1.3.76. **we are confident:** It is likely that Agamemnon is using the royal plural (i.e., the royal **we**) here and in line 78, and elsewhere in the play. He does not use this form consistently—i.e., he often uses "I" in referring to himself, and he often uses **we** as a simple plural pronoun. But, in 2.3, several of his speeches are more intelligible if we assume that his **we** is to be understood as meaning "I, speaking as king." The present speech (1.3.74–78) seems also to be spoken in a royal vein. And his exchange with Aeneas at 1.3.219–21 ("AGAMEMNON What would you 'fore *our* tent? AENEAS Is this great Agamemnon's tent, I pray you? AGAMEMNON Even this.") almost demands that we read "our" as the royal plural. Agamemnon was indeed a king (as were other of the Greek commanders), and he is clearly the commander in chief of the Greek forces. Shakespeare may give him on occasion the speech of a royal in order to make clear his status among the other Greek kings.

1.3.77. **mastic:** It is unclear what this means as an adjective; used as a noun, it is the name of a resinous gum that drops from trees. Possibly relevant are (1) the suffix *-mastix* (scourge), (2) the verb *masticate* (chew), and (3) a misanthropic character from Sir Philip Sidney's *Arcadia* (1590) named *Mastix.*

1.3.87. **Degree:** Ulysses' famous speech on hierarchy and on the chaos that follows its breakdown echoes any number of earlier philosophers, as well as such poets as Homer and Ovid. Two familiar homilies (i.e., sermons) of the Church of England, "On Obedience" and "Homily against disobedience and willful rebellion," also seem present in Ulysses' speech. These homilies were published, along with several others, under the authority of Queen Elizabeth, with instructions that they be read aloud in every parish church. Shakespeare's audience would therefore have been well acquainted with the ideas put forth so eloquently by Ulysses in one of Shakespeare's best-known passages.

1.3.89. **this center:** In the earth-centered Ptolemaic universe, the sphere of the fixed stars (i.e., the heaven or heavens) and the spheres of the seven planets (the moon, Mercury, Venus, the sun, Mars, Jupiter, and Saturn) circle around the earth. Lines 98–105 describe the supposed effect on the earth when the planets do not follow their proper course. The beliefs detailed in these lines assume that the planets, singly and in conjunction, have a powerful influence on events and on human beings.

2.1.14. **unsalted:** Since leaven is never salted, many editors substitute "vinewed'st" [i.e., moldiest] for **unsalted,** arguing that the Folio's "whinid'st" is a spelling of "vinewed'st."

2.2.65. **I . . . wife:** If Troilus is alluding, in the argument that follows, to Paris's **election** of Helen as the **wife** whom he must defend, the argument is undercut by the fact that Helen is actually the **wife** of Menelaus.

2.2.67–69. **My will . . . judgment:** Troilus here describes human faculties as distorted by humanity's fallen state, in which none of the faculties are operating as they were designed to do. In the psychology of Shakespeare's day (known as "faculty psychology"), as well as in the theology of late-sixteenth-century England, **will** and understanding (or reason), the two faculties of the rational soul, are "the two principal fountains of human action" (Hooker, *Laws of Ecclesiastical Polity* 1.7.2). Understanding finds that which is good, and **will** chooses that good (or would do so had not man fallen as a consequence of original sin). **Will** is supposed to govern man's appetites. According to Hooker, "of one thing we must have special care, as being a matter of no small moment, and that is, how the **will** . . . differeth greatly from that inferior natural desire we call appetite. . . . [A]ppetite is the will's solicitor, and the will is the appetite's controller" (1.7.3). Or, as Iago puts it: "Our bodies are our gardens, to the which our **wills** are gardeners. So that if we will plant nettles or sow lettuce, . . . the power and corrigible authority of this lies in our **wills**" (*Othello* 1.3.362–68).

Because, in Judeo-Christian thought, **will** (along with reason) was corrupted at the Fall, the **will**, "prone to evil, . . . [is] egged on by our natural concupiscence," and "lust . . . we cannot resist" (Burton, *Anatomy of Melancholy* 1.1.2.11). "The seat of our affections captivates and enforces our **will.** . . . Lust counsels one thing, reason another," and the "depraved **will**" often yields to passion (1.1.2.11). Again to quote Iago, the "lust of the blood" is often granted the "permission of the **will**" (1.3.377–78).

Troilus, in describing the hypothetical choosing of a wife (and by implication describing the way in which Paris chose Helen), presents the **will** as subject to, rather than controller of, the appetites. The **eyes and ears,** in his description, inflame the **will** and then act as pilots of ships going between **will** and **judgment.** Troilus thus eliminates reason and allows the "lust of the blood" to gain the "permission of the **will,**" which in turn leads **judgment** to select a particular **wife.** Troilus's flawed characterization of the workings of **will**, reason, and appetite invalidates the argument that he then builds on the basis of this characterization. (While it is true that **will** can also mean "desire," Troilus's linking of **will, election,** and **honor** [line 72] makes it unlikely that his argument could stand on a definition of **will** as desire.)

2.2.88. **Whose . . . ships:** This line seems to echo Christopher Marlowe's *Doctor Faustus,* where Faustus says of Helen of Troy "Was this the face that **launched a thousand ships**?" Lines 87–89 have also been linked to Matthew 13.45–46: "the kingdom of heaven is like to a merchant man that seeketh good pearls, Who having found **a pearl** of great **price,** went and sold all that he had, and bought it."

2.3.137. **humorous predominance:** This phrase, which draws on both humor theory and astrology, may mean the "humor that is predominant" in Achilles, or the "capricious superior influence" that Achilles exerts. In astrology, the word **predominance** refers to the ascendancy or superior influence of a given planet. In humor theory, the word is used to describe the given humor or element (choler, blood, bile, or black bile; earth, air, fire, or water) that has superior influence or preponderance within a body.

2.3.180–84. **Imagined . . . himself:** Achilles' inner turmoil is here described in terms of the faculty psychology of the time. According to Ulysses, imagination so heats Achilles' **blood** that he is caught between **his mental and his active parts** (presumably his reason and understanding, on the one hand, and, on the other, "the moving faculty" of "the sensitive soul," which includes the power of appetite, by which "for the most part" "men are led like beasts by sense, giving reins to their concupiscence and several [various] lusts" [Burton, *Anatomy* 1.1.2.8]). He is thus like a kingdom in turmoil, "batter[ing] **down himself.**"

3.2.74–75. **In . . . monster:** The term **Cupid's pageant** would suggest an allegorical tableau or procession of aspects of romantic love. Kenneth Palmer, editor of the Arden 2 edition of *Troilus and Cressida,* notes that Spenser's *Faerie Queene,* III.xii, includes such a pageant, which contains many monsters. Palmer suggests that an audience probably would not notice Troilus's error in saying that **there is presented**

no monster in Cupid's pageant. It seems more likely to us that both Troilus and the audience would be well aware of the "monsters" associated with love. Spenser's pageant presents a "jolly company / In manner of a maske, enranged orderly," a company that includes Fancy, Desire, Doubt, Danger, Fear, Hope, Dissemblance, Suspect (i.e., suspicion), Grief, Fury, Displeasure, Pleasance (i.e., pleasure), Despite, and Cruelty. These figures are followed by Cupid himself, riding on a ravenous lion, followed in turn by Reproach, Repentance, Shame, Strife, Anger, Care, Unthriftihead (i.e., Unthriftiness), "Lewd Loss of Time," Sorrow, Disloyalty, "Consuming Riotise [i.e., dissolute conduct], and guilty Dread / Of heavenly vengeance, faint Infirmity, / Vile Poverty, and lastly Death with infamy." The audience would also have known that Cressida's fears are prophetic, since the familiar story of her life after Troilus reads very like this list of "monsters."

3.2.82–83. **the will . . . limit:** In these lines and in the following two speeches (lines 84–95), the seemingly apparent topic is the discrepancy between sexual desire (**will**) and sexual performance (**act**). Lines 96–98, though, and the subsequent speeches make it clear that a concurrent and more significant topic is the discrepancy between promises of faithfulness (the **will** to love forever) and the performance (**act**) of that faithfulness over time.

3.2.91–92. **our . . . bare till merit crown it:** For a similar association of earning merit and therefore earning the right to cover one's head in public or in company, see *The Merchant of Venice* 2.9.44–47: "O . . . that clear honor / Were purchased by the **merit** of the wearer! / How many then should cover that stand **bare**?"

3.2.190. **characterless:** If this word means, as editors tend to believe, "unrecorded," it would refer to *character* as "graphic sign or symbol, element of a written language," and would suggest a fallen city or empire whose written or carved records have been obliterated. It is also possible, though, that **characterless** suggests, instead or in addition, a fallen city or empire that no longer retains its character, its "distinctive features or qualities."

3.3.208. **Keeps place with:** For Shakespeare's apparent use of **keeps place** to mean "adhere," see *The Merry Wives of Windsor*: "But they do no more adhere and keep place together than the Hundredth Psalm to the tune of 'Greensleeves' " (2.1.60–63).

4.4.85. **godly jealousy:** The eighteenth-century editor Lewis Theobald noted that this phrase quotes St. Paul's Second Epistle to the Corinthians 11.2, where Paul admits to the Corinthians that he is jealous of them with a **godly jealousy.** He has won them for Christ, but he fears that as Eve was seduced by the serpent, so they may be seduced by other preachers or other gospels.

4.4.156–60. **Let . . . chivalry:** As Kenneth Palmer, editor of the Arden 2 *Troilus and Cressida,* points out, a primary weakness of the lines is the use of the metaphor of a bridegroom's alacrity (presumably in rushing to his bride's bed) to describe the eagerness of Aeneas to support Hector. Shakespeare elsewhere employs this metaphor with great power. In *Measure for Measure,* for example, Claudio says "If I must die, / I will encounter darkness as a bride, / And hug it in mine arms" (3.1.93–95); and in *Antony and Cleopatra,* Antony says of his attempted suicide "I will be / A bridegroom in my death and run into 't / As to a lover's bed" (4.14.119–21). King Lear, too, says "I will die bravely like a smug [i.e., neat, trim] bridegroom" (4.6.218). In comparison with these speeches, Aeneas's "Yea, with a bridegroom's fresh alacrity / Let us address to tend on Hector's heels" seems bathetic and rather silly.

4.5.8. **brazen pipe:** The term **pipe** applies literally not to metal instruments like the trumpet but to wind instruments such as the oboe or flute, which are made of wood, reed, or straw. The trumpet here is **brazen** in that it is made of brass and is shameless or insolent.

4.5.9–10. **thy . . . Aquilon:** Ajax here grotesquely piles metaphor upon metaphor (from bowling, from early medicine, and from mythology) in depicting the puffed-out cheeks of a trumpeter. The **spherèd bias cheek** alludes to the ball in the game of bowls, which is weighted or protuberant on one side to make the ball roll obliquely. (The swelling, as well as the course of the ball, is called the **bias.**) The name **Aquilon** is another name for the mythological Boreas, both god of the north wind and the north wind itself. The word **colic** refers to wind-colic (i.e., wind or gas trapped in the stomach or intestines, causing bloating). In *Henry IV, Part 1,* Shakespeare has Hotspur mock Glendower's claim that "the earth did shake [in fear] when I was born" by diagnosing the earth as sick with wind-colic:

> Diseasèd nature oftentimes breaks forth
> In strange eruptions; oft the teeming earth
> Is with a kind of **colic** pinched and vexed
> By the imprisoning of unruly wind
> Within her womb, which, for enlargement striving,
> Shakes the old beldam earth and topples down
> Steeples and moss-grown towers. At your birth
> Our grandam earth, having this distemp'rature,
> In passion shook.
>
> (3.1.28–36)

4.5.64–66. **There's . . . body:** This description of Cressida as a "daughter of the game" (line 72) echoes familiar passages from the Bible and from the church fathers. See, e.g., Isaiah 3.16: "the daughters of Zion . . . walk with extended necks and wanton eyes, walking and mincing as they go, and making a tinkling with their feet." See also Saint John Chrysostom's *Sermone* (quoted by Burton, *Anatomy of Melancholy* 3.2.2.3): "though they say nothing with their mouths, they speak in their gait, they speak with their eyes, they speak in the carriage of their bodies."

4.5.69. **wide unclasp the tables of their thoughts: Tables** were writing tablets consisting of one or more pieces of coated vellum, folded and stitched and sometimes elegantly bound; the coating on the vellum allowed it to be written on with a stylus and then erased with a moistened cloth or by scraping. In this line, flirting women are imaged as opening the clasps that bind the **tables** in which they write out **their thoughts** and spreading the books open before "every tickling reader." The metaphor of spreading open the mind like a book calls up an inevitable sexual image as well.

4.5.75–76. **What . . . commands:** As was pointed out by the eighteenth-century editor George Steevens, the phrase "**what shall be done to him**" echoes the biblical account of the slaying of Goliath (1 Samuel 17.26), where David uses this formula in asking about the reward he might get if he succeeds: "**What shall be done to** the man that killeth this Philistine . . . ?"

4.5.159. **Not . . . mirable: Neoptolemus** was the name of Achilles' son, whose presence at Troy was prophesied to be essential to the city's defeat. It is possible, therefore, that Hector alludes to this son who will one day prove **mirable** (marvelous). It seems more likely, though, that Shakespeare read **Neoptolemus** as Achilles' family name, and that Hector's allusion is to Achilles, the only Greek thought to be the equal of Hector himself.

4.5.197. **By Mars his gauntlet:** This oath is complexly pertinent as addressed to Menelaus. **Mars,** god of war, committed adultery with Vulcan's wife **Venus,** thus making Vulcan the most infamous of cuckolds. A **gauntlet** was commonly used as a gage to challenge an adversary.

5.1.55–58. **the primitive . . . leg:** Menelaus is here imaged as the very symbol, **statue,** or **memorial of cuckolds,** but a **primitive** (early, ancient) and **oblique** (indirect) one—perhaps because of his ridiculousness, since he hangs **at his brother's leg** like a **shoeing-horn** (i.e., a person used as a tool by another, with wordplay on the **horn** from which the shoehorn is made).

5.2.27. **secretly open:** It is difficult to limit, or to pin down, the possible wordplay here. **Secretly** could mean not only "modestly" but also "covertly," "clandestinely," and "stealthily," and could carry the meanings of "in private," "hidden, concealed, disguised." **Open** could mean "generally available," "generally accessible," "unconfined, unenclosed," "bare, exposed," "spread out," "unobstructed," "evident," "acting without concealment," "frank, candid," and "bounteous, generous." What is clear is that **secretly** and **open** stand in opposition to each other, and to be both would be indeed **a juggling trick.**

5.2.170. **rule in unity:** The philosophical problem of the indivisibility of **unity** dominates this speech by

Troilus. The basic question he poses is how Cressida can be two persons in one. In lines 176–81, he puts the argument in terms of a unity separated by infinite space that is divided and that is at the same time indivisible.

5.2.181. **Ariachne's broken woof:** This phrase alludes to the threads in a tapestry being woven by the maiden Arachne, crosswise threads (**woof**) broken when the tapestry is destroyed by the angry goddess Minerva, who turns Arachne into a spider. Shakespeare's spelling "Ariachne" also suggests the maiden "Ariadne," who gave a coil of thread to Theseus to guide him out of the Minotaur's labyrinth.

5.3.121. **turn and change:** David Bevington, editor of the Arden 3 edition of the play, suggests that Troilus "plays on multiple meanings" of these two words: "*turn* (revolve, reverse position, mislead, beguile, desert) and *change* (exchange, alter, change countenance, quit one thing for another, remove to another place)."

5.5.28–29. **Art . . . honor:** That is, are you of the proper social rank to fight with Hector (a question appropriate to the rules of sixteenth- and seventeenth-century codes of **honor**).

Textual Notes

The reading of the present text appears to the left of the square bracket. Unless otherwise noted, the reading to the left of the bracket is from **Q,** the First Quarto text of 1609 (upon which this edition is based). The earliest sources of readings not in Q are indicated as follows: **F** is the First Folio of 1623; **F2** is the Second Folio of 1632; **F3** is the Third Folio of 1663–64; **F4** is the Fourth Folio of 1685; **Ed.** is an earlier editor of Shakespeare, beginning with Rowe in 1709. No sources are given for emendations of punctuation or for corrections of obvious typographical errors, like turned letters that produce no known word. **SD** means stage direction; **SP** means speech prefix: ***uncorr.*** means the first or uncorrected state of Q or of F; ***corr.*** means the second or corrected state of Q or of F; **~** stands in place of a word already quoted before the square bracket; **^** indicates the omission of a punctuation mark. **1st setting** refers to the first attempt to set into type the first page of the play for F; **2nd setting** refers to the second attempt (for discussion of this matter, see "An Introduction to This Text," page li).

A never] *This preface is only in* Q. 19. witted] *wittied* Q 41. *Vale.* | *Troilus and Cressida*] Ed.; *Vale.* | The history of Troylus and Cresseida. Q

Prologue] *The 31-line prologue is only in* F. 1. SP PROLOGUE] Ed.; The Prologue. F 12. barks] F2; *Barke* F 17. Antenorides] *Antenonidus* F 19. Spar] Ed.; *Stirre* F 31. Now, good] ~^~, F 31. war.] *Warre.* | The Tragedie of Troylus and Cressida. F

1.1 15. must] Q; must needes F (1st setting) 20. SP PANDARUS] *Paude*. Q 20–21. leavening] Q; leau'ing F (2nd setting) 25. heating] Q; heating of F (2nd setting) 26. you] Q (yea) 26. burn] Q; to burne F (1st setting) 31. When] Ed.; then Q, F 31. is she] Ed.; she is Q, F 71. travail] Q, F (trauell) 72. on] F *only* (1st setting) 77. not] F *only* (2nd setting) 78. o'] Q (a); on F (1st setting) 79. care] F *only* (1st setting) 82. SP PANDARUS] Q (*Pan.*); *Troy.* F (2nd setting) 84. her.] F (~:); ~∧ Q 90. SD *He exits.*] Q; *Exit Pandar.* F (1st setting); *Exit Pand.* (2nd setting) 92. Helen] *Helleu* Q 100. Daphne's] *Daphues* Q 102. pearl.] ~, Q, F 103. resides] F; reides Q

1.2 0. SD *Cressida*] Cressid Q, F 2 *and hereafter.* SP ALEXANDER] Ed.; *Man.* Q, F 8. chid] Q; chides F 21. they] F; the Q 34. purblind] Q; purblinded F 38. disdain] Q; disdaind F 40. SD *Enter Pandarus.*] F *only* 49. Ilium] Illum Q 52. you] Q (yea) 73. nor Hector] Q; not *Hector* F 74. just ∧ to each of them;] ~, . . . ~∧ Q, F 81. end.] ~∧ Q; ~: F 87. come] F; eome Q 89. wit] Ed.; will Q, F 104. much.] ~, Q, F 108. lief] Q, F (lieue) 113. SP PANDARUS] Q; *dan.* F 119. will he] will hc Q 120. lift] F; liste Q 121. he] Q; he is F 123. came] F; eame Q 129. valiantly] valianty Q 134. the] F2; thee Q, F 151. a] Q *only* 152. pot] F; por Q 154. this] rhis Q 172. chafed] chaf t Q 173. for it] Q; For is F 177. do] Q; does F 180. tears] Q; reares F 181. SD *Sound a retreat.*] *1 line earlier in* Q *and* F 184. Ilium?] ~, Q, F 190. SD *Enter Aeneas*] *1 line earlier in* Q *and* F 192. tell] Q *only* 193. SD *Enter Antenor*] *1 line later in* Q *and* F 196. a] F *only* 197. judgments] Q; judgement F 200. him] Q; him him F 205. fellow] Q, F *corr.*; flelow F *uncorr.* 208. a] Q *only* 209. man's] F; man Q 212. there's laying] Q; laying F 212. will] Q; ill F 217. SD *Enter Paris*] *3 lines earlier in* Q *and* F 223. see] Q *only* 223. SD *Enter Helenus*] *1 line* *later in* Q *and* F 223. SD *Helenus*] Q, F *corr.*; *Hellenuss* F *uncorr.* 229–30. indifferent∧ well] ~, ~ Q, F 231. hear] Q (here); haere F 231. SD *Enter Troilus*] *1 line later in* Q *and* F; *Trylus* F 237. Note] Q *only* 244. choice] choiee Q 246. an eye] Q; money F 246. SD *Enter . . . Soldiers*] F *only* 247. comes] Q; come F 254. amongst] Q; among F 262. such-like] Q; so forth F 262. season] Q; seasons F 265. a woman] Q; another F 265. a man] Q; one F 271. at] Q; at, at F 278. SD *Enter Troilus's Boy.*] *1 line earlier in* F (*Enter Boy.*) 281. There . . . him.] Q *only* 288. SD *Pandarus exits.*] F *only* (*Pand.*) 296. prize] Q (price); prize F 301. Then] Q; That F 301. content] Q; Contents F

1.3 0. SD *Sennet.*] F *only* 1. the] F; these Q 1. jaundice] Q, F (Iaundies) 1. o'er] Q; on F 5. largeness.] ~, Q; ~: F 6. reared,] ~. Q, F 8. Infects] Q; Infect F 13. every] F; euer Q 19. call them shames] Q; thinke them shame F 27. broad] Q; lowd F 28. winnows] winnowss Q 31. thy] F; the Q 31. godlike] Q; godly F 36. patient] F; ancient Q 51. flee] Ed.; fled Q, F 55. Retorts] Ed.; Retires Q, F 57. nerves] Q; Nerue F 60. speaks.] ~, Q, F 62. which,] ~∧ Q, F 62–64. mighty∧ . . . reverend∧] F; ~ (. . . ~) Q 64. thy] F; the Q 71. On] Q; In F 71. heaven rides] Q; the Heauens ride F 71. all the Greekish] Q; all Greekes F 74–78. SP AGAMEMNON Speak . . . oracle.] F *only* 79. SP ULYSSES] F *only* (*Vlys.*) 79. basis] F; bases Q 84. factions.] F; ~, Q 87. expected] expccted Q 96. influence of evil planets] Q; ill Aspects of Planets euill F 98. check,] F; ~∧ Q 106. of] Q; to F 110. primogeneity] Q (primogenitie); primogenitiue F 114. meets] F; melts Q 122. their] Q; her F 123. includes] F; include Q 131. it is] Q; is it F 132. with] Q; in F 141. stands] Q; liues F 153. silly] Q; aukward F 161. o'erwrested] Q, F (ore-rested) 163. unsquared] F; vnsquare Q 165. seem] Q; seemes F 165. hyperboles.] F; ~, Q 168. right] Q; iust F 169.

hem] Q; hum F 194. keeps] Q; and keepes F 199. and] F; our Q 204. hand.] ~, Q; ~: F 206. calls] Q; call F 211. swinge] Q; swing F 213. fineness] F; fincsse Q 216. SD *Tucket.*] F *only* 218. SD *Enter Aeneas*] F *only* 223. eyes] Q; eares F 225. host] Ed.; heads Q, F 232. bid] Q; on F 235. god∧] ~, Q; ~∧ F 242. great] Q *only* 247. that the] Q; that he F 253. affair] F; affaires Q 256. with] Q *only* 258. sense] F; seat Q 258. the] F; that Q 264. loud] F; alowd Q 267. SD *Sound trumpet.*] Q; *The Trumpets sound.* F 270. this] F; his Q 271. resty] Q; rusty F 273. among] Q; among'st F 275. That seeks] F; And feeds Q 284. couple] Q; compasse F 292. Aeneas.] ~, Q, F 297. or] F; a Q 298. I am] Q; Ile be F 301. host] Q; mould F 302. A] Q; One F 302. one] F; no Q 305. put my] Q; put this F 305. brawns] Q; brawne F 306. will] F *only* 309. prove] Q; pawne F 309. troth] Q; truth F 310. forfend] Q; forbid F 310. youth] F; men Q 312. SP AGAMEMNON] F *only* (*Aga.*) 313. sir] Q; first F 317. SD *All . . . exit.*] F *only* (*Exeunt. Manet Vlysses, and Nestor.*) 323. This 'tis] F *only* 333. True] Q *only* 333. as] Q; euen as F 336. Achilles,] F; ~∧ Q 336. were] Q (weare); were F 342. Why] Q; Yes F 343. his honor] F; those honours Q 345. the] Q; this F 349. vile] Q; wilde F 361. receives . . . a] Q; from hence receyues the F 363–65. Which . . . limbs.] F *only* 363. are his] F2; are in his F 368. First show foul] Q; shew our fowlest F 369. shall exceed] Q; yet to shew F 370. By . . . first] Q; Shall shew the better F 374. eyes.] ~∧ Q; ~: F 375. Hector,] F; ~∧ Q 376. share] Q; weare F 378. it] Q; we F 381. do] Q; did F 384. Hector.] ~, Q; ~: F 385. for the better] Q; as the worthier F 387. fall∧] F; ~, Q 393. assumes:] ~∧ Q; ~, F 396. thereof] Q; of it F 397. straight.] ~∧ Q; ~: F 399. tar] F; arre Q 399. a] Q; their F

2.1 6. then] Q *only* 8. there] F *only* 11. SD *Strikes him.*] F *only* 14. thou unsalted] Q; you whinid'st F

17. oration] F; oration without booke Q 18. a] F *only* 19. o'] F3; ath Q; o' th F 20. Toadstool] Q; Toads stoole F 24. a] F *only* 28. Greece.] ~, Q 28–30. When . . . another.] Q *only* 37–42. him— . . . do.] F; him. *Aiax Coblofe,* Hee . . . bisket, you horson curre. Do? Do? Q 46. thou] F; you Q 47. thrash] Q; thresh F 56. SD *Enter . . . Patroclus.*] F *only* 58. thus] Q; this F 65. so I do] Q; I do so F 74. I] F; It Q 77. I'll] F; I Q 91. The] Q; for a F 92. Thersites] *Thesites* Q 94. the vile] Q; thee vile F 104. an] Q; if F 104. he] F *only* 104. out] F; at Q 105. brains] beains Q 109. your] Ed.; their Q, F 109–10. on their toes] F *only* 111. wars] Q; warre F 117. Peace] Q *only* 118. brach] Ed.; brooch Q, F 121. clodpolls] Q (Clatpoles) 126. fifth] F (fift); first Q 134. SD *He exits.*] F *only* (*Exit.*)

2.2 4. travel] Q; trauaile F 6. cormorant] Q; comorant F 9. toucheth] Q; touches F 14–15. surety, | Surety] F; surely | Surely Q 17. worst.] F; ~∧Q 28. father's] Q; Father F 29. sum∧] F; ~. Q 32. diminutive] dyminutue Q 34. at] F; of Q 35. them.] ~∧ Q; ~, F 36. reason] Q; reasons F 37. tell] Q; tels F 47–48. And . . . reason] *lines reversed in* F 49. Let's] F; Sets Q 50. hare] Q; hard F 53. Make] Q; Makes F 55. keeping] Q; holding F 60. mad] Q; made F 62. attributive] Q; inclineable F 65. election∧] F; ~: Q 68. shores] F; shore Q 71. choose] Q; chose F 74. soiled] Q; spoyl'd F 76. unrespective] vnrespectue Q 76. sieve] Q; same F 78. Paris] *Pa is* Q 79. with] Q; of F 80. truce] ttuce Q 85. pale] Q; stale F 92. he] F; be Q 92. worthy] Q; Noble F 96. never Fortune] Q; Fortune neuer F 107. Cassandra] *Crssandra* Q 107. SD *raving*] Q; *with her haire about her eares* F (*5 lines earlier in* Q, F) 111. elders] Q; old F 112. canst] Q; can F 113. clamors] Q; clamour F 189. each] eaeh Q 194. nations] Q; Nation F 220. strike] F; shrike Q

2.3 1. SP THERSITES] Ed.; *not in* Q, F 3. worthy] worrhy Q 13. you] Q; thou F 17. their] Q; the F 19. Neapolitan] Q *only* 20. depending] Q; dependant F 27. couldst] Q; would'st F 33. a] F; not a Q 35. SD *Enter Patroclus.*] F *only, after "Achilles!" in line* 23 *above* 37. in] Q; in a F 40. SP PATROCLUS Amen.] Q *only* 43. O, where?] Q *only* 43. SD *Enter Achilles.*] Q (*after line* 40); F (*after line* 39) 44. come?] F; ~^ Q 50. Thersites] Q; thy selfe F 53. must] Q; maist F 58–64. SP PATROCLUS You . . . fool.] F *only* 59. SP THERSITES] *Ter.* F 67–68. of Agamemnon] F *only* 69. this] Q *only* 71. of] Q; to F 71. creator] F; Prouer Q 72. SD *Enter . . . Calchas.*] *1 line later in* Q (*Agam: Vliss: . . . Diomed.*); *2 lines earlier in* F 72. SD *Nestor*] *Nəstor* Q 74. Patroclus] F; Come *Patroclus* Q 75. SD *He exits.*] F *only* (*Exit.*) 77–78. whore . . . cuckold] Q; Cuckold . . . Whore F 78. emulous] Q; emulations F 79–80. Now . . . all] F *only* 84. shent] Ed.; sate Q; sent F 85. appertainments] F; appertainings Q 85 him.] ~^ Q; ~: F 86. so, lest] Q; of, so F 89. say so] Q; so say F 93. if you] Q; if F 94. 'tis] Q; it is F 94. a] Q; the F 95. A . . . lord] F *only* 105. their] theit Q 105. composure] Q; counsell that F 108. SD *Enter Patroclus.*] F *only* 110. him.] Q; ~, F *uncorr.*; ~? F *corr.* 112. legs are] Q; legge are F 112. flexure] Q; flight F 121. But] Q, F *corr.*; ut F *uncorr.* 125. on] Q; of F 127. and] F *only* 129. come] Q; came F 134. tend] Q; tends F 134–35. on, | Disguise^] F; ~^ | ~, Q 138. course and time] Q; pettish lines F 138. and flows] Q; his flowes F 138. as] F; and Q 139. carriage of this action] F; streame of his commencement Q 144. Bring] Q, F *corr.*; ring F *uncorr.* 148. second] Q, F *corr.*; fecond F *uncorr.* 149. enter you] F; entertaine Q 149. SD *Ulysses . . . Patroclus.*] F *only* (*Exit Vlisses.*) 153. am?] Q, F *corr.*; ~. F *uncorr.* 160. pride] Q; it F 161. Ajax] F *only* 166. I hate] F; I do hate Q 168. And] Q *only* 168. SD *Enter Ulysses.*] *3 lines earlier in* Q, F 180. worth] Q; wroth F 184. down himself] Q; gainst it selfe F 191. SP ULYSSES] Q, F *corr.* (*Vlis.*); *Vis.* F *uncorr.* 196. doth] Q; doe F 200. Shall] Q; Must F 202. titled] F; liked Q 207. him?] F *corr.*; ~, F *uncorr.*; ~. Q 210. this] F; his Q 212. pash] F; push Q 221. let] F; tell Q 221. humorous] Q; humours F 229–30. SP ULYSSES He . . . shares. | AJAX I] F; *Aiax* A . . . shares. I Q 231. SP NESTOR He's . . . warm. Force] Ed.; he's . . . warme? | *Nest.* Force Q, F 232. praises] F; praiers Q 232. Pour in, pour in] F *corr.* (poure in, poure in); poore in, poore in F *uncorr.*; poure in, poure Q 235. You] Q *corr.*; Yon Q *uncorr.* 236. does] Q; doth F 242. with us thus] Q; thus with vs F 252. Famed] Q; Fame F 253. beyond, beyond] F; beyond all Q 253. thy] Q; all F 259. bourn] F; boord Q 260. Thy] F; This Q 268. SP NESTOR] Q; *Ulis.* F 270. here;] ~∧ Q; ~, F 271. great] Q *only* 276. cull] F; call Q 278. boats] Q; Botes may F 278. hulks] Q; bulkes F

3.1 0. SD *Music . . . within.*] F *only, at the end of* 2.3 0. SD *and Paris's Servingman*] Ed.; *and a Seruant* F; *not in* Q 1. you not] Q; not you F 3 *and hereafter.* SP MAN] Q; *Ser.* F 6. notable] Q; noble F 17. titles] Q; title F 25. friend] F *only* 28. art] F *only* 32–33. visible] Ed.; inuisible Q, F 35. not you] Q; you not F 36. attributes] ac- | tributes Q 37. that] F *only* 52. SP HELEN] Ed.; *Nel.* Q; *Nel*, F 78. queen, my] Queenem,y Q 85. I'll . . . life] Q *only* 86. matter;] ~∧ Q; ~, F 88. make 's] Q; make F 90. poor] F *only* 96. horribly] Q; horrible F 101. twain] tawine Q 106. lord] F; lad Q 112. Love, love] Q *corr.*; loue, lone Q *uncorr.* 113. SP PANDARUS] F *corr.*; *omit* F *uncorr.* 113. In . . . so] F *only* 114. *Love*] F *corr.*; Pand. *Loue* Q; Pan. *Loue* F *uncorr.* 114. *still love*] Q *only* 115. bow∧] ~. Q; ~, F 117. *shaft confounds*] F; shafts confound Q 131.

deeds?] ~∧ Q *uncorr.*, F; ~, Q *corr.* 134. Deiphobus, Helenus] Q *corr.*; *Deipholus, Helenes* Q *uncorr.* 147. They're] F; Their Q 147. the] Q *only* 150. these] F; this Q 158. SP PARIS] Q *only* 158. thee] F *corr.*; the F *uncorr.*; her Q

3.2 0. SD *Enter . . . Man,*] F; *Enter. Pandarus Troylus, man.* Q 3. he] F *only* 3. SD *Enter Troilus.*] F *only* 8. Like] F; Like to Q 10. those] F; these Q 12. Pandar] Q; *Pandarus* F 16. SD *Pandarus exits.*] F *corr. only* (*Exit Pandarus.*); *Exeunt Pandarus.* F *uncorr.* 20. palate] Ed.; pallats Q, F 21. thrice-repurèd] Q; thrice reputed F 22. Swooning] Q, F (Sounding) 23. tuned] Q; and F 28. SD *Enter Pandarus.*] F *only* 32. spirit] Q; sprite F 33. as short] Q; so short F 33. SD *Pandarus exits.*] F (*Exit Pand.*); *not in* Q 37. unawares] F *corr.*; vnwares Q, F *uncorr.* 38. SD *Pandarus . . . Cressida*] *pandar . . . Cressid* Q 45. thills] Ed.; filles Q, F 68. fears] Ed.; teares Q, F 72. safer] Q; safe F 76. Nor] Q; Not F 81. is] F *only* 85. than] Q *corr.* (then); thene Q *uncorr.* 92. crown it. No perfection] F; louer part no affection Q 95. words to] Q *corr.*; wordes to to Q *uncorr.* 99. SD *Enter Pandarus.*] F *only* 110. be wooed] Q; are wooed F 118. glance∧] ~; Q *corr.*, F; ~: Q *uncorr.* 120. till now not] Q; not till now F 120. much∧] Q *corr.*; ~; Q *uncorr.* 122. children] Q *corr.*; chilPren Q *uncorr.* 122. grown] Q; grow F 131. silence] Q *corr.* (sylence); scylence Q *uncorr.* 132. Cunning] Ed.; Comming Q, F 133. very] Q *only* 133. counsel] Q; counsell from me F 150–51. I . . . wit] Q; Where is my wit? | I would be gone F 151. know . . . speak] Q; I speake I know not what F 152. that speak] Q; that speakes F 154. confession∧] ~. Q; ~, F 157. might.] ~∧ Q; ~, F 158. woman—] ~. Q; ~: F 160. aye] F; age Q 160. love,] ~. Q, F 161. youth,] F; ~. Q 167. purity] Q; puriritie F 175. truth] Q; truths F 181. Yet] F *only* 182. authentic] anthentique Q 187. and] F; or Q 194. wind . . . sandy] Q; as Winde, as sandie F 195. or] Q; as F 202. pains] F; paine Q 210. with a bed] Ed.; *not in* Q, F 212. SD *Troilus . . . exit.*] Q *only* (*Exeunt.*) 214. pander] Q; and Pander F 214. SD *He exits.*] Q (*Exit.*); *Exeunt*. F

3.3 0. SD *Diomedes . . . Agamemnon*] Q (*Diomed . . . Agamem*); *Enter Vlysses, Diomedes, Nestor, Agamemnon, Menelaus and Chalcas. Flourish*. F 1. you] F *only* 3. your] F *only* 4. come] F4; loue Q, F 5. possessions] Ed.; possession Q, F 14. benefit‸] ~. Q; ~: F 21. Cressid] Q *uncorr*. (Cressed); *Cressed* Q *corr*. 22. denied;] Q *corr*. (~,) F(~:); ~‸ Q *uncorr*. 34. fairly] Q *corr*. (farely); farrly Q *uncorr*. 38. SD *Achilles . . . tent.*] Q; *Enter* Achilles *and* Patroclus *in their Tent*. F 38. SD *Patroclus*] Q (Patro) 38. SD *stand*] Q *only* 40. pass] Q; to passe F 43. me‸] ~. Q; ~, F 44. unplausive] F; vnpaulsiue Q 50. pride,] Q *corr*. (~:); ~‸ Q *uncorr*.; ~: F 66. cuckold] Cnckould Q 71. SD *He exits.*] *Exeunt*. Q, F 75. use] Ed.; vs'd Q, F 84. but honor] Q; but honour'd F 104. shining] F; ayming Q 106. giver] F; giuers Q 109. itself‸] ~. Q; ~, F 110–11. To . . . itself] Q *only* 115. mirrored] Ed.; married Q, F 117. strain] Q; straine it F 120. man] Q; may F 121. be] Q; is F 124. applause‸] ~. Q; ~, F 131. what!] ~‸ Q; ~. F 132. are‸] ~. Q, F 133. abject] F; obiect Q 142. fasting] Q; feasting F 146. shrieking] Q; shrinking F 157. mail] Ed.; male Q, F 163. turn] Q; hedge F 165–68. hindmost . . . on] F; him, most Q 167. rear] Ed.; neere F; *not in* Q 170. past] F; passe Q 174. Welcome] Ed.; the welcome Q, F 175. Farewell] Q; farewels F 175. Let] Q; O let F 180. calumniating] calumniati g Q 184. give] Ed.; goe Q, F 189. sooner] Q; begin to F 190. Than] F; That Q 190. stirs not] Q; not stirs F 190. once] Q; out F 205. providence] prouidencc Q 206. grain of Pluto's gold]

F; thing Q 207. deep] Ed.; depth Q; deepes F 219. our islands] Q; her Iland F 233. a] F *only* 234. air] Q; ayrie ayre F 241. necessary∧] ~. Q; ~, F 244. they] Q; we F 252. SD *Enter Thersites.*] *1 line later in* Q; *2 lines earlier in* F 267. this] Q; his F 279. to him] F *only* 281–82. professes] profefses Q 284. his] F *only* 287. most] F *only* 291. Grecian] F *only* 291. army, Agamemnon,] ~. ~, Q; ~∧~, F 292. *et cetera*] F *only* (& c.) 307. b' wi' you] Q, F (buy you) 309. of the] Q; a F 315. he's] F *only* 321. bear] Q; carry F 324. myself] myselse Q

4.1 0. SD *Antenor*] *Autemor* Q 0. SD *Diomedes and Grecians*] Ed.; *Diomed the Grecian* Q, F 5. you] F; your Q 9. wherein∧] Q; within; F 10. a] Q; in a F 18. But] F; Lul'd Q 18. meet] Q; meetes F 22. backward.] ~, Q, F 34. despiteful] Q; despightful'st F 38. 'Twas] Q; it was F 39. Calchas'] Calcho's Q; Calcha's F 43. believe] Q; doe thinke F 47. whereof] F; wherefore Q 55. SD *Aeneas exits*] F *only* (*Exit Aeneas.*) 57. the] F *only* 58. deserves . . . best] Q; merits . . . most F 62. soilure] F; soyle Q 71. nor less] Q; no lesse F 72. the] Q; which F 75. false] falfe Q 82. they] Q; you F 84. that not] Ed.; what we Q, F

4.2 13. joys] Q; eyes F 17. tediously] Q; hidiously F 23. SD *within*] F *only* 23. doors] doorcs Q 26. SD *Enter Pandarus.*] F *only* (*2 lines earlier*) 35–36. *capocchia*] Ed.; chipochia Q, F 38. SD *One knocks.*] *1 line later in* Q; *1 line earlier in* F 43. SD *Knock.*] *1 line later in* Q, F 45. SD *Troilus and Cressida exit.*] Ed.; *Exeunt.* Q, F 59. Ho] Ed.; Who Q, F 62. SD *Enter Troilus.*] F *only* 68. us] F; him Q 68. for him] F *only* 72. so concluded] Q; concluded so F 78. nature] F; neighbor *Pandar* Q 79. SD *Troilus and Aeneas exit.*] *Exeunt.* Q; *Exeunt. Enter Pandarus and Cressid.* F 83. SD *Enter Cressida.*] Q *only* (*Cress.*) 84. SP CRESSIDA] F *only* (*Cres.*) 87. sweet] sweeet Q 94–95. I beseech you] F *only* 107.

force] Q; orce F 108. extremes] Q; extremitie F 111. I'll] Q; I will F 115. SD *They exit.*] F *only* (*Exeunt*)

4.3 0. SD *Enter . . . Diomedes.*] Q (*Deiphob, Anth. Diomedes.*) 0. SD *and*] F *only* 2. For] Q; Of F 10. own] Q *only*

4.4 4. violenteth] Q; no lesse F 6. affection] F; affections Q 9. dross] Q; crosse F 10. SD *Enter Troilus.*] Q, F (*1 line earlier in* F) 11. Ah] Ed.; a Q, F 12. ducks] Q; ducke F 24. strained] Q; strange F 43. one] Q; our F 50. Distasted] Q; Distasting F 50. tears.] Q; teares. *Enter Aeneas*. F 52. genius] Q; genius so F 53. so] Q; come F 55. tears?] F; ~∧ Q 56. the root] F; my throate Q 60. When] Q; *Troy*. When F 61. my] F *only* 81–82. Their . . . flowing] F *only* 82. flowing] F2; Flawing F 84. novelty] Q; nouelties F 84. person] F; portion Q 87. afeard] Q; affraid F 109. true?] Q; true? *Exit*. F 116. SD *Enter . . . Diomedes.*] Ed.; *Enter the Greekes.* F (*2 lines earlier*); *not in* Q 128. usage] Q; visage F 131. zeal] Ed.; seale Q, F 131. to thee] Q; towards F 132. In] Q; I F 142. you] Q; my F 145. I] Q; Ile F 149. SD *Sound trumpet*] F *only* 154. to the] Q; in the F 156–60. SP DEIPHOBUS Let . . . chivalry.] F *only* 156. SP DEIPHOBUS] Ed.; *Dio*. F 160. *They exit.*] *Exeu*. Q; *Exeunt*. F, *in both texts 5 lines earlier*

4.5 0. SD *Agamemnon*] Q (*Agam.*) 0. SD *Nestor, etc.*] Ed.; *Nester, Calcas, &c.* Q, F 2. time∧ . . . courage.] ~. . . . ~, Q, F 15. yond] Q; yong F 32. And . . . argument.] Q *only* 36. Patroclus] *Patrolus* Q 41. SP MENELAUS] Ed.; *Patr.* Q, F 48. not] F; nor Q 50. o'] Q, F (a') 56. two] Ed.; then Q, F 64. language] Q; a language F 68. accosting] Ed.; a coasting Q, F 69. unclasp] vnclapse Q 70. tickling] F; ticklish Q 72. SD *Diomedes . . . exit.*] Ed.; *Exeunt*. F; *not in* Q 73. SD *Enter . . . Attendants.*] *1 line earlier in* Q (*enter all of Troy.*), F (*Enter all of Troy, Hector, Paris, Aeneas,*

Helenus and Attendants. Florish.) 75. the] Q; you F 79. they] Q *only* 85. SP ACHILLES But] Ed.; but Q, F 86. misprizing] Q; disprising F 91. Achilles] *Achillei* Q 106. breath] Q; breach F 108–9. SP ULYSSES . . . already. | AGAMEMNON] F; *Vlisses:* Q 110. knight] Q; Knight; they call him *Troylus* F 112. in] F; *not in* Q 130. disposed] dispo'd Q 148. Of . . . feud] F *only* 149. drop] F; day Q 161. could] Q; could'st F 177. SD *Agamemnon . . . rest*] F (*Enter Agamemnon and the rest.*); *not in* Q 182. all] Q; of F 184–89. But . . . integrity] F *only* 198. Mock . . . oath] F; (Mock not thy affect, the vntraded earth) Q 199. quondam] quandom Q 208. Despising many] Q; And seene thee scorning F 209. thy] F; th' Q 211. to some] Q; vnto F 214. hemmed] F; shrupd Q 220. O] Q *only* 227. As . . . courtesy] F *only* 278. an] Q; the F 281. stithied] F; stichied Q 281. helm,] F; ~. Q 290. have] Q *only* 301. we] Q; you F 304. Beat . . . taborins] F; To taste your bounties Q 305. SD *All . . . exit.*] Ed.; *Exeunt.* Q, F 310. upon . . . earth] Q; on heauen, nor on earth F 313. you] Q; thee F 317. As] F; But Q 322. she loved] F; my Lord Q

5.1 5. core] F; cur re Q 6. botch] Ed.; batch Q, F 13. need these] F; needs this Q 15. boy] F; box Q 16. said] Q; thought F 19. the guts-griping] Q; guts-griping F 19. guts-griping, ruptures] ~∧ ~∧ ~ Q, F 20. catarrhs] F *only* 20. o'] Q, F (a) 21–24. palsies . . . tetter] Q; palsies, and the like F 30. no] Q *only* 32. sleave-silk] Q; Sleyd silke F 32. sarsenet] sacenet Q 33. tassel] toslell Q 47. banqueting] banquctting Q 48. SD *He exits*] F *only* (*Exit.*) 55. brother] F; be Q 57. shoeing-horn] Q *corr.* (shooing-horne); shooing-horue Q *uncorr.* 57. hanging] F *only* 58. brother's] F; bare Q 59. forced] F; faced Q 61. he is] F; her's Q 62. dog] F; day Q 62. mule] F; Moyle Q 62. fitchew] Q (Fichooke) 65. not] F *only* 67. SD *Enter . . . lights.*] Q (*Enter Agam:*

Vlisses, Nest: and Diomed with lights.); *Enter Hector, Aiax, Agamemnon, Vlysses, Nestor, Diomed, with Lights.* F (*1 line later in* Q, F) 68. Sprites] Q; spirits F 70. lights] Q; light F 72. SD *Enter Achilles.*] F *only* 75. good] Q (God) 83. at once] F *only* 85. SD *Agamemnon . . . exit.*] Q (*Exeunt Agam: Menelaus.*); *not in* F 86. Nestor] *Nector* Q 95. SD *Achilles . . . exit.*] *Exeunt.* Q, F 101. foretell it] Q; foretell it, that F 105. his] F *only* 106. SD *He exits.*] Ed.; *Exeunt* F

5.2 0. SD *Diomedes*] Q, F (*Diomed*) 3. your] Q; you F 5. SD *Enter . . . Ulysses*] F *only* 6. SD *Enter Cressida.*] *1 line later in* Q; *Cressid* Q, F 13. sing] Q; finde F 14. clef] Q; life F 16. SP CRESSIDA] F2; *Cal.* Q, F 19. should] F; shall Q 25. forsworn] Q; a forsworne F 30. do] Q; do not F 37. a] Q; one F 39. you] F *only* 44. Nay] F; Now Q 45. distraction] F; distruction Q 48. all hell's] Q; hell F 54. How now, my] Q; Why, how now F 57. Adieu] F *only* 67. these] F *only* 69. But] F *only* 70. la] Ed.; lo Q, F 74. my] Q; sweete F 76. SD *Enter Cressida*] Q (*Cress.*) 82–83. I . . . CRESSIDA] F *only* 95. on] Q; in F 100. doth take] Q; rakes F 103. SP CRESSIDA] F *only* 108. one's] Q; one F 111. By] F; And by Q 112. will] wlll Q 123. do] doc Q 124. SP TROILUS] Ed.; *Ther.* Q, F 124. you] Q; me F 129. SD *He exits.*] F (*Exit.*), *1 line earlier*; *not in* Q 137. said] Q; say F 143. co-act] F; Court Q 147. th' attest] Q; that test F 148. had deceptious] F; were deceptions Q 161. soil] F; spoile Q 168. be sanctimonies] Q; are sanctimonie F 171. is] F; was Q 172. itself] Q; thy selfe F 173. Bifold] Q; By foule F 181. Ariachne's] Q *corr.* (*Ariachna's*); *Ariathna's* Q *uncorr.* 187. five-finger-tied] F (fiue finger tied); finde finger tied Q 190. given] Q; bound F 197. as] F2; *not in* Q, F 199. on] Q; in F 203. sun] Q; Fenne F 207. SP THERSITES] *Thier.* Q 220. SD *Aeneas*] *Eeneas* Q 227. SD *He exits.*] Q *only* (*Exit.*)

5.3 4. in] Q; gone F 5. all] Q *only* 8. brother] brothet Q 9. intent] intenr Q 16. SP CASSANDRA] F; *Cres.* Q 22–25. To . . . CASSANDRA] F *only* 23. give much, to use] Ed.; count giue much to as F 33. SD *Cassandra exits.*] Q (*Cassan.*) 44. sword,] ~. Q; ~: F 50. mother] Q; Mothers F 64. But . . . ruin] F *only* 88. SD *Andromache exits.*] Q (*Androm.*) 93. do] Q; doth F 95. dolor] F; dolours Q 96. distraction] F; destruction Q 100. Yet] Q; yes F 101. SD *She exits.*] F *only* (*Exit.*) 104. worth] Q; of F 107. SD *Pandarus*] *Pandar.* Q, F 115. o' these] ath's Q; o' th's F 123. deeds] Q; deedes. | *Pand.* Why, but heare you? | *Troy.* Hence brother lackie; ignomie and shame | Pursue thy life, and liue aye with thy name. F

5.4 0. SD *Alarum.*] F *only* (*before "Exeunt"* [*They exit*] *at the end of* 5.3) 0. SD *Excursions. Enter Thersites.*] Ed.; *Enter Thersites: excursions.* Q; *Enter Thersites in excursion.* F 4. young] F *only* 9. O' th'] Q (Ath') 10. stale] Q; stole F 12. proved not] Ed.; not prooued Q, F 16. begin] Ed.; began Q, F 18. SD *Enter . . . Troilus*] F *only* (*Diomed*) 28. thou, Greek] F; Greeke Q

5.5 0. SD *Enter Diomedes and Servingman.*] Q (*Diomed, Seruant*); F (*Diomed, Seruants*) 6. SD *Enter Agamemnon.*] Q (*Agamem.*) *1 line earlier* 7. Polydamas] Q (Polidamas) 8. Margareton] Ed.; *Margarelon* Q, F 12. Epistrophus and Cedius. Polyxenes] Q (*Epistropus* and *Cedus, Polixines*) 13. Amphimachus and Thoas] Q (*Amphimacus* and *Thous*) 22. here] Ed.; there Q, F 23. scalèd] F; scaling Q 25. strawy] Q; straying F 26. a] Q; the F 37. lost] loft Q 43. luck] F; lust Q 45. SP AJAX] F *only* 46. *He exits.*] Q, F *both 1 line later* (*Exit.*)

5.6 1. SP AJAX] F *only* 1. SD *Enter Diomedes.*] Q (*Diom.*) 2. SP DIOMEDES] F *only* (*Diom.*) 8. the] Ed.; thy Q, F 12. SD *Enter . . . exits*] Ed.; *not in* Q; *Exit*

Troylus. | *Enter Hector.* F 13. SD *Enter Achilles.*] Q (*Achil:*) 14. SP ACHILLES] F *only* (*Achil.*) 14. Ha] Q *only* 23. SD *Enter Troilus.*] Q (*Troyl:*) F, *1 line later* 29. I end] Q; thou end F

5.7 1. SP ACHILLES] F *only* (*Achil.*) 6. arms] Q; arme F 8. SD *They exit.*] *Exit.* Q, F

5.8 0. SD *Enter Thersites; then Menelaus fighting Paris.*] Ed.; *Enter Thersi: Mene: Paris.* Q; *Enter Thersites, Menelaus, and Paris.* F 3. double-horned] Ed.; double hen'd Q, F 3. Spartan] Q; sparrow F 4. SD *Menelaus*] *Menelus* Q 9. bastard begot] Q; a Bastard begot F 15. *He exits.*] Q (*Exit.*); *Exeunt.* F

5.9 3. my] Q; good F 4. SD *his*] F *only* 7. dark'ning] Q; darking F 11. next! Come] Q; now F 13. and] Q *only* 15. retire] Q; retreat F 15. part] prat Q 16. SP A MYRMIDON] Ed.; *One:* Q; *Gree.* F 16. Trojan trumpets] F; Troyans trumpet Q 16. sound] Q; sounds F 20. bait] Q; bed F

5.10 0. SD *Sound retreat.*] F *only* 0. SD *Enter . . . marching*] Q (*Agam: . . . Mene: . . . Diom:*) 0. SD *Shout.*] F *only* 1. shout] F *only* 1. this] Q; that F 3. SP SOLDIERS] Q (*Sould:*) 6. was . . . as] Q; was a man as good as F

5.11 0. SD *Deiphobus*] Q (*Diephobus*); *and Deiphoebus* F 2. Never] F; *Troy.* Neuer Q 2. SD *Enter Troilus.*] Q (*1 line earlier*), F 3. SP TROILUS] F *only* 8. smite] Ed.; smile Q, F 13. fear,] F; ~ ∧ Q 17. screech-owl] scrich-ould Q 18. their∧] Q; there, F 21. Cold] Q; Coole F 22–23. But . . . dead] F *only* 24. vile] F; proud Q 25. pitched] Q; pight F 30. still,] ~. Q 35. Ignomy and] F; ignomyny Q 36. SD *All . . . exit.*] Q; *Exeunt.* F 38. world [3rd]] F *only* 41. loved] Q; de-sir'd F 53. your] F; my Q 54. hold-door] Q (hold-ore) 59. SD *He exits.*] Ed.; *Exeunt.* F; *not in* Q

Appendix on the Characters in the Play

Achilles: son of the mortal Peleus and the sea nymph Thetis; leader of the Myrmidons, a people created by Zeus (the Romans' Jove, king of the gods) from ants. He brought fifty ships to Troy. In Homer he was famous for his anger and at odds with **Agamemnon,** who had taken his concubine slave from him. Achilles, the main Greek warrior, refused to fight until **Patroclus** was killed by **Hector.** (For more, see **Hector.**)

Aeneas: son of the Trojans' patroness Aphrodite (the Romans' Venus, goddess of love) and the human Anchises, thus descended from the younger branch of the Trojan royal family (**Priam** being from the elder branch). Not an important hero for Homer, Aeneas is made famous in Virgil's epic, the *Aeneid,* for escaping Troy's destruction and founding Rome.

Agamemnon: in Homer, king of Mycenae, elder brother of **Menelaus,** and general of the Greek forces during the ten-year-long Trojan War.

Ajax: leader of the men of Salamis against Troy. In Homer, a warrior of great size and determination who often led the Greek forces into battle. (For more, see **Hector.**)

Antenor: an elder of Troy. Later legend made him a traitor to Troy for telling the Greeks how to destroy

Troy by stealing the Palladium and by building the Trojan Horse. The Palladium was an image of the goddess Pallas Athena; its presence in Troy ensured the survival of the city, and it was stolen by the Greeks **Ulysses** and **Diomedes.** The Trojan Horse, a great wooden horse left behind by the apparently departing Greeks, was accepted by the Trojans, who brought it into their city. At night the Greeks came out of it and destroyed Troy.

Calchas: See **Cressida.**

Cassandra: in Homer, the most beautiful daughter of **Priam** and Hecuba. In later legend, she was loved by Apollo, who granted her the gift of prophecy. When she rejected the god, Apollo avenged himself by ensuring that her prophecies were never believed.

Cressida: in Boccaccio's *Il Filostrato* and Chaucer's *Troilus and Criseyde,* daughter of Calchas, a Trojan prophet who foresaw the fall of Troy and fled the city to the Greeks, leaving his widowed daughter to the wrath of the Trojans. Cressida sought the aid of **Hector,** who shielded her. Her name, which derives from that of Chryses in Homer, had by Shakespeare's time become a byword for the false woman, thanks in part to poems like Robert Henryson's *The Testament of Cresseid.*

Diomedes: in Homer, leader of the men of Argos and Tiryns against Troy. He was a fierce fighter who wounded in battle even the gods, namely the Trojans' patroness Aphrodite (the Romans' Venus, goddess of love) and Ares (Mars, god of war). (See also **Antenor.**)

Hector: in Homer, the eldest and greatest of the sons of **Priam** and Hecuba. He was leader of the Trojan forces, but not a match for the greatest of the Greek fighters. In single combat, the Greek **Ajax** proved equal to Hector. Then the Greek **Achilles** slew him single-handedly after Hector chose to fight him in the belief, into which Hector was misled by the patron goddess of the Greeks, Athena, that his brother Deiphobus was at hand to assist.

Helen: in Homer, the most beautiful woman in the world. Daughter of Zeus (the Romans' Jove, king of the gods) and the human Leda, Helen was queen of Sparta, wife to **Menelaus.** In Homer's account, she fell in love with **Paris** under a divine spell, when he was an ambassador to Sparta, and he carried her off to Troy. (For more, see **Paris.**)

Helenus: son of **Priam** and Hecuba, priest and prophet.

Menelaus: king of Sparta, husband of **Helen,** younger brother of **Agamemnon.** In Homer, a successful fighter who beats **Paris** in single combat and who would have killed him, had not the Trojans' patroness Aphrodite (the Romans' Venus, goddess of love) saved him.

Nestor: in Homer, king of Pylos, and of a great age, having outlived two generations, but still both mentally and physically vigorous, if long-winded in giving counsel.

Pandarus: in Homer, son of Lycaon and, during the Trojan War, leader of the Trojans who lived around the base of Mount Ida. He was made famous by Boccaccio's *Il Filostrato* and Chaucer's *Troilus and Criseyde* as **Cressida**'s uncle and the go-between who brought her to her lover **Troilus.** His role as go-between was granted a dignity in medieval courtly romance that it has subsequently lacked.

Paris: in Homer, son of **Priam** and Hecuba, who, when she was carrying him in her womb, dreamed that she would give birth to a firebrand. Thus Paris was exposed to die in the wilderness. Saved by shepherds, he later won acceptance back into the royal family with his athletic prowess. When he was sent on an embassy to Sparta's King **Menelaus, Helen** fell in love with him, and he took her back to Troy, thereby bringing about the Trojan War. In later legend, his capture of **Helen** was put into a larger context of the story of the Judgment of Paris. According to this story, Paris, the most handsome man in the world, was chosen by the goddesses Hera (the Romans' Juno, queen of the gods), Athena (or Minerva, goddess of wisdom), and Aphrodite (Venus, goddess of love) to determine which of them was the most beautiful. Choosing Aphrodite, Paris was rewarded by being given the most beautiful woman in the world—**Helen.**

Patroclus: in Homer, **Achilles**' favorite companion. (For more, see **Achilles.**)

Priam: in Homer, the very old king of Troy and husband to Queen Hecuba; father of fifty sons and many daughters, he was killed by Neoptolemus (**Achilles**' son) at the fall of Troy.

Thersites: in Homer, a lowborn, ugly, and abusive critic of the Greek leaders.

Troilus: hardly mentioned by Homer, but made famous by Chaucer's *Troilus and Criseyde* as the betrayed yet faithful lover of Criseyde and an accomplished knight.

Ulysses: king of Ithaca. In Homer, he was the one who persuaded all **Helen**'s other suitors to join him in swearing an oath that should she be taken from the man she chose to be her husband, all would join her husband in recovering her. Thus he was obliged, along with so many others, to fight at Troy. Nonetheless, he tried unsuccessfully to avoid the Trojan War by pretending to be mad. During the war, he was a great fighter and councillor, tactful and shrewd. (See also **Antenor.**)

Troilus and Cressida: A Modern Perspective

Jonathan Gil Harris

Troilus and Cressida is the trickiest of Shakespeare's plays to classify by genre. The title page of the 1609 Quarto edition brands it a "Historie," but the Quarto's preface to the reader markets it as a "Commedie." The 1623 Folio edition of Shakespeare's works complicates matters further. The play appears there as *The Tragedie of Troylus and Cressida,* but the Folio's table of contents doesn't include it among the opening lists of histories, comedies, or tragedies. Instead, the play-text is inserted indeterminately between *Henry VIII,* the last play in the section for histories, and *Coriolanus,* the first play in the section for tragedies.

As a result, *Troilus and Cressida* can resemble the famous anamorphic image of an animal that looks from one perspective like a rabbit and from another like a duck. That indeterminacy is why the play, even more than the similarly slippery *All's Well That Ends Well* and *Measure for Measure,* has become the chief representative of the antigenre called the Shakespearean "problem play." *Troilus and Cressida*'s failure to fit into any one conventional category irked some of its earliest readers and critics, who judged it to be neither rabbit nor duck, but simply turkey. In 1679, for example, John Dryden described the play as a "heap of rubbish," an assessment he offered as justification for his adaptation in which Cressida—improbably transformed into a conventional romantic heroine—remains faithful to Troilus.[1]

Yet *Troilus and Cressida*'s genre troubles confirm one of the play's most distinctive preoccupations. When Troilus, spying on the supposedly false Cressida in the Greek camp, says "This is and is not Cressid" (5.2.175), he typifies the play's insistence that everything can simultaneously be what it is not, that every object on which we gaze can hold several contradictory values, that the singularity we think we see (or *want* to see) is a naive but violent simplification of an altogether more complex plurality. For some readers, this insistence makes *Troilus and Cressida* a decidedly modern play—modern, that is, in the sense of displacing absolute truths with multiple and even paradoxical perspectives, like the modernist European Cubist canvases of the 1910s and 1920s. Hence the title of this essay, "*Troilus and Cressida*: A Modern Perspective," might be taken as referring not just to a modern perspective *on* the play but also to the curiously modern perspective *of* the play.

This modern perspective—or rather, this modern *multiplication* of perspective—becomes apparent from the play's outset. If, as is likely, *Troilus and Cressida* was written in 1601–02, the Prologue's opening speech seems custom-made to quicken the pulse of an audience used to stirring war scenes from such recent plays as Shakespeare's *Henry V*, performed in 1599, and perhaps also Thomas Dekker and Henry Chettle's play about the Trojan War from the same year. The Prologue says:

In Troy there lies the scene. From isles of Greece
The princes orgulous, their high blood chafed,
Have to the port of Athens sent their ships
Fraught with the ministers and instruments
Of cruel war.

(Pr. 1–5)

Fittingly, the Prologue tells us that he is "armed" and "suited / In like conditions as our argument" (Pr. 23–25). All this would seem to promise an action drama modeled on the events described in Homer's *Iliad.* Yet what do we get once we reach the play's first scene? Troilus's opening words are "Call here my varlet; I'll unarm again" (1.1.1). Speaking in the conventionally paradox-ridden language of the Petrarchan lover, Troilus presents himself as a refugee from the Prologue's martial universe, refusing war with the Greeks as long as another is waged in his heart over his love for Cressida. But this generic volte-face is itself reversed. When we next hear from the supposedly pacifist Troilus in Act 2, scene 2, he has become a strident apologist for war. So which play is he in? Is he a Romeo or a Hotspur, a romantic comedian or a bellicose tragedian? He is, of course, all these; the Troilus we first see in Act 1, then, is and is not Troilus.

Such multiplication of perspective typifies the play's constant reframing of its characters. No sooner has the reader made an apparently decisive evaluation of a character than another perspective presents itself. Cressida parries with ribald prose Pandarus's attempts to woo her for Troilus, but then poetically proclaims herself in love with him. Hector argues thoughtfully against keeping Helen and continuing the war, but on a whim says she should not be returned to the Greeks. Troilus describes himself as a paragon of constancy, but seems oddly disinclined to dispute the Trojans' decision to hand Cressida over to the Greeks. The Greek characters are just as prone to such reversals. Ulysses is one minute the fierce defender of hierarchy and the puritanical adversary of the theatrically inclined Achilles and Patroclus, but resorts the next to Machiavellian scheming and carefully crafted histrionics. Achilles scandalously cavorts with "his masculine whore" Patroclus (5.1.18), but refuses to fight the Trojans because of his courtly love for King Priam's daughter Polyxena. And Helen is described as "a theme of honor and renown" (2.2.208), but comes across as a vapid nymphomaniac in her one onstage appearance.

Some of these contradictions can be chalked up to the many competing versions of the Trojan story with which Shakespeare and his audiences might have been familiar. Ajax is "a man into whom nature hath . . . crowded humors" (1.2.25–26), a description that hints at the unlikely quilt-work of literary materials Shakespeare stitched together to produce his character: the valiant Ajax of Homer's *Iliad,* the blockheaded Ajax of Ovid's *Metamorphoses,* even the scatological Ajax—a pun on "jakes," or toilet—of Sir John Harrington's 1596 satire on sanitary plumbing, *The Metamorphosis of Ajax.* Odysseus in Homer is a brilliant military strategist, but he becomes in Ovid a dangerously deceptive politician; both avatars seem to inform Shakespeare's Ulysses. Even his Helen is a composite of competing literary traditions: the beauty memorialized by Christopher Marlowe's legendary "face that launched a thousand ships,"[2] and reprised by Shakespeare as the "pearl / Whose price hath launched above a thousand ships" (2.2.87–88), is eclipsed in Act 3, scene 1, by the sluttish "Nell" of contemporary popular ballads. This yoking of competing sources is exemplified also by Troilus when he claims that the enigma of Cressida's identity "Admits no orifex for a point as subtle / As Ariachne's broken woof to enter" (5.2.180–81). "Ariachne" is, like the play's Trojan and Greek characters, a conflation of different mythological figures—proud Arachne the weaver, turned into a spider by Athena, and Ariadne of Minos, who helped Theseus out of the labyrinth with a ball of thread.

But the impression of Cubist characters with multiple selves—underlined not just by Troilus's "This is and is not Cressid" but also by Cressida's own claim to "have a kind of self resides with you" and "an unkind self that itself will leave" (3.2.148–49)—has less to do with Shakespeare's diverse source materials than with his treatment of a more modern phenomenon: the fluctuations of desire and value in the marketplace. Even though it is set in the Homeric age of heroes, *Troilus and Cressida* brims with mercantile imagery of a kind that belongs more to Shakespeare's own time. In his first scene, Troilus describes Cressida as "a pearl" in "India" and himself as a venturing "merchant" (1.1.102, 105). This strain of imagery is developed throughout the rest of the play, and with extraordinary persistence; as a consequence, a profiteering mercantile impulse rather than the martial valor or chivalry that we might expect from the Homeric world comes to shape the characters' actions and identities. The supposedly principled Ulysses, scheming to replace the sulking Achilles with Ajax in the proposed duel with Hector, says "Let us like merchants / First show foul wares and think perchance they'll sell" (1.3.367–68). Troilus refers not to Helen's face but her "price," which he claims has transformed "crowned kings to merchants" (2.2.88–89). Paris, in his discussion with Diomedes of Helen's worth, praises him for doing "as chapmen [i.e., merchants] do, / Dispraise the thing that they desire to buy" (4.1.81–82). The standoff between the Trojans and the Greeks increasingly comes across not as an epic struggle between heroic figures, but rather as a mercantile competition to "buy," and favorably manipulate the market value of, hotly desired commodities.

Cressida in particular displays a keen sensitivity to the market forces that shape her own identity as a commodity. Upon revealing to the audience that she does indeed love Troilus, she explains why she is wary about admitting as much to him:

> Women are angels, wooing;
> Things won are done; joy's soul lies in the doing.
> That she beloved knows naught that knows not this:
> Men prize the thing ungained more than it is.
> (1.2.293–96)

Although Troilus repeatedly insists that both he and Cressida possess an intrinsic and fixed value, she fears that her value is variable, and in ways that she can only partially control. Cressida realizes that she is subject to re- and devaluation according to laws of supply and demand; so long as she remains "ungained" or in scarce supply, she believes she will be an "angel"—also an Elizabethan term for a valuable coin—highly "prize[d]" by Troilus. But she is afraid that her value will depreciate if and when she makes herself available to him. The play hints that her fears are justified. After Cressida relents and gives herself sexually to Troilus, Shakespeare presents us with a morning-after exchange that can come across as a cruel parody of *Romeo and Juliet*'s famous aubade scene. Romeo and Juliet cannot bear to be separated from each other after their first night together; Troilus seems in a hurry to leave his newly bedded love. Romeo and Juliet try to will the morning larks into nightingales; Troilus complains impatiently that the lark "hath roused the ribald crows" (4.2.12). Little wonder Cressida laments that "I might have still held off, / And then you would have tarried" (4.2.21–22).

Cressida's experience of her fluctuating market value, and of the different commodified selves these fluctuations produce, is ingeniously anticipated by the extended debate between Troilus and Hector about the nature of value. Troilus argues that value originates in the evaluator; Hector counters that

value dwells not in particular will;
It holds his [i.e., its] estimate and dignity
As well wherein 'tis precious of itself
As in the prizer. 'Tis mad idolatry
To make the service greater than the god;
And the will dotes that is attributive
To what infectiously itself affects
Without some image of th' affected merit.
(2.2.57–64)

Hector here presents extrinsic value as an infection that passes from the sick appetite to an object without regard for the object's inherent "merit." This literally pathological vision of valuation resonates with that of the English mercantile writer Gerard de Malynes in his treatise *The Canker of England's Commonwealth*, published in the same year—1601—that Shakespeare most likely began writing *Troilus and Cressida.* Malynes endeavors to explain the causes of England's economic problems, which he attributes to a crisis in understandings of value. According to Malynes, money *should* have an intrinsic value and serve as a universal gold standard for measuring the value of everything else. But thanks to the new markets in foreign currencies, which take advantage of fluctuating exchange rates generated by the local scarcity or abundance of national denominations, money's value has become extrinsic, variable, and dependent on the greedy whims of bankers. Malynes regards this usurpation of intrinsic value by individual appetite as a sickness, one that he calls a "canker"—a term, we might note, that serendipitously rhymes with *banker.*

While Malynes's treatise provides a key with which to unlock Hector's critique of infectious valuation, it also helps illuminate Ulysses' famous speech about why the Greeks have failed to win the war. Like Malynes, Ulysses is nostalgic for a lost gold standard—in his case, "degree" or hierarchy—with which the fixed value of everything else was once measured. Also like Malynes, Ulysses sees this loss of "fixture" (1.3.105) as a disease that frays the cohesiveness of the Greek army: it prompts "plagues," for without degree, "The enterprise is sick" (1.3.100, 107). And like Malynes, Ulysses attributes this illness to the unrestrained appetites of individuals who disrespect the supposedly natural order of things:

> Then everything includes itself in power,
> Power into will, will into appetite,
> And appetite, an universal wolf,
> So doubly seconded with will and power,
> Must make perforce an universal prey
> And last eat up himself.
>
> (1.3.123–28)

Ulysses describes a world within which the only constant is appetite, a force that unsettles all stable identities by transforming everyone into what they are not. His vision sheds light on the play's self-contradictory characters. *Troilus and Cressida* may materialize what it means to be both rabbit and duck at once; but this animal plurality is itself the outcome of the "universal wolf" Ulysses identifies.

The character who most insistently recognizes the "universal wolf" of infectious appetite is not Ulysses, however, but the misanthropic fool Thersites. He repeatedly insists that appetite is the corrosive force that unites the seemingly lofty pursuits of war and love. In the process, he offers a quasi-Freudian interpretation of human behavior: all socially valued actions are merely sublimated expressions of sexuality. Thersites sees both war and love as "Nothing but lechery" (5.1.106), and the play bears him out on both fronts. Troilus's supposedly pure love for Cressida is shown to be a raging lust hurtling toward the "little death" of sexual climax ("What will it be," Troilus asks, "When that the wat'ry palate taste indeed / Love's thrice-repurèd nectar? Death, I fear me" [3.2.19–21]). And Hector's much-vaunted chivalry reveals its appetitive underbelly, thereby costing him his life, when he is seduced into pursuing the "goodly armor" of a soldier who turns out to be nothing but a "putrefied core" (5.9.1–2). Shakespeare uses that most Freudian of devices—the pun—to suggest the Janus-faced conjunction of chivalry and lust: after the Greek generals have welcomed (or, depending on one's perspective, collectively molested) Cressida upon her entrance to their camp, they pause to note the clarion call of "The Trojan's trumpet" (4.5.73). When we *read* this line, we might see in it only a reference to a martial ritual; but in performance, we can *hear* the play's reevaluation of Cressida as "the Trojan strumpet." With this pun, the shadow of appetitive sexuality—the Greeks' as much as Cressida's—is shown to lurk beneath the performance of chivalry.

Thersites' vision of the sexual appetite, like Hector's understanding of the evaluative appetite and

Ulysses' of the appetite for power, is relentlessly pathological. Sexual appetite, in Thersites' view, leads inexorably to venereal disease. He wishes "the Neapolitan bone-ache"—a common term for syphilis—on his fellow Greeks, "For that, methinks, is the curse depending on those that war for a placket [i.e., a petticoat, woman, or female genitalia]" (2.3.19–21). And in one particularly splenetic tirade, he wishes the full range of syphilitic symptoms on his lecherous companions:

> Now the rotten diseases of the south, the guts-griping, ruptures, catarrhs, loads o' gravel in the back, lethargies, cold palsies, raw eyes, dirt-rotten livers, whissing lungs, bladders full of impostume, sciaticas, limekilns i' th' palm, incurable bone-ache, and the rivelled fee-simple of the tetter, take and take again such preposterous discoveries.
>
> (5.1.18–25)

With these rants, Shakespeare expresses more fully the disgust at sexuality and "the thousand natural shocks / That flesh is heir to" that had characterized his previous play *Hamlet* (3.1.70–71). But whereas Hamlet's flight from flesh leads him eventually to an intuition of transcendence—the "special providence in the fall of a sparrow" (5.2.234)—*Troilus and Cressida* offers no such solution. This play ends not with the redemptive fall of a sparrow but with the sick actions of another bird: a goose.

It is Pandarus who introduces this odd bird. After accusing the audience of being, like him, syphilitic whoremongers, he tells them he expects to die soon:

> Some two months hence my will shall here be made.
> It should be now, but that my fear is this:

Some gallèd goose of Winchester would hiss.
Till then I'll sweat and seek about for eases,
And at that time bequeath you my diseases.
(5.11.55–59)

Pandarus's "goose of Winchester," slang for both prostitute and pustule of syphilitic infection, conflates the marketplace, sexual appetite, and venereal disease, all of which he "bequeath[s]" to the audience. Nowhere else does Shakespeare spit so much bile at his paying customers. Some readers have therefore speculated that *Troilus and Cressida* was performed only for a private audience—perhaps lawyers at the Inns of Court—who were more accustomed to vitriolic satire in this vein. But the mere fact that most of Shakespeare's audiences *were* paying customers engaged in the appetitive act of evaluation—as the Prologue says, "Like, or find fault; do as your pleasures are" (Pr. 30)—must have made them an inescapable target in a play so horrified by the pathological effects of the marketplace and sexuality.

Pandarus's final speech anachronistically brings the Trojan past into Shakespeare's present. But *Troilus and Cressida* looks forward to our own time as well. The play's fiercely skeptical view of the reasons leaders take their citizens to war, its obsession with sexuality and venereal disease, and its compulsive reduction of everything to market forces all potentially speak to the play's modern readers. Some of these themes are uncannily reflected in the newer connotations of the play's most famous names-cum-commodities. For most Americans, "Trojans" suggest sexual accessories rather than doomed Homeric heroes, and the name "Cressida" calls to mind a marketable brand of Toyota rather than an unfortunate young woman. Perhaps, then, *Troilus and Cressida* is no longer a "heap of rubbish" in need of generic discipline, but a play whose problematic time has come.

---

1. John Dryden, *Troilus and Cressida, Or Truth Found Too Late, A Tragedy* (London, 1679), sig. A4v.

2. Christopher Marlowe, *Doctor Faustus,* ed. Roma Gill, 2nd ed. (London: A & C Black; New York: Norton, 1989), 12.81.

Further Reading

Troilus and Cressida

Abbreviations: *Ant.* = *Antony and Cleopatra;*
Cym. = *Cymbeline; Ham.* = *Hamlet;*
John = *King John; H5* = *Henry V;*
MM = *Measure for Measure; R3* = *Richard III;*
RSC = The Royal Shakespeare Company;
Temp. = *The Tempest; Tit.* = *Titus Andronicus;*
Tro. = *Troilus and Cressida*

Adelman, Janet. " 'This Is and Is Not Cressid': The Characterization of Cressida." In *The (M)other Tongue: Essays in Feminist Psychoanalytic Interpretation,* edited by Shirley Nelson Garner, Claire Kahane, and Madelon Sprengnether, pp. 119–41. Ithaca, N.Y.: Cornell University Press, 1985. (Revised and reprinted in *Suffocating Mothers: Fantasies of Maternal Origin in Shakespeare's Plays, Hamlet to the Tempest* [New York: Routledge, 1991], pp. 38–75.)

Adelman contends that up to 4.4 Cressida is not a stereotype of wantonness but a whole character. In 1.2 we are encouraged to speculate about her motives, and in 3.2, a scene that "clearly focuses on her inner state," we witness her fear of betrayal and her vulnerability. To the extent, however, that the play embodies Troilus's ambivalent fantasies concerning desire for union with the separated mother and fear of maternal engulfment, Cressida's characterological integrity needs to be sacrificed, something that begins in 4.4 when she moves suddenly into an "opacity" from which she never recovers.

"Insofar as [Troilus's] union with Cressida is an attempt to recapture the infantile fusion with a maternal figure, the rupture of the union threatens to soil the idea of the mother herself . . . [and] threaten[s] . . . to dissolve a universe felt as coherent into fragmented bits of spoiled food" (see 5.2.156–63, 182–90). Thus, Troilus can preserve his union with Cressida and his idealized sense of her only by splitting her in two, a shift in "the mode of characterization [that] forces us to participate in his fantasy about her." For Adelman, Cressida's loss of interiority does not constitute an artistic failure, because both her inconstancy and "radical inconsistency of characterization" occur simultaneously as "reflections of the same fantasy."

Apfelbaum, Roger. *Shakespeare's Troilus and Cressida: Textual Problems and Performance Solutions*. Newark: University of Delaware Press, 2004.

Seeking a way of balancing editorial and theatrical choices, the author brings stage history to bear on eight passages that have challenged editors of the play: the Prologue; Cressida's "Who were those went by" (1.2.1); the stage directions regarding the entrances of Cassandra at 2.2.107 and of Patroclus at 2.3.24 ("Good Thersites, come in and rail"); the implications of music and extras in "Who play they to" (3.1.21); Cressida's exit and the interpretations of Diomedes' "Lady, a word. I'll bring you to your father" (4.5.61); "They call him Troilus" (4.5.122), Ulysses' secondhand account of a Troilus who presumably stands before him; and the play's multiple and disruptive movements of closure as manifest in Troilus's final speeches and Pandarus's final appearance ("Hence, broker, lackey" [5.11.35]). Each chapter tackles the editorial and performance history of the passage in question but "the focus remains on the method of interrogating textual problems with performance decisions." While many productions from William Poel's (1912) to Peter Hall's (2001) are discussed, the author pays extensive attention to Sam Mendes's *Tro.* for the RSC in 1990. Since there is no real performance history to speak of until the twentieth century, Apfelbaum finds a "substitute for an early theater history" in John Dryden's adaptation (1679), J. P. Kemble's promptbook (c. 1795), and the acting editions of the eighteenth and nineteenth centuries. Apfelbaum's intertextual approach to *Tro.* raises "many questions about what the text of a play can be and how editors, directors, and performers are special kinds of readers and shapers of the text." Two appendices dealing with editions and productions of *Tro.*, respectively, round out the volume.

Barfoot, C. C. "*Troilus and Cressida:* 'Praise us as we are tasted.' " *Shakespeare Quarterly* 39 (1988): 45–57.

Barfoot explores the valuations that characters in *Tro.* offer of each other and themselves. His examination of the criteria for these valuations, the assumptions informing them, and their consequences leads him to conclude that neither the state of the valuer nor the conditions surrounding the valuation remain constant. As 5.2 makes clear, "the person valued is able to rate him or herself differently from the valuation attributed by another; and the individual, as distinct from an object, is capable of opposing his own estimation of his value to that of an outside observer, and has the authority of self-esteem or self-distrust to do so." Within the oft-noted complex of mercantile imagery that shows interpersonal relationships to be transactional at their core is both a pervasive imagery of food and appetite and "a foregrounding of words based on 'praise,' 'prize,' and 'price' (including 'pride' and 'place')." Taken together, these image and word clusters articulate closely related themes "that question the stability of value and the reliability of attribution, despite the constant assumption of the former and the assertion of the latter." With so many characters constantly being called on to introduce themselves, "conscious that their names are one of their major attributes[,] . . . [*Tro.*] leads us to the conclusion that we can no more trust our heroes, or even our anti-heroes, than we can trust our words."

Bradbrook, Muriel C. "What Shakespeare Did to Chaucer's *Troilus and Criseyde.*" *Shakespeare Quarterly* 9 (1958): 311–19.

Bradbrook claims that *Tro.* differs from most of Shakespeare's plays in that it "was designed to be read as Literature and not only for the Boards." She cites its many formal debates and complex vocabulary as marks of "conscious labor and effort." Her chief concern is with the ways in which, by comparison with Chaucer's poem, Shakespeare's governing intention is revealed, an intention she sums up as one of inversion, speed, and compression. "The tone and flavor of the play, disturbing and ambiguous, controls and directs the response." Shakespeare's counterparts to Chaucer's Troilus, Cressida, and Pandarus are less sympathetic, and with respect to the latter two, more distorted. Cressida, for example, is not as delicate or innocent as Criseyde, and the Pandarus of the play is more wily and raw, as evidenced in the "brutal exchange" between him and Cressida in 4.2.27–37. The epilogue exemplifies Shakespeare's overall deflation of Chaucer's "high and heroic romance": whereas Chaucer concludes with a prayer that subsumes the human tragedy into something larger and beautiful, Shakespeare concludes with a deflating reference to brothels. And where Chaucer tells the tale in a leisurely, protracted manner, Shakespeare emphasizes the haste of "Injurious Time" (4.4.44) in both the courtship and the betrayal. The strength of Shakespeare's play "lies in a vision not of the grandeur but the pettiness of evil; the squalor and meanness and triviality of betrayal, which here enjoy their hour."

Bruster, Douglas. " 'The alteration of men': *Troilus and Cressida,* Troynovant, and Trade." Chapter 7 of *Drama and the Market in the Age of Shakespeare,* pp. 97–117. Cambridge: Cambridge University Press, 1992.

Bruster explores how early modern English drama "responded to the market, even as it sprang from it." Three strategies proved especially useful for playwrights trying to cope with the dynamics of a changing social and financial economy: the first connected identity with ownership, thereby "rendering the relationship between property and person as one of almost complete interdependence"; the second exploited the economic basis of the cuckold myth; and the third used urban tales of international cities, past and present, to stage the London market. Linking "the sexual and the economic, the urban and the rural, and the ancient with the modern" enabled playwrights to define the nature of those changes affecting the socioeconomic structure of London. In the chapter on *Tro.,* Bruster demonstrates how Shakespeare used the Troy story "to mythologize the elaborate realities of London's material base." In 1602 (the year Bruster assigns to the play), tensions were mounting over military and mercantile supremacy involving England and Spain; at a time when war and trade were "inextricably entwined" and piracy and privateering dominated English foreign policy and politics, an ancient tale of national conflict rooted in an act of theft resonated historically and morally in the imaginations of Elizabethan playwrights. Bruster singles out the "sleeve business" in 5.4 to make the point that "the drama continually concerns itself with problems of the material, with exchange and its effects on action, language, and thought." Because the "parlance of the market" informs matters of love and war in a world "unsettled by commodity," the romantic treatment of Troy found in earlier writers gives way to cynicism in Shakespeare's play. At the turn of the century, pessimism prompted by Elizabeth I's age and illness and by the economic toll of wars with Spain, Ireland, and the Low Countries led many to see London's decline as mirroring Troy's final moments. Shakespeare's *Tro.* is about "the passing of the old and the coming of the new"—i.e., about an economic system "that apparently distorts human relationships and actively encourages the lapses in morality once ascribed to the machinations of abstract sins and commodities."

Charnes, Linda. " 'So Unsecret to Ourselves': Notorious Identity and the Material Subject in *Troilus and Cressida.*" Chapter 3 of *Notorious Identity: Materializing the Subject in Shakespeare,* pp. 70–102. Cambridge, Mass.: Harvard University Press, 1993. (An earlier version of the chapter appeared in *Shakespeare Quarterly* 40 [1989]: 413–40.)

In her discussion of the ideological foundations of "notorious identity" (the pathological form of fame) in *R3*, *Tro.*, and *Ant.*, Charnes explores how Shakespeare is less interested in "reproducing cultural mythography" than in demonstrating what is involved in the "experience of being reiterated," that process through which each "notorious" figure confronts the determinant power of an infamous name as he or she self-fashions a new identity. In the chapter on *Tro.*, she uses the line "This is and is not Cressid" (5.2.175) to argue that the problem of self-identity is a "phenomenon that haunts" the play. "Subjectivity crippled by cultural inscription" is the particular neurosis represented in *Tro.*—"arguably . . . the most 'neurotic' " work in the canon. Although the end is always known—Troilus will always feel betrayed and fail to trust, and Cressida will always be false—the play's legendary characters do have moments of subjectivity, i.e., other selves determined "to lay to rest the haunting sense that they are, and are not, 'themselves.' " Charnes examines in some detail 1.3 and 2.2 (the play's "two major ideological" episodes). She finds in Helen a paradigm for the way characters attempt to subvert their official names and origins in a struggle to be mimetically spontaneous figures rather than rhetorical ones exploited by others. By deconstructing the "legend of Troilus and Cressida," Shakespeare "reconstructs theater and drama as a new site not for representing 'identity' but for staging 'kinds of selves.' "

Cook, Carol. "Unbodied Figures of Desire." *Theater Journal* 38 (1986): 34–52.

Cook invokes the theories of Jacques Lacan and Luce Irigaray to examine the disproportion between anticipation and achievement that links the Greek and Trojan competition for Helen in the war plot and Troilus's quest for Cressida in the love plot. The play's entanglement in the "deeply problematic relation between desire and representation" is most clearly defined in the "problematic status of women as objects of desire" within a "heterosexual economy" that intersects with what Luce Irigaray labels "hom(m)o-sexuality." That heterosexuality founded on a traffic in women "is a mediated homosexuality" can be seen in Troilus's coming to Cressida by Pandar, and Pandar's coming to Troilus by Cressida. In the war plot, this same structure of homosexual desire is repeated as

Greeks and Trojans depend on the "mediation of a woman to 'come by' one another." Masculine desire puts woman in the place of "that unbodied figure of the thought / That gave 't surmisèd shape" (1.3.16–17); the female body thus becomes the means by which masculine desire represents itself to itself. But because the image proves insufficient, violence results, often in a rage expressed through the imagery of a woman's fragmented body. Helen and Cressida "can be enjoyed in fantasy as disbursed and fetishized signs, flickering images, unbodied figures of the thought, but as bodies they threaten a monstrous entrapment in finitude, repetition, representation." *Tro.* intermittently reveals and masks the "dependency of its parallel fables of masculine enterprise on this textual aperture—the feminine absence upon which masculine desire and truth are erected."

Elton, W. R. "Shakespeare's Ulysses and the Problem of Value." *Shakespeare Studies* 2 (1966): 95–111.

In this influential essay on the play's value context, Elton focuses on Ulysses' degree speech (1.3.85–141) and his "mystery of state" speech (3.3.205–13) to argue that they reveal not an absolute, fixed hierarchal order but a relativistic, unstable world subject to market fluctuations and changing opinions. The "evaluative discourse" of the first two scenes shows that theatrically the play advances "by a process of multiplying perspectives"; those scenes, along with the Prologue, place Ulysses' speech on degree in a context that encourages similar weighing of views. To emphasize the speech's relation to orthodox Elizabethan political ideology, as so many past scholars have done, is to miss the "ironies of its dramatic context," for what the pragmatic rather than idealistic Ulysses is saying is that "observance of degree is the best we can hope for in a self-devouring world." Elton considers the play's value context in light of the transformation of value philosophy from Aquinas—who saw value as inherent, fixed, and absolute—to Hobbes, who viewed it as external, quantified, and relative to a market economy of appreciation and depreciation that assigns each man or woman his or her fluctuating price; see, for example, Achilles' sense of honor as an accidental attribute (3.3.83–86) and Agamemnon's comment on Achilles' quantifiable worth (2.3.141–42). In the mutable world of *Tro.*, where nothing survives flux (3.3.153–55), Shakespeare shows that all the world is "a market place."

Freund, Elizabeth. "'Ariachne's broken woof': The Rhetoric of Citation in *Troilus and Cressida.*" In *Shakespeare & the Question of Theory,* edited by Patricia Parker and Geoffrey Hartman, pp. 19–36. New York: Methuen, 1985.

In a deconstructionist reading of the play's allusions and rhetoric, Freund uses the Ariachne reference (5.2.181) to gloss Shakespeare's treatment of the powerful and canonical story of Troy. Whether the conflation of two distinct classical allusions—Arachne (who bested Athena in a weaving contest and was, consequently, turned into a spider) and Ariadne (whose thread guided Theseus out of the Cretan maze)—was deliberate on Shakespeare's part or the result of compositorial error, the resulting confusion is paradigmatic of the split signifiers informing the play, as in the frequently cited "This is and is not Cressid" (5.2.175). An "aporetical figure in Shakespeare's tapestry of citations," "Ariachne" points us toward "the major labyrinth of citation and the travesty of citation that is the 'stuff' out of which [*Tro.*] 'make[s] paradoxes' [1.3.188]." Persistently emphasizing its intertextuality and anachronicity, *Tro.* illustrates the dilemma facing

Renaissance artists who wished to balance reverence for classical texts with the privileging of new values associated with originality. Freund concludes that in no other play does Shakespeare "strip *both* his sources *and* his own text of their 'original' substance with such spirited iconoclasm." As a result, *Tro.* is "probably Shakespeare's most daring experiment in defensive self-presentation, and perhaps his noblest failure."

Girard, René. "The Politics of Desire in *Troilus and Cressida.*" In *Shakespeare & the Question of Theory*, edited by Patricia Parker and Geoffrey Hartman, pp. 188–209. New York: Methuen, 1985.

Girard examines *Tro.* in accordance with his theory of "mimetic" desire, i.e., a "mediated" desire prompted not by anything intrinsic to the one being desired but by a rivalry with someone else for the same object, which cannot be shared. Shakespeare's goal in writing *Tro.* was not "good theater" but rather the creation of "circumstances favorable to the genesis and revelation of . . . configuration[s] of mimetic desire" in both the erotic and political plots. Troilus, for example, loses interest in Cressida after their one night together (4.2.1–39), only to find a new desire awakened when he imagines her surrounded by "merry Greeks" (4.4.59–87)—namely, the desire to possess what they possess. Even the initial desires of Troilus and Cressida for each other are rooted in mimetic impulses: Pandarus entices Troilus to woo Cressida in the first place by comparing her to Helen (1.1.42–44, 76–80), and the rumor that Troilus is desired by Helen serves as Pandarus's bait to attract Cressida to Troilus (1.2.95–177). In the political plot, desire also coincides with emulative rivalry. For just as Troilus needs the admiring look of other men in the love plot, Achilles needs the same among his fellow warriors. Achilles' wish to replace

Agamemnon, along with the desires of Agamemnon and Ajax to be Achilles, reveals that each man "wants to *be* the other man without ceasing to be himself" (see, e.g., 1.3.133–38, 189–94). And just as Helen was central to the mimetic desires of Troilus and Cressida, so she embodies a typically vicious circle of mimetic desire at the center of the Trojan War: the more people die for her, the more valuable she appears to be and vice versa. As the play demonstrates, "it always takes other men to make an erotic or a military conquest truly valuable in the eyes of the conqueror himself." From a dramatic standpoint, the two plots do not really come together, and that is one of the play's failures. "But from the standpoint of the mimetic plague"—all those twists and turns of human desire in a world of competing desires—"they marvelously mirror each other."

Grady, Hugh. " 'Mad idolatry': Commodification and Reification in *Troilus and Cressida.*" In *Shakespeare's Universal Wolf: Postmodernist Studies in Early Modern Reification,* pp. 58–94. Oxford: Clarendon Press, 1996.

The writings of Jacques Lacan and Michel Foucault, along with the Frankfurt School's analysis of reification (i.e., "the property of social systems to act through their own objective logic, as if they possessed an autonomous intentionality"), are central to Grady's postmodernist interpretation of *Tro.* as a "cheerless" and "nearly nihilistic" play that "present[s] a complexly organized, mirrors-within-mirrors exploration of mutually metaphoring systems of power, desire, market-value, and instrumental reason." The result is a "full thematic development of . . . the basis of an implicit notion of Renaissance reification." Through the "dizzying set of interactions" one can construe from the play's elaborate parallels and contrasts, Shakespeare demonstrates "how it is possible to 'think' concepts analogically in poetry and drama that were not available in the (nascent) theoretical discourses of the time." For Grady, the central organizing duality of the play is not that of Trojans versus Greeks, as many have argued, but "the mutual metaphor between love and politics, eros and power, lechery and war." He contends that the play's analogical system, through a sustained deflation of love/lechery and honor/power, collapses the very ideas that "inspirited" both the love story and the political story. Grady spends considerable time analyzing Ulysses' speech on degree (1.3.85–141) because it reveals "ideology in the service of reified systems of instrumental thought." Appearing as a traditionalist on the surface but really an "incipient modern," Ulysses seeks to instrumentalize rationality as a strategic means to an end (see 1.3.204–14); his "universal wolf" (1.3.125) of will (understood as desire) and power—reification itself—drives the play, infecting with a contagious negativity human relations and interactions. In *Tro.*, where all is war and lechery, the destruction of honor, romance, and chivalry "is a triumph of instrumental reification in which the final self-destruction of the universal wolf is only deferred through an apparently endless play of destruction."

Greene, Gayle. "Shakespeare's Cressida: 'A kind of self.'" In *The Woman's Part: Feminist Criticism of Shakespeare*, edited by Carolyn Ruth Swift Lenz, Gayle Greene, and Carol Thomas Neely, pp. 133–49. Urbana: University of Illinois Press, 1980.

In this frequently cited essay, an early foray into feminist criticism of the play, Greene uses *Tro.*, perhaps Shakespeare's most misogynistic work, to further the argument that gender is a social construct—or, in the words of Simone de Beauvoir (*The Second Sex*), that "one is not born, but rather becomes a woman[;] . . . it is civilization as a whole that produces this creature."

Although Cressida is the "clearest representative of woman's 'frailty' " in Shakespeare, the playwright "provides a context that exonerates [her]." That context, one of "relativistic and mercantile standards," subjects all the characters in the play to appearances and to the vacillations of Time (see 3.3.177–80). Women, however, are even more dependent than men on "external supports for identity, more vulnerable to 'opinion' [as] they are 'formed in th' applause' [3.3.124] of others, 'in the glass' of others' 'praise' " [1.2.292]. What explains "the conspicuous disjunction between Cressida's words and actions" is not a lack of coherent characterization but rather her required compliance with " 'opinion,' with the assumption of her society that [an individual's worth lies] in the eye of the beholder: and, as opinion changes, so does she." Her characterization thus reveals "several principles we have come to understand as crucial to women's psychology—the tendency of a woman to define herself in 'relational' capacities, to derive self-esteem from the esteem of others, and to 'objectify' herself." The society represented in the play, so modern and familiar in its reduction of people to terms of appetite and trade, "prompts a powerful indictment of the mercantilism of the age, and Cressida reminds us of the effects of capitalism on woman." Greene cautions against taking the identifying tags for Troilus, Cressida, and Pandarus in 3.2.204–6 as the last word: they are "stylized, simplistic definitions" that need to be understood in context. Cressida's inconstancy is qualified by the world of the play, as is Troilus's "truth."

Greenfield, Matthew. "Fragments of Nationalism in *Troilus and Cressida*." *Shakespeare Quarterly* 51 (2000): 181–200.

If Shakespeare's histories invest in some healing idea of national community, *Tro.* is more pessimistic in its political argument, as it programmatically reveals the nation to be "a collection of fictions." Instead of constructing a genealogy for England, something crucial to the history play, *Tro.* "attacks the very idea of genealogy" as it undoes or empties out the chroniclers' efforts to establish Troy as the point of origin for the English nation. Unlike the bastard Faulconbridge in *John,* who incarnates England and the principle of legitimacy in every sense but the biological, the bastard Thersites "speaks from a cosmopolitan, extranational perspective." Where Faulconbridge functions "as a synecdoche for the nation, Thersites stands outside its border" to "emblematize" the play's "relentless attack on nationalism's narratives, its tropes, its strategic amnesia, and its assumptions about human character and agency." The defecting Calchas succinctly describes (3.3.3–12) "the division of identity that the war eventually effects in almost all of the play's characters," who embody "in microcosm not one but both communities": e.g., the Cressida split between Troilus and Diomedes; the Iliadic Achilles in love with Patroclus versus the medieval romantic Achilles in love with Priam's daughter, Polyxena; the hybrid Ajax—half Trojan and half Greek; and finally, the ambiguously heroic Hector, both disturbingly acquisitive and nobly chivalric. "With its procession of bastards, cuckolds, exiles, traitors, and racial hybrids, the play persistently undermines the idea that national identity is an unambiguous aspect of self-definition." Noting that Shakespeare's skepticism about the possibility of the nation varies from play to play, Greenfield calls for a more extensive examination of the "variety of [those] skepticisms."

Harris, Jonathan Gil. "Canker/Serpego and Value: Gerard Malynes, *Troilus and Cressida.*" Chapter 4 of *Sick Economies: Drama, Mercantilism and Disease in Shake-*

speare's England, pp. 83–107. Philadelphia: University of Pennsylvania Press, 2004. (An earlier version of the chapter appeared as "The Enterprise Is Sick: Pathology of Value and Transnationality in *Troilus and Cressida,*" *Renaissance Drama,* n.s., 29 [1998]: 3–37.)

The chapter revises and expands Harris's initial study of the early modern linkage between discourses of economics and pathology by way of an intertextual analysis of Gerard de Malynes's *Treatise of the Canker of England's Commonwealth* (1601) and *Tro.* (written soon after). Both works reveal strikingly similar concerns with the migrations of disease and value across national borders. When compared with Shakespeare's "light-hearted, mercantile comedies" of the 1590s, his problem plays written in the early seventeenth century, of which *Tro.* is one, appear "morbidly sick." Finding the two dominant approaches to the disease discourse of these plays wanting—one engaged in speculation about Shakespeare's physical or mental health at the turn of the century, and the other viewing the disease imagery as metaphorically figuring social decline—Harris proposes an alternative "mercantile and transnational framework" as a way of decoding *Tro.*'s preoccupation with a host of illnesses. He argues that the contest in the play between endogenous (humoral) and exogenous (infectious) models of disease (i.e., disease as resulting either from an imbalance of bodily fluids or from the invasive agency of foreign bodies) "bespeaks a larger tension between differing paradigms of not just disease but also value—a tension strained to the breaking point by the growth of global trade and foreign currency exchange"; the play's pathological imagery thus manifests "an uncertainty specific to the mercantilist moment of early seventeenth-century England." Both *Tro.* and the mercantile culture of the time grapple with similar questions: Can one determine whether the origins of disease and value are endogenous/intrinsic or exogenous/extrinsic? And if, as Ulysses suggests, "The enterprise is sick" (1.3.107), what exactly is the nature of economic illness and from where does it come? Harris contends that the play gestures toward an alternative model of value that is neither simply intrinsic to the object nor "derived from the external imposition of the wills of multiple, potentially competing subjects"; according to the new paradigm, value in *Tro.* is fixed by a single sovereign will synonymous with public authority. But as with its "double coding of 'infectious' valuation" as both endogenous and exogenous, *Tro.*'s presentation of the sovereign will—its authority questionable in the figures of both Agamemnon and Priam—is "mediated by a conflicted pathological vocabulary." The chapter's expansion of the original essay includes discussion of the early modern association of usury with "canker" and greater attention to the turbulent economic environment that gave rise to Malynes's treatise.

James, Heather. " 'Tricks we play on the dead': Making History in *Troilus and Cressida*." Chapter 3 of *Shakespeare's Troy: Drama, Politics, and the Translation of Empire*, pp. 85–118. Cambridge: Cambridge University Press, 1997.

James investigates the ways in which Shakespeare's dramatic translations of the Troy legend in *Tit.*, *Tro.*, *Ant.*, *Cym.*, and *Temp.* served to legitimate the cultural place of the theater in late Elizabethan and early Stuart London. "Collectively the plays meditate what might constitute an English national politics rather than a narrow courtly politics; individually, they vary according to the historical stimuli that prompt Shakespeare to renew negotiations with court or city and produce a given 'translation of empire.' " The cultural conditions leading to the composition of *Tro.* include (1) the appearance of Chapman's Homer and (2) the fall of the earl of Essex and the "simultaneous collapse of the aristocratic culture of honor." In contrast to Chapman's Homer, Shakespeare's play reveals the social mobility and economic tensions of a developing capitalist society. With respect to Essex, James takes 3.3.205–15 as a point of departure to argue that *Tro.* "engages the aftermath of the Essex rebellion," when a "pall of suspicion and surveillance" engulfed London as censors and state officials adopted such theatrical tactics as disguise, plots, and entrapping dialogue "to keep citizens from overmighty lords [for whom Achilles provides a model] to recusants, printers, players, or rogues and vagabonds from 'meddling' with state practices." Shakespeare's interrogative rather than encomiastic treatment of the Troy legend robs it of both authority and integrity. By asking "what happens when subjects . . . perceive themselves as diminished and altered copies of a lost original," and by investigating "the degree to which identity and thought are impinged on by politically authoritative codes ranging from statutes to hortatory norms," Shakespeare "extends the destabilizing function of literary history from a single hero to the entire Troy legend: and when a writer demands that we confront the divisions internal to the myth of national origins itself, then the very authority which is its theme and *raison d'être* can only emerge as vitiated." The scene between Helen and Paris (3.1) "typifies the way the play destabilizes generic, evaluative, and characterological categories."

Mallin, Eric S. "Emulous Factions and the Collapse of Chivalry: *Troilus and Cressida.*" *Representations,* no. 29 (Winter 1990): 145–79. (Slightly revised and reprinted in his *Inscribing the Time: Shakespeare and the End of*

Elizabethan England, New Historicism: Studies in Cultural Poetics 33 [Berkeley: University of California Press, 1995], pp. 25–61.)

Mallin claims that the tense transitional years between the reigns of Elizabeth and James "materially shape . . . and misshape . . . [*Tro.*]." Specifically, he finds in the play a reflection of the political, military, and ideological anxieties associated with the late Elizabethan "neurosis of invasion," when invasion was understood as both a military threat posed by war with Spain and Ireland and an ideological threat to the Virgin Queen herself. As a play dealing with a war precipitated by rape, *Tro.* becomes the perfect vehicle for exploring both senses of invasion. Mallin emphasizes Elizabeth's cultivation of factions as a way of preventing challenges to the monarchy—a strategy, however, that in her final years came to fuel rather than restrain disorder, the most notable example being the anti- and pro-war factions of the Cecil and Essex camps, respectively. The emulative rivalry (1.3.133–38) of the "hollow factions" (1.3.84) among the Greek warriors mirrors late Elizabethan mimetic factionalism (whereby members of the queen's court competed to equal or surpass each other in the quest for social/political advancement—imitation being the key method of rendering one's rival obsolete); and the "antifeminist . . . homoerotic" chivalry of Priam's sons mirrors the decline of chivalric codes of knighthood in Elizabeth's court, where "masculine self-interest took precedence over obligatory chivalric service to a woman." A "repressive misogyny," in fact, infects both Trojan and late Elizabethan chivalry. Central to Mallin's argument is the figure of Essex, who "bifurcates" into both Achilles and Hector: the former inscribes the earl's aggressive militarism and surly reclusiveness; the latter, his status as the "final flawed representative of [a waning] martial, chivalric glory." Just as violent emulation in Elizabeth's court "wrought havoc on cultural templates such as honor, nobility, and distinction," so Shakespeare's "emulation" of the "overtold" Troy story "contaminates what it copies."

Martin, Priscilla, ed. *Troilus and Cressida: A Casebook.* London: Macmillan, 1976.

The book is divided into two parts. The first extracts commentary written between 1679 and 1939 from such critics as John Dryden, Samuel Johnson, William Hazlitt, S. T. Coleridge, G. G. Gervinus, A. C. Swinburne, G. B. Shaw, A. C. Bradley, G. Wilson Knight, Oscar Campbell, and Mark Van Doren. The second half focuses on studies spanning the years 1945 to 1975 and includes excerpts from essays and books by Una Ellis-Fermor, Kenneth Muir, Alvin Kernan, A. P. Rossiter, David Kaula, Clifford Leech, Willard Farnham, Jan Kott, R. J. Kaufmann, Joyce Carol Oates, Northrop Frye, Arnold Stein, T. McAlindon, and John Bayley. A select bibliography rounds out the volume. In the introduction, Martin charts the play's critical reputation from its first appearance (1609) until 1975. Among the topics discussed are differences between the Quarto and Folio texts; the play's disputed generic classification (as either tragedy, comedy, or heroic farce); the transmission of the Troy story from Homer to Shakespeare by way of Chaucer, Lydgate, Henryson, Caxton, and Chapman; and *Tro.*'s affinity with the modern, post–World War I temper as found in its "bitter, anti-heroic elements" and "relativistic philosophy of value." Martin briefly comments on performance history, citing the first known revival at Munich in 1898 and stagings at London theaters in 1907 (with Lewis Casson as Troilus), 1912 (with Edith Evans as Cressida), and 1938 (Michael MacOwan's "terrifyingly contemporary" interpretation).

Weimann, Robert. "Bifold Authority in Shakespeare's Theatre." *Shakespeare Quarterly* 39 (1988): 401–17.

Weimann's focus is "that disparate set of relationships between language, power, and authority best exemplified" in the plays of Shakespeare. The collision in Shakespeare's theater between the early modern modes of negotiating authority and "a mimesis of premodern circumstances of authorization" results in the "text's projection of two different . . . locations of authority: the represented *locus* of authority, *and* the process of authorization on the platform stage." Central to this discussion of the bifold authority of the object represented and of the agency representing—i.e., of the script and performance, writing and stagecraft—is the division of the Elizabethan platform stage into *locus* and *platea:* the *locus,* "associated with the localizing capacities of the fictional role[,] . . . tended to privilege the authority of what and who was *represented* in the dramatic world"; the *platea,* "associated instead with the actor and the neutral materiality of the platform stage, tended to privilege the authority of what and who was *representing* that world." Where the primary concern of the *locus* is "playing for an audience," that of the *platea* is "playing with an audience." This spatial division, mutable rather than rigidly fixed, demonstrates that the "authority" of theatrical mimesis ultimately requires validation by an audience willing to cooperate with the "imaginary forces" of author's pen and actor's voice. Although the term "bifold authority" derives from *Tro.* (5.2.173), the play at the center of the essay is *H5.* The findings related to that play's "redefinition and use of 'distance' " in the process of theatrical representation may open up "a perspective on a more highly experimental and self-conscious use of the *platea* projection of complementary authority" in subsequent plays such as *Ham., Tro.*

and *MM,* "where divided uses of authority appear most centrally to involve a changing use of *locus* and *platea* conventions."

Yachnin, Paul. " 'The Perfection of Ten': Populuxe Art and Artisanal Value in *Troilus and Cressida.*" *Shakespeare Quarterly* 56 (2005): 306–27.

Yachnin uses Cressida's "cheeky" remark at 3.2.84–88 ("They say all lovers swear more performance than they are able . . . vowing more than the perfection of ten and discharging less than the tenth part of one") to begin his discussion of the "populuxe and artisanal dimensions" of *Tro.* "Populuxe" (a term coined by the cultural critic Thomas Hine to describe the "deluxe dressing up" of consumer goods in the 1950s and '60s) denotes something that is "both popular and deluxe." The "perfection" comment is popular because it can be enjoyed at the Globe, a public theater open to anyone with a penny and a couple of hours to spare; Cressida's wisecrack is deluxe because of her "canonical pedigree" dating back to the twelfth century and because her "edgy wit" recalls the verse satires fashionable in the 1590s and the satirical plays by Jonson and Chapman (among others) performed at the private playhouses. "Classy but common," Cressida embodies "one of the most salient and formative features of Shakespeare's art": an artisanal ethos, defined by Yachnin as "the ethos of theatrical labor," i.e., the working conditions and stagecraft responsible for translating script into performance. If Cressida's comment is read not simply as referring to sexual performance but as suggesting dramatic performance—the collective ability of ten engaged in the "work" of bringing a dramatic performance to completion—we begin to see not only that "playing" is an organized, goal-oriented undertaking but also that an artisanal ethos is present in "this up-market satire of classical, canonical, and aristocratic value-claims." A socioeconomic approach that attends to the working conditions of the theater company in the course of production and to the players as craftsmen "yield[s] a fuller and more historical account of Shakespeare's ideas about value" within this play, as well as a "more satisfactory account of his drama's politics in general."

Shakespeare's Language

Abbott, E. A. *A Shakespearian Grammar.* New York: Haskell House, 1972.

This compact reference book, first published in 1870, helps with many difficulties in Shakespeare's language. It systematically accounts for a host of differences between Shakespeare's usage and sentence structure and our own.

Blake, Norman. *Shakespeare's Language: An Introduction.* New York: St. Martin's Press, 1983.

This general introduction to Elizabethan English discusses various aspects of the language of Shakespeare and his contemporaries, offering possible meanings for hundreds of ambiguous constructions.

Dobson, E. J. *English Pronunciation, 1500–1700.* 2 vols. Oxford: Clarendon Press, 1968.

This long and technical work includes chapters on spelling (and its reformation), phonetics, stressed vowels, and consonants in early modern English.

Hope, Jonathan. *Shakespeare's Grammar.* London: Arden Shakespeare, 2003.

Commissioned as a replacement for Abbott's *Shakespearian Grammar,* Hope's book is organized in terms of the two basic parts of speech, the noun and the verb. After extensive analysis of the noun phrase and the verb phrase come briefer discussions of subjects and agents, objects, complements, and adverbials.

Houston, John. *Shakespearean Sentences: A Study in Style and Syntax.* Baton Rouge: Louisiana State University Press, 1988.

Houston studies Shakespeare's stylistic choices, considering matters such as sentence length and the relative positions of subject, verb, and direct object. Examining plays throughout the canon in a roughly chronological, developmental order, he analyzes how sentence structure is used in setting tone, in characterization, and for other dramatic purposes.

Onions, C. T. *A Shakespeare Glossary.* Oxford: Clarendon Press, 1986.

This revised edition updates Onions's standard, selective glossary of words and phrases in Shakespeare's plays that are now obsolete, archaic, or obscure.

Robinson, Randal. *Unlocking Shakespeare's Language: Help for the Teacher and Student.* Urbana, Ill.: National Council of Teachers of English and the ERIC Clearinghouse on Reading and Communication Skills, 1989.

Specifically designed for the high-school and undergraduate college teacher and student, Robinson's book addresses the problems that most often hinder present-day readers of Shakespeare. Through work with his own students, Robinson found that many readers today are particularly puzzled by such stylistic devices as subject-verb inversion, interrupted structures, and compression. He shows how our own colloquial language contains comparable structures, and thus helps students recognize such structures when they find them in Shakespeare's plays. This book supplies worksheets—with examples from major plays—to illuminate and remedy such problems as unusual sequences of words and the separation of related parts of sentences.

Williams, Gordon. *A Dictionary of Sexual Language and Imagery in Shakespearean and Stuart Literature.* 3 vols. London: Athlone Press, 1994.

Williams provides a comprehensive list of the words to which Shakespeare, his contemporaries, and later Stuart writers gave sexual meanings. He supports his identification of these meanings by extensive quotations.

Shakespeare's Life

Baldwin, T. W. *William Shakspere's Petty School.* Urbana: University of Illinois Press, 1943.

Baldwin here investigates the theory and practice of the petty school, the first level of education in Elizabethan England. He focuses on that educational system primarily as it is reflected in Shakespeare's art.

Baldwin, T. W. *William Shakspere's Small Latine and Lesse Greeke.* 2 vols. Urbana: University of Illinois Press, 1944.

Baldwin attacks the view that Shakespeare was an uneducated genius—a view that had been dominant among Shakespeareans since the eighteenth century. Instead, Baldwin shows, the educational system of Shakespeare's time would have given the playwright a strong background in the classics, and there is much in the plays that shows how Shakespeare benefited from such an education.

Beier, A. L., and Roger Finlay, eds. *London 1500–1700: The Making of the Metropolis.* New York: Longman, 1986.

Focusing on the economic and social history of early modern London, these collected essays probe aspects of metropolitan life, including "Population and Disease," "Commerce and Manufacture," and "Society and Change."

Bentley, G. E. *Shakespeare's Life: A Biographical Handbook.* New Haven: Yale University Press, 1961.

This "just-the-facts" account presents the surviving documents of Shakespeare's life against an Elizabethan background.

Chambers, E. K. *William Shakespeare: A Study of Facts and Problems.* 2 vols. Oxford: Clarendon Press, 1930.

Analyzing in great detail the scant historical data, Chambers's complex, scholarly study considers the nature of the texts in which Shakespeare's work is preserved.

Cressy, David. *Education in Tudor and Stuart England.* London: Edward Arnold, 1975.

This volume collects sixteenth-, seventeenth-, and early-eighteenth-century documents detailing aspects of formal education in England, such as the curriculum, the control and organization of education, and the education of women.

Dutton, Richard. *William Shakespeare: A Literary Life.* New York: St. Martin's Press, 1989.

Not a biography in the traditional sense, Dutton's very readable work nevertheless "follows the contours of Shakespeare's life" as he examines Shakespeare's career as playwright and poet, with consideration of his patrons, theatrical associations, and audience.

Honan, Park. *Shakespeare: A Life.* New York: Oxford University Press, 1998.

Honan's accessible biography focuses on the various contexts of Shakespeare's life—physical, social, political, and cultural—to place the dramatist within a lucidly described world. The biography includes detailed examinations of, for example, Stratford schooling, theatrical politics of 1590s London, and the careers of Shakespeare's associates. The author draws on a wealth of established knowledge and on interesting new research into local records and documents; he also engages in speculation about, for example, the possibilities that Shakespeare was a tutor in a Catholic household in the north of England in the 1580s and that he played particular roles in his own plays, areas that reflect new, but unproven and debatable, data—though Honan is usually careful to note where a particular narrative "has not been capable of proof or disproof."

Schoenbaum, S. *William Shakespeare: A Compact Documentary Life.* New York: Oxford University Press, 1977.

This standard biography economically presents the essential documents from Shakespeare's time in an accessible narrative account of the playwright's life.

Shakespeare's Theater

Bentley, G. E. *The Profession of Player in Shakespeare's Time, 1590–1642.* Princeton: Princeton University Press, 1984.

Bentley readably sets forth a wealth of evidence about performance in Shakespeare's time, with special attention to the relations between player and company, and the business of casting, managing, and touring.

Berry, Herbert. *Shakespeare's Playhouses.* New York: AMS Press, 1987.

Berry's six essays collected here discuss (with illustrations) varying aspects of the four playhouses in which Shakespeare had a financial stake: the Theatre in Shoreditch, the Blackfriars, and the first and second Globe.

Cook, Ann Jennalie. *The Privileged Playgoers of Shakespeare's London.* Princeton: Princeton University Press, 1981.

Cook's work argues, on the basis of sociological, economic, and documentary evidence, that Shakespeare's audience—and the audience for English Renaissance drama generally—consisted mainly of the "privileged."

Greg, W. W. *Dramatic Documents from the Elizabethan Playhouses.* 2 vols. Oxford: Clarendon Press, 1931.

Greg itemizes and briefly describes many of the play manuscripts that survive from the period 1590 to around 1660, including, among other things, players' parts. His second volume offers facsimiles of selected manuscripts.

Gurr, Andrew. *Playgoing in Shakespeare's London.* 2nd ed. Cambridge: Cambridge University Press, 1996.

Gurr charts how the theatrical enterprise developed from its modest beginnings in the late 1560s to become a thriving institution in the 1600s. He argues that there were important changes over the period 1567–1644 in the playhouses, the audience, and the plays.

Harbage, Alfred. *Shakespeare's Audience.* New York: Columbia University Press, 1941.

Harbage investigates the fragmentary surviving evidence to interpret the size, composition, and behavior of Shakespeare's audience.

Hattaway, Michael. *Elizabethan Popular Theatre: Plays in Performance.* London: Routledge and Kegan Paul, 1982.

Beginning with a study of the popular drama of the late Elizabethan age—a description of the stages, performance conditions, and acting of the period—this volume concludes with an analysis of five well-known plays of the 1590s, one of them (*Titus Andronicus*) by Shakespeare.

Shapiro, Michael. *Children of the Revels: The Boy Companies of Shakespeare's Time and Their Plays.* New York: Columbia University Press, 1977.

Shapiro chronicles the history of the amateur and quasi-professional child companies that flourished in London at the end of Elizabeth's reign and the beginning of James's.

The Publication of Shakespeare's Plays

Blayney, Peter W. M. *The First Folio of Shakespeare.* Hanover, Md.: Folger, 1991.

Blayney's accessible account of the printing and later life of the First Folio—an amply illustrated catalog to a 1991 Folger Shakespeare Library exhibition—analyzes the mechanical production of the First Folio, describing how the Folio was made, by whom and for whom, how much it cost, and its ups and downs (or, rather, downs and ups) since its printing in 1623.

Hinman, Charlton. *The Norton Facsimile: The First Folio of Shakespeare.* 2nd ed. New York: W. W. Norton, 1996.

This facsimile presents a photographic reproduction of an "ideal" copy of the First Folio of Shakespeare; Hinman attempts to represent each page in its most fully corrected state. The second edition includes an important new introduction by Peter W. M. Blayney.

Hinman, Charlton. *The Printing and Proof-Reading of the First Folio of Shakespeare.* 2 vols. Oxford: Clarendon Press, 1963.

In the most arduous study of a single book ever undertaken, Hinman attempts to reconstruct how the Shakespeare First Folio of 1623 was set into type and run off the press, sheet by sheet. He also provides almost all the known variations in readings from copy to copy.

Key to
Famous Lines and Phrases

The heavens themselves, the planets, and this center
Observe degree, priority, and place[.]
[*Ulysses*—1.3.89–90]

O, when degree is shaked,
Which is the ladder of all high designs,
The enterprise is sick.
[*Ulysses*—1.3.105–7]

Take but degree away, untune that string,
And hark what discord follows.
[*Ulysses*—1.3.113–14]

And, like a strutting player whose conceit
Lies in his hamstring and doth think it rich
To hear the wooden dialogue and sound
'Twixt his stretched footing and the scaffollage . . .
[*Ulysses*—1.3.157–60]

Pride is his own glass, his own trumpet[.]
[*Agamemnon*—2.3.163]

To fear the worst oft cures the worse.
[*Cressida*—3.2.73]

This is the monstruosity in love, lady, that the will is infinite and the execution confined[.]
[*Troilus*—3.2.81–82]

[T]o be wise and love
Exceeds man's might. That dwells with gods above.
[*Cressida*—3.2.156–57]

Time hath, my lord, a wallet at his back
Wherein he puts alms for oblivion[.]
[*Ulysses*—3.3.150–51]

Love, friendship, charity are subjects all
To envious and calumniating Time.
[*Ulysses*—3.3.179–80]

One touch of nature makes the whole world kin[.]
[*Ulysses*—3.3.181]

The grief is fine, full, perfect that I taste[.]
[*Cressida*—4.4.3]

Injurious Time now with a robber's haste
Crams his rich thiev'ry up, he knows not how.
[*Troilus*—4.4.44–45]

There's language in her eye, her cheek, her lip;
Nay, her foot speaks. Her wanton spirits look out
At every joint and motive of her body.
[*Ulysses*—4.5.64–66]

What's past and what's to come is strewed with husks
And formless ruin of oblivion[.]
[*Agamemnon*—4.5.185–86]

The end crowns all,
And that old common arbitrator, Time,
Will one day end it.
[*Hector*—4.5.245–47]